Let Your Light Shine

Bruce McNab

To order additional copies of this book, contact:
Xlibris Corporation
1-888-795-4274
www.Xlibris.com
Orders@Xlibris.com
90505

THE SERMONS

These sermons are organized according to the ordinary calendar year, not the church year. Therefore, the first in the collection is an Epiphany sermon and the last is a sermon for Christmas Day.

This book is gratefully dedicated to the loving people
of Christ Episcopal Church in Aspen, Colorado,
who "let their light shine" in ways that
give glory to our Father in heaven.

I have been blessed to be their priest and pastor.

FOREWORD

About Christ Church and these Sermons.

About Christ Church

The sermons in this book were all preached in Christ Church, the only Episcopal church in Aspen, Colorado, where I have served as rector since the beginning of 2004. Aspen is a resort community to which people come from all over the United States and around the world to enjoy the recreational and cultural opportunities the area provides. Many people who live in Aspen and Snowmass are relatively affluent, and a number of celebrities have homes in the area, but there are also many hard-working middle class families and even a number of homeless people living here. Despite being labeled "Glitter Gulch" by snarky out of town newspapers, Aspen is not just a getaway spot for Hollywood types and corporate moguls. It is a "real" town—and a small one at that.

Aspen is a place where there's always something intellectually stimulating, entertaining, or just plain fun to do, including on Sunday mornings. That was one of the qualities which attracted me to a parish ministry in this place, because it meant that those who came to church on Sundays would be there because they felt *serious* about their relationship with God. I thought: if someone has chosen to take a job and raise a family in Aspen, or has come across the country and paid the stiff price for a vacation in this place where there are scores of alluring alternatives to Sunday worship, yet this person chooses to come to church, he or she probably arrives in the pew with a high sense of commitment, spiritual curiosity, or both. That's the sort of people we have here, and that's the sort of person to whom the sermons in this book were directed.

As is typical of resort community congregations, Christ Church in Aspen experiences seasonal fluctuations in attendance. The church is full in the summer months, as people from southern climes flee triple-digit temperatures at home to find relief in the cool of Aspen's 7,900 foot elevation and low humidity. In August when it's 105 degrees in Houston or Birmingham, people are sleeping under blankets in Aspen.

Many of the people from other places who sojourn in Aspen and worship in Christ Church have acquired homes in the area. A significant number of them have become part of the congregation. Some are not Episcopalians, but Christ Church welcomes associate members from any church background, without trying to turn them into Episcopalians. People who are Presbyterians or Lutherans or Roman Catholics back home can be Episcopalians while they're here with us. The diversity they bring makes our life more interesting.

Tourists, visitors, and part-time members alike slowly start to drift away as autumn comes on, until by late October and November the town is empty and church services are populated only by permanent residents. We have two "mud seasons," October-November and April-May. These are times of the year when the priest can usually call everyone in church on Sunday by name. By Thanksgiving, the mountains and the valley alike are blanketed in snow and the ski slopes open for the new season. From that holiday straight through early April the town is bustling again with seasonal visitors, and numerous guests show up in church for Sunday services.

About these sermons

When I took a leave of absence from grad school to go to seminary in 1969, I intended only a brief detour from my pursuit of a doctorate and the credentials required to be a college teacher. I anticipated a lifetime of scholarship, teaching and research in some academic environment. The last thing I wanted to do was become a preacher—maybe an academic lecturer, but not a preacher. God's ways, however, are higher than our ways. So, from 1974 when I returned home from dissertation research in Britain until the present I have been engaged in full-time parish ministry in six different congregations, five in the USA and one overseas. Rather than being my bread and butter, academic pursuits have been more of a hobby for me, avocational and sporadic. Ministry to and with the people of God in local parish churches has been my life, and everywhere I have served, preaching has been the heart of my work.

I do not regard preaching as primarily an educational enterprise, although education might indeed be a by-product of preaching. I was raised as an evangelical protestant (a Presbyterian) in the middle years of the twentieth century, and I was taught very early that Scripture is a revelation of the Word of God. For me, preaching is an occasion for bringing that Word to bear on the circumstances of human life. I believe every sermon should at least in some way be a call to action. It needs to demand an active response: change of mind or change of life (usually both), deepened devotion to prayer, fresh commitment to service, renewed compassion for the marginalized, or a more generous and selfless way of living in the world.

My personal theology and devotion focus on the person of Jesus Christ. Understanding Jesus as God-with-us is what makes Christianity unique. If those who preach in the church do not "know him and make him known," then in my understanding of the mission of the church, they have failed. For better, for worse, I am a "Jesus person." There are very few sermons in this collection that do not, in some way, invite the hearers to know Christ.

This book brings together sixty-seven sermons from all the seasons of the Christian year. There are sermons for Epiphany, Ash Wednesday, Good Friday, Easter, Pentecost and Christmas as well as for Sundays. Mothers' Day and Fathers' Day are not part of the church calendar, but they are important to families in the church and sermons for those days are included, as well as for other occasions in ordinary parish life such as the Sunday nearest Independence Day. I was not trying to pick out a sermon for each Sunday in the church year, although every season is represented and, in some cases over-represented, since this book contains sixty rather than only fifty-two Sunday sermons.

Readers will discern some common themes in these sermons. A few thoughts and specific phrases recur, and this is not by accident. I believe that one of the ways a preacher can be most effective in a congregation that hears only him (or her) week after week is to practice consistency and circle back, year after year, to repeat key ideas in easily memorable, even aphoristic forms. In time, these pastoral maxims "take" and become engrafted into a congregation's collective understanding of God's will and God's ways.

The sermons in this book are published exactly as they were delivered. None has been edited to make it more applicable to a general audience. I consider this my own small way of participating in what students of Christology have called "the scandal of particularity." Those from different backgrounds can read words that were addressed to my own unique, small church here in the heart of the Rockies within the context of its congregational life and, I hope, extrapolate truths from those words that will apply in their own situations. All local references have been retained. For example, we radically remodeled and enlarged our physical facilities in 2008-9, and while our new building was under construction we held services in the historic Aspen Community United Methodist Church, erected in 1891. The pastor and congregation there made us feel very welcome. Sermons from that year can be easily identified by references to our host church or the building project.

I often feel inspired, and I know that is the work of the Holy Spirit, but I lay no claim to being a particularly original thinker. I tell people who compliment my preaching, "Thank you very much, but I doubt that I have ever had an original thought. Most of my ideas have come from somebody else, but I can't remember exactly which idea came from whom." This book of sermons is not a work of scholarly research; therefore, it omits citations of sources. But readers of the book are hereby warned that I read widely and borrow freely from many different sources in preparing sermons. If I find an apt story or good illustration somewhere I make use of it. When I quote someone directly I name the person sometimes, especially if the name is one that people in the congregation might recognize. But other times I just say, "I ran across this great quotation in my reading this week."

I think it's a sufficient disclaimer for me to acknowledge that the words I am speaking came from someone else. If I'm recounting a story to illustrate a point, I will usually say, "There's a story about . . ." When I borrow a story, I will almost always re-write it in my own style so that when I tell the story it sounds like me instead of someone else.

I have profound respect for the original thinkers, the distinguished preachers, theologians, and writers on spirituality from whom I have borrowed ideas or from whom I have quoted a sentence or two in these sermons. I am grateful for the insights and stories offered by such contemporary American preacher-writers as Frederick Buechner, William Willimon, John Ortberg, Barbara Brown Taylor, William Bausch, Fred Craddock, and Tony Campolo, online journalists like Tom Ehrich and Daniel Clendinin, and theologians such as N.T. Wright, Alan Jones, Parker Palmer, Richard Rohr, Thomas Merton, Henri Nouwen, and C.S. Lewis.

Finally, I want to acknowledge the unfailing love and help of my wife and ministry partner, Joan. A seminary-trained vocational deacon, Joan and I have had a joint ministry in every parish I have served since we were married in 1992. Mention of her appears in sermon after sermon. She read them all in rough form before they were first delivered from the pulpit and—without once being critical—she regularly gave me gentle hints on how to make them more effective, such as "Do you have to say it just that way?" Or "I think this point needs a story." And most often, "This is really long!" Joan is my best friend, copy editor, encourager, and most attentive listener. This volume is dedicated to the saints of God in Christ Church, Aspen, but the book exists at all because my beloved wife encouraged me to produce it and spent long hours helping with the most tedious aspects of the work.

—Bruce McNab, All Saints Day 2010

1. FOLLOW THE LIGHT.

The Feast of the Epiphany
Matthew 2:1-12

When I was a little kid, I used to go out in the mild southern night at this time of year and scan the skies, looking for the star of Bethlehem. I was sure it would look like the star on a Christmas card: hanging low in the sky, with rays streaming down from it towards the earth. I was smart enough to know that the star had shone a long time ago and had served its purpose, but I hoped that somehow, maybe, it would shine again—and I would get to see it. I would get to follow it.

We're all familiar with the song that goes, *"On the twelfth day of Christmas my true love gave to me twelve drummers drumming, eleven pipers piping, ten lords a-leaping, nine ladies dancing"* . . . etcetera. Well, today is the Twelfth Day of Christmas. In Merrie Olde England, Twelfth Night was an occasion for revelry the way New Year's Eve is today. It was party-time. The lords were really leaping and the ladies were really dancing. Epiphany itself was one of the great festivals of the Church. Nowadays, though, most people don't go to church on Epiphany—except every six years, when it falls on a Sunday. So the day doesn't get much attention.

The *magi*—the so-called Wise Men from the East—are the main actors in Matthew's Epiphany story. They weren't kings. That idea came from a medieval misunderstanding of the Bible. And there may have been three, or seven or any number. Matthew only says that they brought three kinds of gifts to give the Newborn King, but not how many there were who brought them. We know that the magi were astrologers, who saw significance in the conjunctions of certain planets in particular constellations in the night sky. They saw such a conjunction—a new star—in the sky and identified it as a sign from God, a sign that a new king had been born in Judea. So they came from their homes—which were probably in Persia—to Jerusalem. And they were sent from Jerusalem out to Bethlehem, where they found the baby Jesus and worshiped him, offering gifts of gold, frankincense, and myrrh. Then, the Bible says, when the time had come for them to return home, an angel warned them not to go back to see Herod again, but instead to go back to their homes "by another road."

I want to point out four things from the story of the Wise Men that I believe offer guidance for us in our time. *First:* THE WISE MEN WERE TEACHABLE; they were seekers. The magi were important people in their native land. Neighbors came to them to get help with personal problems and looked to them for direction in religion, business, and even romance. But although they were wise leaders and very learned, they were conscious that they didn't already "know it all." There was more to life and the mysteries of the universe than they already comprehended. When the new star appeared, there were no doubt others who saw it, but as far as we know only these few followed it. The Wise Men were brave enough to follow the new star. Truly wise people know when to lead and when to follow.

Humility is a virtue. Arrogance is a flaw. Nobody, *nobody* is so wise, experienced, or brilliant that he (or she) can't learn something new. The number one lesson for us from the Wise Men is *to stay teachable.* Jesus told his disciples that they needed to "become like little children." The universally true thing about little children is that they all have a lot to learn. So do we.

The story of the Wise Men also tells us that God has more to reveal than we've already seen. I'm a pretty conservative person myself, especially in matters of faith. I'm a student of history and I value tradition in the family, in the church, and in the nation. But I believe that what God said to the prophet Isaiah five hundred years before Christ is still valid today. God said, "Forget about what's happened; don't keep going over old history. Be alert, be present. I'm about to do something brand-new. It's bursting out! Don't you see it?" (*THE MESSAGE,* Isa. 43:18-19)

We want to have eyes to see the new things God is doing in our time and the wisdom to know the difference between new things *God* is doing and new things that are merely human novelties. The Wise Men in Matthew's story were learned men, but they were teachable too. They saw a new star and it told them that God was doing something new. They wanted to be part of it.

Here's the second aspect of this story that can guide us: THE WISE MEN FOLLOWED THE LIGHT. Jesus is the Light of the World. The main symbol of the Feast of the Epiphany is *light*. That's why we have all the candles down the church aisle this morning, just like we did on Christmas. When John wrote about the birth of Jesus in his gospel, he said, "The true light that enlightens everyone was coming into the world." At the end of this service, we're going to sing: "As with gladness men of old did the guiding star behold; as with joy they hailed its light, leading onward, beaming bright; so, most gracious Lord, may we evermore be led to thee." The light of the wonderful star guided the Wise Men to Jesus, and the light of Jesus is still shining in the dark night of our world, just as it has been shining since he was born in Bethlehem ages ago. The question is: *Where do we see his light shining today?* Like the Wise Men who found the newborn King not in Herod's palace but in a humble house in Bethlehem, so we have to be prepared to find the light of Christ shining in an unexpected place.

Where is the light of Christ shining for you? Look in the places you least expect. Is it in discovering contemplative prayer? Is it in giving yourself to serve the poor? Is it in a call to ordained ministry as a deacon or priest? Is it in loving people who have only been treated as outcasts, rejects, by society? Or, is it in the most unexpected place of all: right in your own home and your own family, where you spend most of your life? It's your job to discern where the light of Christ is shining for you, so keep your eyes open to see it.—It's there.

The third aspect of the story to think about is this: WHEN THE WISE MEN FOUND THE ONE WHO WAS THE OBJECT OF THEIR SEARCH, THEY WORSHIPED HIM. The Wise Men offered the newborn King gifts of gold, frankincense, and myrrh. These were mystical gifts which some people say were symbols of the office of the *magi*, elements essential to the rituals of their exotic priesthood. This kind of gift-giving tells us that when we come to Christ, the True Light, the object of our life-long search, the fundamental imperative for us is *worship*. Authentic worship, whatever shape it takes, is the recognition of God's ultimate value, God's worth. Our worship (and

I'm not just talking about what we do in church on Sunday)—if it really is worship—has to focus on giving Christ the most precious gifts we can offer: our true selves, our hearts and minds, our natural endowments and skills. True worship entails the offering of a sacrifice, a costly gift, joyfully given.

The final thing we learn from the Epiphany gospel is this: AFTER THE WISE MEN HAD FOUND CHRIST AND WORSHIPED HIM, THEY RETURNED TO THEIR HOMES "BY ANOTHER ROAD." If we're teachable, like the Wise Men were . . . If we, like them, are able to see the new thing that God is doing in our lives and in his world . . . If we come to Christ, the True Light, and offer our whole being to him in love . . . then *we're going to be changed.* Real worship always changes us. And if we're truly changed by our experience of Christ, then we're going to find ourselves taking "another road," a new road, a new way of moving forward with our lives. We're not going to be satisfied with things the way they used to be before we offered ourselves to Christ. We're not going to be content to stay in our comfortable rut, whatever it might have been—not if we have found him and truly worshiped him. We're going to "go back home by another road."

We'll go back to our jobs, our families and friends, and the occupations of daily life on a new and different path. This fresh path will vary somewhat for each of us. That's only natural. But our various personal paths will have this much in common: they will all be new to us, and on each of them the True Light of Christ will be shining to show the way forward. Follow that Light.

2. I'VE JUST GOT TO BE ME.

Matthew 3:13-17

Have you noticed that film-makers seem to have a fresh interest in the genre we usually call The Western? They haven't gone back to John Wayne-style formula flicks, but stories set in the Old West, like last year's *3:10 to Yuma,* or *Open Range* three years earlier (featuring Aspen's own Kevin Costner), have made a comeback. They tell a timeless human story with a theme going all the way back to the Greek classics: the hero's struggle to claim and live into his identity.

In these westerns, there always comes a scene where the peace-loving main character straps on his six-guns, saddles his horse, and gets ready to ride out to confront the bad guys. As he's about to mount up, his sweet wife comes out and throws her arms around him and begs him to save his life by staying home with her and the kids. But he tells her, "I couldn't hold my head up in this valley if I didn't go out there and face 'em. It's somethin' I have to do. I've just got to be me."

"I've just got to be me." Here's a question to think about: *When do you become who you are?* Or: *when in your life is it clear who you're meant to be and what you're meant to do?*

There's a wonderful time in childhood when we can play around with all kinds of possibilities. Our imaginations let us see ourselves in many different guises: as astronauts, scientists, athletes, explorers, or super-heroes with cool masks and capes. We have two grandsons up in Montana—aged nine and eleven—and they're pretty sure they're going to be professional freestyle skiers or pilots when they grow up. (Do kids ever fantasize about being CPAs or corporate trainers? Do you know any nine year-olds who have friends over to play lawyer and client?)

When kids get older they get serious about their life and their life's work—especially what they're going to do when they grow up. Of course, you know, the age of being grown up seems to be fairly flexible these days. I'm not sure it comes much earlier than 30. Sometimes we become adults, get graduate degrees, get married, have a career (maybe even a very successful career in a financial sense), but then one day we wake up to the fact that *we really don't know who we are*. We have a job, maybe even a well-paying job, but we don't have a deep sense of identity. That's what some people label the mid-life crisis.

If we're going to be spiritually whole, there's a basic need we all have: a need to know *who we are* (our identity) and understand *what we're meant to do* (our life purpose or mission). And I say "meant to do" very intentionally, because for most of us there are a variety of things we could do (or could have done when we were younger), different kinds of jobs or careers in which we could perform well. But what were we *meant to* do? What were we *created* to do? What's the essential purpose of our life here on earth? It's the classic religious question: *What am I here for?*

If life is meaningless, then every religion is a waste of time. But if every life has meaning, then religion is essential for every human being. Since Christmas, the Church has been offering us passages from the Bible that invite us to deal with these fundamental questions—*Who am I?* and *What am I meant to do?*—through reflection on how Jesus dealt with the same questions himself.

When Jesus at the age of thirty went down to the Jordan River where his cousin John was preaching and baptizing, I think he was doing what we do: he was struggling with the big questions of identity and purpose. This is sheer speculation on my part, but I believe Jesus had been wrestling with these questions for years, trying to make some sense out of his personal history and the stories that Mary and Joseph told him about his birth. What did it mean to him to be told that he was *the Son of The Most High*, as well as the son of Joseph the carpenter and his wife Mary? (What does it mean to you to be told that you're a "child of God"?)

Jesus clearly had a deep, inner relationship with God. He even called God his *Abba*—a word that means "dear Father." It's the same intimate name he'd used for Joseph, the name an affectionate Jewish child of the first century used in addressing his dad. But if God was Jesus' Father, what did that mean about Jesus' life-work, his purpose? In those days Jewish boys always took on their fathers' trade. If Jesus owned *God* as his Father, and not just Joseph, should he continue to be merely a village carpenter? Or was there something more for him, some higher calling, some larger purpose in life?

We don't know exactly what led Jesus to ask John to baptize him with his baptism of repentance for the forgiveness of sins, but I believe that decision was a key moment in Jesus' working out his answer to the big questions of identity and purpose: *Who am I?* And *what am I meant to do?*

Many different sorts of people were going to John for baptism, repenting of their sins and promising to lead a new life. I think there came a moment when Jesus said to himself, as he stood watching the crowds of ordinary people—tradesmen and farmers and housewives and soldiers—coming down to the water confessing their sins and asking God's forgiveness, "These are my Abba's people. If they're his people, then they're my people. My life's work must be for them."

Jesus was a righteous man, but he chose to identify with sinners and outcasts; therefore, he plunged into the waters of the Jordan as a sign of his new self-understanding. It was a fundamental decision about his identity and purpose, a commitment he made in faith and love for God. In a sense, Jesus got baptized in order to take upon himself the burden of sin that the others were laying down. He went into the water and *took on* what the others had washed off. That's why John later pointed to him and said to bystanders, "Look! There's the Lamb of God who takes away the sins of the world."

I believe that for many years Jesus had been praying, "Father, show me what you want me to do." I think he went into the water and let John baptize him because he felt God prompting him to do it right at that moment. When he had been baptized and was coming up from the river, Matthew tells us the heavens opened, and as the Spirit of God descended on him as a dove, the voice of his Father, his Abba, spoke to everyone: "This is my Son, my Beloved, with whom I am well pleased." Jesus' struggle with the questions of identity and purpose had reached its turning point, its moment of resolution. His prayers had been answered. Finally he owned the truth of who he was and what he was meant to do.

All of us need *affirmation* and *reassurance*. We need someone very important to us, someone very powerful in our lives, to say "I believe in you. You're on the right track. Just keep going. You make me very happy." The Voice of God came to Jesus at the moment he needed to hear it the most. And this Divine affirmation launched him on his mission as the Lamb of God who takes away the sin of the world.

All of us wrestle with the need to be recognized, validated, and told that we're significant. But our lives have shown us that the recognition we seek from others can quickly be withdrawn. One day we're popular; the next day we're ignored. One day we're the hero; the next day we're the goat.

A sense of our true identity and purpose demands grounding deep within—in the depths of our souls, where the Voice of God speaks. It demands an understanding of the life of Christ as the pattern for our own being. This enables us to claim our identity, discover our own True Self, and grasp the purpose of our existence—despite even the well-intentioned pleas of people who love us, but want to save us from ourselves, like the sweetheart of our western movie hero, or—in the gospel—Jesus' Mother, who begged him to come back home to Nazareth and not get himself in trouble with powerful and important people.

The Voice of God spoke to Jesus and the Spirit of God rested on Jesus. That Voice and that Spirit still come to those who are in love with God and ask, "Who am I, Father? . . . What is my life all about?"

The One who spoke to Jesus will speak to us, if we love him enough to ask him our questions and trust him enough to wait for his answer.

3. BY FAITH WE UNDERSTAND.

Hebrews 11:1-2

I want to show you something. Here's a Bible. *This* much of it is what we call the Old Testament, the Hebrew Bible, the Bible of Jesus and Peter and Paul and the first Christians. The most important human character in *this* Bible is the man called Abraham. Three great religious communities—Jews, Christians, and Muslims—revere Abraham as their primary spiritual ancestor. Did you know that? Christians take Abraham as the example of what we mean when we talk about *faith*.

As the story goes, Abraham was born and lived for the first part of his life in a place called Ur, one of the oldest cities we know about. We don't know what Abraham did for a living there, but he seems to have been a city boy, not a country boy. Maybe he was a gentleman farmer, or a merchant, or a potter, or a banker, or a camel trader. Nobody knows. We *do* know from the Bible that he had an elderly father named Terah, a wife named Sarah, and a nephew named Lot who lived with them because his father, Abraham's brother, had died. But Abraham and Sarah had no children of their own.

One day Abraham had an experience unlike any he'd ever had before. He heard God speaking to him. We don't know how Abraham heard God, but the Bible tells us what he heard God saying: "Leave this place, your family and your father's house, and go to the land which I am going to show you. And I will give you that land to be a heritage for you, and I will make you a great nation. Your descendants will be as numerous as the sands of the seashore or the stars of the sky. I will bless you to be a blessing, and by you shall all of the nations of the earth bless themselves."

In the part of the Letter to the Hebrews that we read today, it says "By faith, Abraham obeyed . . . and he set out, not knowing where he was going." Notice this: "by *faith*, Abraham obeyed."—Not by logic, not by social pressure, not by force, not by any other inducements, but by *faith*. By faith, Abraham the city boy became a tent-dwelling nomad for the rest of his life—entirely in response to the Voice of God—departing on a journey with no established destination.

Abraham just packed up and left town. I wonder what the neighbors said. What did they think when Abraham left his historic, family home and his established business, and took off? And what do you suppose he said to them? It's not an everyday event for any of us to tell our friends, "I'm moving away because God told me to. Yes, that's right; GOD spoke to me. God told me to pack up and go to, uh . . . somewhere. Somewhere. To a place he's going to show me when I get there."

For those of you with a nice home here in Aspen or anyplace else, what would your friends think if you told them you were selling your house and buying a Winnebago so you could be free to go wherever God told you whenever God had a mind to tell you to move on?—Most people we know would be pretty skeptical if a practical, mentally stable neighbor not only said that he'd heard God, (which, by itself is very out of the ordinary), but that God told him to sell his house, close down his office, liquidate his assets, pack up his family, and travel to some destination to be named later.

The Bible says that by faith Abraham obeyed God. But it was a long time before he got to the place God had promised—a *really* long time. However, not only had God promised Abraham a land, he'd also promised him an heir, a son. He'd promised to make him "the father of a great nation." Abraham and Sarah were childless, and by the time they got to the Promised Land, they were very old . . . far beyond the normal age of becoming parents. But when Abraham was a hundred years old and Sarah was not much younger, the Child of the Promise arrived.—Living in faith includes *waiting* in faith. People of faith learn to be patient.

Abraham truly is the great hero of the Bible, and not just the Old Testament. The New Testament points to him as the perfect example of faith and obedience. *Faith and obedience.* Those two go hand-in-hand.

Please hear this: *There's a message for you and me in the story of Abraham.* And the message is about the life journey you're on. You can go your own way, or you can go God's way. You can make your own plans, or you can follow God's plans. You can trust your own wisdom, or you can rely on the wisdom of God. You and I have a choice. We always have a choice.

Abraham had a choice too. When God spoke to him, Abraham could have said, "This is nuts. It's just a dream. There can't be anything to this. Why on earth should I leave behind everything I have to follow a dream?"—But Abraham believed what God said, and he acted. He believed God, and he obeyed God. He had faith. He was a city fellow, but when God said so he became a tent-dwelling nomad. You might say he sold his house on Red Mountain, bought a motor home, and hit the road—for the rest of his life. Now *that's* obedience.

Faith is a decision. It's a choice. I have said this before and you'll hear me say it again because it bears repeating: *the opposite of faith isn't doubt; it's certainty.* As the Bible tells us today, "Faith is the assurance of things hoped for, the conviction of things not seen." Abraham heard God calling him to set out on the road to an unknown destination. He had no GPS. He had no map. There were no road signs. Travel directions would be supplied by God on an as-needed basis. Did Abraham worry? Did he have doubts? You bet. Lots of doubts. (Just read Genesis. But doubt can be the midwife of faith.)—By faith, Abraham spent a lifetime on the road.

So, what is God's call to us? Is God saying something to you and me about where he wants us to go with our lives? God is speaking to us. Are we listening? Jesus has given voice to God's call to you and me. And this is what he's said: "Follow me. Follow *me.*"

Jesus came to Peter and Andrew as they were casting their nets in the Sea of Galilee, and he said, *"Follow me."* He came to James and John, who were in the boat with their father, and he said, *"Follow me."* He came to Matthew the tax collector, sitting at his desk, and he said, *"Follow me."* They didn't ask him, "Where are you going?" They just dropped everything and went with him.

The first disciples learned the lesson of Abraham. On the way . . . through a lifetime . . . Peter and Andrew and James and John and Matthew and the others learned what the journey was about. They learned to live in faith and hope—just like Abraham. They learned the law and the language of the Kingdom of God along the road, on the journey, following Jesus. And that's what God is calling us to do. That's what God is calling our church to do: *discover the meaning of the Kingdom of God as we follow Jesus.*

A sermon needs to be at least a little bit practical, so I'll try. In practice, what do you think it means to follow Jesus? I don't think it's mainly about Sunday church attendance. That's very good, but it's not the main thing.

Following Jesus is not mainly about religious practices. Rather, it's about believing Jesus, trusting Jesus, obeying Jesus—pondering his words, patterning your life according to his example, yielding yourself to his Spirit, and expecting that *as you do this*—step by step, day-by-day—one day you'll wake up and realize that you've crossed the frontier and you're living in the Kingdom of God.—But you weren't aware of exactly when that cross-over from the kingdom of this world to the Kingdom of God happened.

This is a process. God is calling you to discover what the Kingdom of God is AS you follow Jesus. Do you remember Jesus' first words in the gospel lesson this morning? "Fear not, little flock, it is your Father's good pleasure to *give* you the Kingdom." The Kingdom is God's gift to us, but we don't know exactly when we're going to receive it. We don't know exactly when we're going to enter it. We just keep believing and keep moving on.

Here's the point of this sermon, and you've probably guessed it already. *It's in the journey itself that you find the destination.* It's in believing God, staying on the road with Jesus, moving on, moving on, that you discover, all of a sudden—even while you still feel like a homeless nomad—that you've crossed an invisible frontier and entered the Kingdom of God. You entered the inheritance God promised you long ago, and you didn't even know when it happened.

You're in the Promised Land—regardless of where you might be on a map of the world. But you can only *live* in the Kingdom of God if you keep moving on, trusting God to give you directions for the next day's journey.

Faith is the assurance of what we hope for, the conviction of what we can't yet see.

4. WINE FOR THE WEDDING.

John 2:1-11

Christians have an undeserved reputation in some circles for being party-poopers. No fun. Wet blankets. Killjoys. Prudes. Some of you have probably had to deal, at some time, with secular friends wondering why you would want to be a part of a movement which they think discourages its members from enjoying life. I hope you directed them to the gospel for this morning, because it's a simple lesson on the joy of believing.

Today's gospel is about a wedding. Weddings are supposed to be happy occasions—for lots of different reasons. They're meant to be a celebration for the couple getting married, joyful for their families, and a party for their friends. Clergy go to more weddings than anybody else except event planners and caterers. But the happiest, most joyful wedding I ever participated in wasn't a Christian wedding. It was a Jewish wedding, the only one I've ever been invited to. It was held at the Queens Jewish Center in Forest Hills, New York, when I was a seminarian—back around 1970. A good friend from graduate school was getting married.

My friend's family was from Israel, though he had been born in Ithaca, where his father was a distinguished professor at Cornell. The bride was from Queens. Both families were serious about their religion, and the marriage rite was very conservative—all in Hebrew. And the wedding party was traditional too. (Wow, the Jews have great traditions!) The service was at noon and the party began by 2:00 in the afternoon and lasted until late, late. They provided an incredible quantity of food and drink and a live orchestra. There was lots of dancing—both the conventional kind and the

Israeli type, where men and women dance separately in circles with lots of clapping and high kicks, like in *Fiddler on the Roof.* It was fun, especially for gentiles like me who'd never seen anything like it before.

When Jesus and his disciples were invited to a wedding in the tiny village of Cana in Galilee, a kind of suburb of Nazareth, they took part in an occasion which was a prototype for the kind of wedding I attended. But in Jesus' day, if there was a wedding, everybody in the village was invited—as well as family members from all around. Nobody was excluded. And the festivities didn't just last a day, they lasted a week. It was held in the home of the bridegroom, and the groom's family put on the party. Every day there would be more food and drink and dancing—lots of food, and lots of drink. And they didn't drink Fiji water, either. The rabbis said, "Where there is no wine, there is no joy." These people were mostly poor, and for many of the poor the only times in the year when they had meat to eat or wine to drink was at Passover and weddings.

In fact—and the New Testament demonstrates this in a number of places—the wedding feast came to be a metaphor for life in heaven. The age to come, life in the Kingdom of God, was going to be like an everlasting marriage party, because that was the most fun anybody could think of. The redeemed were not going to sit on clouds and play harps. That would be boring.—They were going to eat and drink and have a joyful time together. (Hang on to that image.)

O.K., have I set the stage well enough for you to understand what was going on when Jesus' mother took him aside from the other guests and told him, "They're out of wine"? If the wine was gone, *this* party would be over. The joy would evaporate. Perhaps this was the marriage of one of Jesus' cousins, so his mother couldn't stand aside and let her family be embarrassed by not having provided enough wine to last the full week. So she did what came naturally; she told Jesus. Notice that she didn't ask him to do anything in particular. She didn't say, "Why don't you hop on a donkey and ride over to Nazareth and come back with a few skins of wine." She just said, "There's no more wine."

It's hard to translate Jesus' answer into contemporary English. The best version would be something like, "Is that any of our business, Mother—yours or mine? This isn't my time. Don't push me." But she went ahead anyway, and told the servants, "Whatever he tells you, do it." (This is good advice for us too.)

We all know what Jesus did. There were six over-sized stoneware jars set into the ground in the courtyard. An archaeologist would call them *amphorae.* They provided water for the rituals of purification customary in an observant, pharisaical household. (And their presence shows that the bridegroom's family kept the Law of Moses strictly.) Jesus told the servants to fill these *amphorae* to the brim with water. They'd have had to make many trips to the well, because the six jars may have held as much as 180 gallons. Then he told them to take a dipper of the water to the steward of the feast. When he tasted it, it was no longer water, but wine—and better wine than had yet been served. The bridegroom had obviously done the unexpected. He had saved the best vintage for last.—That's a sign of what we Christians call grace.

Near the end of a whole week of celebration, Jesus provided nearly-sated guests with 180 gallons of Dom Pérignon, and the wedding party gained new life. Their joy was complete. And nobody knew what had happened except Jesus' mother, the house-servants, and his disciples. Later on in the gospel of John it says, "Jesus did many signs in the presence of his disciples." But the first sign of all was this one: providing wine for the wedding. It manifested his glory, and his disciples believed in him.

Think what would have happened if Jesus had not intervened. The wedding celebration would have been cut short, and the villagers would have gone home and gossiped for months about the fiasco. The bride and groom and their family were poor people, but they would have been humiliated, the depth of their poverty exposed to everyone. They had tried to throw a good party, and failed. They couldn't even afford enough wine for a wedding.—But Jesus was there, and as John says, *"from his fullness have we all received, grace upon grace."* He met their need, but he didn't draw attention to his role in providing this abundance of good wine. He stayed in the background. Only a handful of people knew the truth; everyone else gave credit to the bridegroom. But this is how God does things; most of the beneficiaries of his grace are unaware of what's going on. We rarely even know enough to say thank you.

A reason I find John's gospel so attractive is that it discloses—in one episode after another—the overflowing love of God, who delights in providing for his children. Matthew, Mark and Luke begin Jesus' ministry with his preaching, saying *"The Kingdom of God is near."* And, surely, he did preach that message. But John shows Jesus beginning his earthly ministry not with a sermon, but by attending a wedding party and providing a wonderful gift—wine for the wedding—a sign of the joyful nature of the Kingdom of God, as well as its arrival. The wedding feast at Cana was a foretaste of heaven, a sign to those with eyes to see and hearts ready to believe in the grace of God. Later in John Jesus says, "I have come so that they might have life, more and better life than they ever dreamed of."

Christians are not party-poopers, wet blankets, or kill-joys. Neither are we tight-fisted. God never meant his Church to be a community of unsmiling faces, stingy dispositions, and no fun. Jesus shows that life among the saints is intended to be full of gladness, delight, and abundance—yes, laughter, wine, and dance music, where a good time is had by all—but also an open-handed, generous, gracious outreach to the world to which God has sent us, especially to the sad, the lonely, the poor and hungry, and those whose lives are empty.

At Cana, Jesus gave a sign: he is with us. His glory and unselfish grace are ours to give away.

5. DISCIPLES NEED DISCIPLINE.

Hebrews 12:1-7, 11-14

There are certain simple phrases or expressions that quickly evoke in us definite thoughts or feelings. For example, if somebody says "warm chocolate chip cookies," you might feel like you'd like to have one right now. (I would.) But if somebody says "tax audit," we'd all probably have instant acid stomach. If I say, "tell me about your Grandma," many of you will have a quick, sweet twinge of nostalgia and maybe feel all warm and happy from the memories.

Let's try another phrase. How would it feel if somebody pointed to you and said, "You need to have some discipline"? Unless you're a Navy Seal or an endurance athlete, when you hear anyone talk about discipline your gut ties in a knot. You tense up. You cringe. *Discipline* is not a feel-good word for most of us. Discipline has all the appeal of a five-day fast. Discipline sounds like punishment: unpleasant, unattractive—and probably painful. Oh, yeah, we all know that discipline is good for us, but so is broccoli. So is plain yogurt. But we'd rather have a Big Mac and a large order of fries—with a chocolate shake. (And you can supersize that.)

I've enjoyed more than my share of chocolate chip cookies over the last few decades, but for a number of years back when I was a skinny guy, I was a runner. I was never good enough to be in the elite group, but I got out there and ran with the pack. One time I won a red ribbon for placing third in the men 35-to-40 age group. That was my one big achievement. (Of course, I think there were only six or seven other guys in my age group.) The rest of the time I was just an also-ran and collected a t-shirt at the finish line.

Truth is, I never would have even bought myself a pair of running shoes if it hadn't been for a friend in college named John who once dragged me out to the college track and alternately either pulled me along by the arm or pushed me from behind to get me through just four laps, one mile. He was a scrappy little guy about two-thirds my size, but he had discipline and commitment, and he believed I could be like that, too, if he could just inspire me. Later on he dropped out of college, enlisted in the Marine Corps and went to serve in Vietnam where he became a master sergeant, so you can guess what kind of person he was.

That brings me to what we can learn from the Bible today. We don't really know who wrote the Epistle to the Hebrews. But whoever the author was, he was clearly an athlete, probably a runner. He knew the value of discipline, commitment, and endurance. And he offers Jesus as an example of those virtues to his readers, to inspire them.

Hebrews gives us a roll call of the heroes and heroines of faith. The author lists one after another, starting with Abel, Enoch and Noah, then going on with Abraham and Sarah, Isaac, Jacob, Joseph, Moses, Rahab, Gideon, Barak, Samson, Jephthah, David, Samuel and the prophets—all of whom endured hardships, achieved great things and won strength out of weakness *through faith.*

He paints a word-picture of those famous men and women of faith assembled the way runners are who have finished a punishing race but stay at the finish line to cheer each successive competitor who makes it all the way. He says, "Since we are surrounded by so great a cloud of witnesses, let us also lay aside every weight and the sin that clings so closely, and let us run with perseverance the race that is set before us, looking to Jesus the pioneer and perfecter of our faith, who for the sake of the joy that was set before him endured the cross, disregarding its shame, and has taken his seat at the right hand of the throne of God."

Today the Bible invites us to answer the question, *"What are you living for?"* I hope it's not just for pleasure, or creature comforts, or personal security, or prescription drug benefits when we retire. Each of us has a race to run, a course to finish. There *is* a glorious goal to the life God has given us. There's an end, a purpose, an ultimate point to it all. Don't be misled by the nihilists and the atheists and the materialists who see no meaning to human existence. They're the ones who coined the expression, "Life is hard and then you die."—What a lousy outlook that is.

Today we're told to keep our eyes on Jesus—who kept the faith, who ran the race, who endured the cross, and who tells us, "In the world you will have troubles. But take courage. I have overcome the world."

In "the race that is set before us"—our great life work, the personal mission that's given to each of us (and, yes, I said each of us, bar none)—God will judge us at the finish line not by our quantifiable achievements, not by our ribbons or trophies or monuments, but by our *faithfulness.* By our sticking with it. We can't compare ourselves to other people. They have their races; we have ours. They have their possibilities; we have ours. They have their challenges; we have ours.

As disciples of Jesus Christ we're participants in what the author of Hebrews calls a great *agōn*—the Greek word for a painful struggle or a strenuous contest. From it comes our word *agony,* which is what even a tough, trained athlete feels coming down to the finish line—lungs burning and legs aching with every step. We are followers of the Christ, and we need to accept his disciplines for disciples, or we'll never finish our race. Jesus is the "pioneer and perfecter of our faith."

That means he's the one who has gone before us to break the trail we're now running on, and he's following behind us to keep us on it. He's like my college buddy who took my hand and pulled me around the track, or got behind me and pushed me along to keep me moving. He's the one whose life gives us the perfect example of faith, courage, perseverance, patience and discipline.

About ten years ago, I noticed that quite a few high schoolers in my youth confirmation class were wearing W.W.J.D. bracelets. (In case you don't know, W.W.J.D. means "What Would Jesus Do?") I told them I was proud of them for wearing those bracelets, especially considering the anti-religious attitudes that can show up in some schools. But I said to them, "A better question for you to ask yourself is *'What does Jesus want* ME *to do?'* We can speculate about what Jesus might do if he were here in the flesh right now. He might well do something we couldn't do. But what would Jesus want *you* to do right now, in whatever situation you're facing? That's the decision you have to make as a believer."

The author of Hebrews doesn't picture the Christian life as a cake-walk. He doesn't see it as sweet and easy. It's not just a matter of coming to church and bringing some canned goods for Loaves and Fishes Sunday or donating money to the capital campaign. The Christian life is an *agōn*. It's a wonderful, great and sacred enterprise—but it's also a struggle. It isn't easy; it's demanding. And Jesus expects us to get in shape for the race. Prepare for it. Train for it. Get tough. "Lay aside every weight and the sin that clings so closely."

So let's lay off the spiritual Twinkies and drop some weight. Let's discipline ourselves to fill up on the Bread of Life first thing every morning by prayer and reflection on God's Word. (It's amazing how many Christians have no disciplined life of prayer.) Let's decide right now to do whatever it takes to get ourselves spiritually healthy.

The "sin that clings so closely" is the kind we won't admit to—usually because we're taking so much pleasure in it. Jesus, the one who broke the trail for us to follow is always going to be there to take our hand and lift us up when we fall, to coach us, inspire us, and cheer for us. He's going to point out our own personal, private "sin that clings so closely," if we're teachable and willing to cooperate with him. He'll point it out, and he'll cleanse us of it too—if we'll let him.

The long-distance runner who wrote Hebrews said: "Endure trials for the sake of discipline. God is treating you as children; for what child is there whom a parent does not discipline. Now, discipline always seems painful rather than pleasant at the time, but later it yields the peaceful fruit of righteousness to those who have been trained by it."

Only parents who really love their children are willing to discipline them. Every good child psychologist will tell you the same thing. Discipline isn't a dirty word; it's a *healthy* word. As a disciple of Jesus, you need to embrace the *disciplines* that go along with being a disciple—the disciplines that will enable you to stay the course and run your race. If you're running with Jesus as your guide and your coach—looking to him, trusting in him, setting your goal to be as much like him as you can be—you'll keep running all the way to this life's end. And you'll cross the finish line in faith, while all the heavenly cloud of witnesses stand around and cheer. Keep running.

6. WHAT'S A *BLESSING*, ANYWAY?

Luke 6:17-26

"**J**esus looked up at his disciples and said,
Blessed are you who are poor, for yours is the Kingdom of God . . .
But woe to you who are rich, for you have received your consolation."

I'm surprised there's not a little sticky note in the margin of my lectionary that says, "Preach on something else.—This is not a suitable text for Aspen."

"Blessed are you who are poor, but woe to you who are rich. "—This makes it seem like it's good to be poor and bad to be rich. I bet if you went into any poverty-stricken neighborhood in any big city in America—like Denver, L.A., Chicago, Detroit, or Miami—and asked people on the street if they thought it was a good thing to be poor and a bad thing to be rich, nobody would say, "Man, it's great to be poor. I am *so* happy. We're so lucky to be on welfare, with no health insurance, living in a rat-trap walk-up apartment. I'd be really bummed if we had to live in a big house and waste all our time having fun and eating in four-star restaurants."

"Blessed are you who are poor . . . Woe to you who are rich. " Jesus did say that.—What was his point? Let's try to understand him this morning, because there's more wisdom here than we're able to grasp right away. (And we need to take not that, according to Luke, the "poor" and the "rich" he was addressing were all *disciples,* that means they were people like us.)

First off, it's really important for us to be *thankful.* Complaining about what we want or need, but don't have, comes a lot more naturally to most of us than giving thanks to God for what we already have.

It's a spiritual commonplace that we ought to count our blessings. But these sayings of Jesus that we read from Luke's gospel today raise a very serious question: Are we able to recognize a real *blessing* when we see one?

First off, notice that Jesus is speaking to his disciples here. He isn't addressing an assortment of people, some of whom were disciples and others of whom were critics or skeptics or naysayers. The audience was composed of people who were disciples, people who had decided to follow Jesus. He spoke to them very personally and very directly, in the second person plural:

"Blessed are you poor . . .
Blessed are you that hunger now . . .
Blessed are you that weep now . . .
Blessed are you when people hate you on account of the Son of Man . . ."

Neither the poor people nor the rich people Jesus was talking to regarded poverty as a blessing. Not any more than we do. . . . Nor hunger.—Of course, for people like me who are carrying a few more pounds around the midsection than are good for us, it *might* be a blessing to go hungry. But when I see a Sudanese baby with the symptoms of severe malnutrition, I don't think of that child's hunger as any kind of blessing.

But maybe Jesus was (and *is*) trying to teach his disciples (then and now) something about what a blessing really is. Usually, I look at our nice new car, this comfortable house the church provides for us to live in, and I say, "We're blessed." I look around at this beautiful place in the heart of the Rockies and at you lovely people in this congregation, and I say, "We're blessed."

Then we go down to Denver and drive through some of the seedy neighborhoods there—like no place in Aspen—where bars cover the windows of old, run-down houses and where the evidence of poverty and deprivation are easy to see, and I think, "These people *need* to be blessed." I'm prosperous and comfortable. They're unemployed and UN-comfortable. So, I'm blessed, and they're *not*.—Right?

Jesus would say, "Not so easy. Think again. . . . Blessed are you poor, for yours in the Kingdom of God. . . . But woe to you that are rich, for you have received your consolation."

Jesus is trying to get his disciples to *think* here. This is wisdom, not social commentary. The word our Bibles usually translate "blessed" is a Greek word that means "happy"—or even "lucky." The *wisdom* in Jesus' saying, the theological point of this, is found here: "Lucky" people, "happy" people are the ones who trust in God, who look to God for their needs to be met, who know—deep in their hearts—that the future is in God's hands, not theirs.

When we Christians (we who might rightly claim to be disciples of Jesus Christ) have things—money, investments, lots of real estate, plenty of toys—we may call these goodies "blessings" and we may say that we really put our trust in God, but in every one of the tests of trust that life brings our way, we are (by reflex) inclined to rely not on God, but on the personal power that comes from affluence. We're hard-wired, you might say, in every time of crisis to put our confidence in ourselves and our material resources, to rely first of all and most of all on what St. Paul (and the prophet Jeremiah, too) would have called "the flesh," rather than on the Spirit. Our reflex is to put our trust in what we can control, rather than in God—who is always *beyond* our control.

But: having an easy, readily available, socially acceptable alternative to God is *not*—in fact—a blessing.—Not, at least, in the eyes of Jesus. (Don't you think that it's wonderfully, deliciously ironic that every coin, every banknote in this country has the words "In God We Trust" stamped on it?)

Jesus wants us—his disciples—to rethink what blessings are, and re-assess what things in life are *means* towards the *end* of a deeper, fuller, more truly God-centered life—a life that's rooted in love for God, love for neighbor, and even love for enemies. All love is a risk. All love demands a leap of faith. Such a risk-taking, loving life is the life of those whose trust is not in their personal resources (whether material or social), but in the God who promised "If you seek me, you shall surely find me, if you seek me with all your heart." Jesus said, "Where your treasure is, there your heart will be also." The challenge is for us to decide what really constitutes our "treasure."

For example: Some good, fiscally conservative, prudent managers might look at the Christ Church budget for 2004, see that it includes about a $20,000 deficit, and begin to worry. In Jesus' way of wisdom, that deficit is not a cause for worry. It's a blessing—*if* it turns our hearts to God, "from whom all blessings flow."

Here's a definition for you. If you don't remember anything else I've said this morning, hang on to this: *Blessings are the experiences in life that toss us into the arms of God, that throw us back upon our need for him. Anything that draws us to God, that causes us to depend on God, is a* blessing. (And anything that does the opposite is a curse.)

We're blessed when we don't have a glib answer to the hard questions, and we have to seek the face of God. We're blessed when we don't have the power to save ourselves or our loved ones, and we have to seek the mercy of God.

Blessings are the experiences in life that force us to say, and truly mean what we say: "There's nothing we can do but pray." When that happens, we're living in the Kingdom of God. And that's the greatest blessing of all.

7. NOTHING IS AS WONDERFUL AS KNOWING CHRIST.

Annual Parish Meeting
Philippians 3:7-11

Since this is the day of our Annual Parish Meeting, I want to share some thoughts about our past and some hopes for our future. Last October, when we were beginning our annual stewardship appeal, I wrote that one of the best ways to understand the Christian life is to see it as an *adventure in faith*—like walking a steep trail up a mountain, led by Jesus. When the Lord called his first disciples—as we talked about last Sunday—he didn't interview them in advance, and he didn't ask them for any commitment up front. Neither did he tell them where he'd be leading them. He just said, "Follow me and I will make you fish for people."

Much later, Jesus made clear to them that continuing to follow him was going to require willingness to put their personal ambitions aside, take up crosses like the one he was about to bear, and keep on walking in his footsteps. But by that time, the little band of his closest disciples had come to love Jesus so much and trust him so completely that they'd have paid any price to stay with him and share his destiny.

From that day to this, Jesus hasn't changed. And I don't think he expects any less of disciples now than he did in the beginning. Maybe we can learn something from Paul. When he met Christ on the Damascus road, Paul was on the fast-track to power and influence in Judea. He was a student of one of the greatest rabbis of his time. He had a brilliant future ahead of him. But he gave all that up—just to follow Jesus, just to be "on the upward way" with him, living the adventure of faith. Paul wrote these words to the little church in Philippi, people to whom he apparently opened his heart more fully than to anyone else: "Christ has shown me that what I once thought was valuable is worthless. Nothing is as wonderful as knowing Christ Jesus my Lord . . . All I want is Christ and to know that I belong to him . . . [So, then] I press on toward the goal for the prize of the heavenly call of God in Christ Jesus. Let those of us then who are mature be of the same mind; and if you think differently about anything, this too God will reveal to you. Only let us hold fast to what we have attained."

I want to use Paul's words as a guide for us today, but I'm going to start at the end, with his closing sentence, "Let us hold fast to what we have attained." By the grace of God some good things happened among us during 2005. We grew, both in full-time resident members and in part-time folks who count Christ Church as their Aspen church home. We had a fifteen per-cent increase in Sunday attendance. Financial support for the church exceeded anything in our history. And—as a part of that—we passed along to others, both nearby and far away, the highest level of charitable outreach giving anybody can remember.

We started the year by raising a lot of money to build homes for people in southern Thailand who'd lost everything in the tsunami. We collected a record amount of food and money to help hungry and homeless people in our own valley through Feed My Sheep. We adopted more needy families through Holiday Baskets this Christmas than ever before. We partnered with other churches to help the devastated Episcopal Church and community in Bay St. Louis, MS, a town where most families lost their homes to hurricane Katrina. And we're committed to helping them straight through 2006 because there's a lot left to do down there. In addition to these special undertakings, we doubled our regular charitable outreach budget. When Jesus began his ministry, he repeated the words of Isaiah, "The Spirit of the Lord is upon me, because he has anointed me to bring good news to the poor." If through our charitable giving in 2006 we can continue bringing good news to the poor, then we'll be following in the Lord's footsteps.

On the home front: if we plunge into the ambitious task of remodeling or rebuilding our church in the years ahead—a project that seems more necessary with every day that passes—we're going to need to keep up or even exceed the high standard of stewardship that we set in 2005. So, as Paul said, *"Let us hold fast to what we have attained."*

I started with his final words, now I want to wrap things up with the first words Paul wrote in the passage I quoted: "Christ has shown me that what I once thought was valuable is worthless. Nothing is as wonderful as knowing Christ Jesus my Lord." Here's the challenge for us. How many of us could say the same thing: "Christ has shown me that what I once thought was valuable is worthless"? That requires a revolution in our thinking, a transformation of our minds.

I love it that our congregation is named Christ Church. I love that name because Christianity doesn't have anything unique to offer the world *except* Jesus Christ. There's a sad tendency in some mainstream churches to be uncomfortable with the Christ of the gospels. But when we get uncomfortable with Jesus it's generally because he's challenging our complacency and our easy, relaxed, anything-goes-as-long-as-we're-all-just-nice brand of relativism.

If we're to be the church the Lord wants, there has to be a deep, personal conversion to Christ in the heart of each of us. How wonderful if we all came to the point where we could honestly make Paul's words our own: "Christ has shown me that what I once thought was valuable is worthless. *Nothing is as wonderful as knowing Christ Jesus my Lord."*—I can stand up here and preach this every Sunday, but only the Holy Spirit can make the words go from our heads to our hearts.

I'm convinced that Jesus is God's answer to the world's needs. He's the Way, the Truth, and the Life. He is Lord, whether other people choose to recognize it or not.—I'm talking about *Jesus* here, not about a specific theological system or a particular denomination within world Christianity. I'm talking about Jesus, the carpenter, the Son of God.

We all know very well that it's much easier to be good church members than to be good disciples of Christ. But in 2006 I want us to move from just being church members to being *disciples*. What will it take to get this transformation going? I suppose there are a variety of things that could kick-start it, but I only want to name two this morning, two things that fall within the realm of the possible for us in 2006.

First, we have to DECIDE TO BE SERIOUS ABOUT WORSHIP. Worshiping the Lord on Sunday is not just an option for disciples. It's an expectation. Worship re-sets our spiritual compass, re-orients our minds, and re-focuses our attention on God and God's will for our lives. Worship reminds us of what has *true* value. Without solid commitment to worshiping God every Sunday in the Church, it's easy to slide into spiritual indifference.—And when I say "worship," I'm not just talking about taking up pew space. And I'm not talking about coming to church mainly to hear a sermon (as flattering as that might be to the preacher). I'm talking about "offering ourselves, our souls and bodies, as a reasonable holy and living sacrifice" to the Lord. I'm talking about coming before God every Sunday morning to report for orders, asking, "Lord, what do you want me to do this week?"—and expecting to hear an answer.

Second, we have to DECIDE TO BE COMMITTED TO ONE ANOTHER. As I said last Sunday, being a disciple of Christ "means living with Jesus day-by-day, and living with Jesus really means living with each other day-by-day, because *we* are the Body of Christ. The Christian life is not about 'Jesus and me.' It's about 'Jesus and US.'" Our mission statement is CHRIST CHURCH: SHARING HIS LOVE. Sharing Christ's love has to begin with one another in the Church. It's not that the Lord doesn't want us to reach out in love to our neighbors, whether they're Christians or non-believers. We know he does. But if we can't love our brothers and sisters in Christ, it's unlikely we'll ever love our neighbors and it's a virtual certainty that we'll never learn how to love our enemies.

Authentic commitment to one another demands that we *know* one another—not superficially, like people who only see each other at parties, but deeply, as people who pray together, work together, and share their lives with one another—good times and bad times, joys and sorrows alike.

Today we're holding our Annual Meeting and moving into 2006. We do so with gratitude for all that God has done in us and through us in the last year, eager to *"hold fast to what we have attained"*—but equally eager to do whatever the Holy Spirit shows will move us from merely being church members to being disciples.

Please pray with me. Lord, we offer ourselves afresh to you this morning. May your Spirit renew our minds, transform our thinking, and empower us to share your love more effectively this year than ever before. We pray in Jesus' name. Amen.

8. IF YOU CHOOSE . . .

Mark 1:40-45

I expect that most of us who are privileged to be parents, and who lived through the teenage years with our progeny, can remember words such as these being uttered—or maybe shouted in anger—by an outraged adolescent just before she ran to her room and slammed the door: "I can't wait 'til I'm out of this house and can do whatever I want!" [*SLAM!*]

Maybe, at the time our dear child blasted us with her indignation, we recalled having said something a lot like it to our own parents. I know I did. When we're fourteen or fifteen we think adults get to do whatever they want, whenever they want. There's nobody to tell *them* that they have to be home by 11:00, or that they can't go to the mall 'til they've cleaned their rooms. Of course, there's a certain sense in which that's true. For example, nobody is going to make me get my sermon planned before Sunday morning. If I choose to, I can wait 'til the moment when I'm supposed to get up here and preach, and then wing it. That might work out o.k. But, then, it also might not. It's my choice: either prepare or don't prepare.

This morning, in the final verses of the first chapter of Mark, we hear about Jesus—who has now left his home in Capernaum and gone on a preaching tour through the towns and villages of Galilee—being accosted by a leper who's sure this carpenter-turned-prophet is a man with the power to cleanse his body of the skin disease that has made him an outcast, condemned to keep away from other people, and to call out a warning to anybody who might accidentally get too close to him, saying (about himself): *"Unclean. Unclean."*

This lonely soul violates the rules and comes right up close to Jesus, groveling in the dust at his feet, and saying: "If you choose, you can make me clean."—"If you *choose*..."—He's saying, "I know it's entirely up to you. If you're willing to deal with the likes of me, you could make this leprosy go away. If you want to, you can change my life. You can take away my shame. You can make it so that I can enter the town, visit my family, and put my arms around my children again. It's in your power, *if* you choose to act." And Jesus, moved with pity, responds to his plea. He says, "I *do* choose to. Be made clean." He reaches down and touches the leper, and the man's diseased flesh is instantly healed.

There are many different lessons we could draw from this story of the cleansing of a defiled man, but what I will focus on today (because I *choose* to!) is the role that *choice* plays in our spiritual life.

I was brought up in a pretty strict conservative, Calvinist church. Did you ever know a twelve year-old who wrote his English term paper in seventh grade on predestination? I did that. O.K., I was a little weird for a 12 year-old, but the subject worried me a lot. I agonized about it.—Was our experience of having choices in life just an illusion? Was everything already determined by God? Were we like puppets manipulated from above by a string-pulling deity who determined every aspect of our existence, including our eternal destiny? If so, what was the point in being alive at all, or in imagining that our anguished choices mattered? I don't think I'm the only kid who ever thought about stuff like that.

Those concerns stayed with me and ultimately led me to the Episcopal fold, where we believe that *freedom to choose* is a gift God has given to all of his children. In the Genesis creation story, where we're told that Adam and Eve were made "in the image and likeness of God," it's the freedom to choose which made them to be, in a sense, "like God." God told the First Man and the First Woman not to eat the fruit of the tree in the center of the Garden, but it remained their choice. They could obey or disobey, eat or not eat. That story is the classic parable of our mortal existence, asking the question: *how will you use your freedom?*

Our choices matter. Sure, the circumstances of our upbringing and various forces in our culture and environment have a huge effect on the choices we make. They incline us to make *these* choices rather than *those*. For instance, people who grow up in America are more likely to be active in a church than people who grow up in Great Britain. Religious Americans are more likely to be either Christians or Jews, while religious Egyptians are almost certain to be Muslims. Culture *always* influences our choices. In some cases there may even be coercion, but we're still making choices. Courage is a decision. So is cowardice.

Shallow-minded skeptics think they've scored big points on us when they say, "How can you believe in God when you see the rampant evil in this world?" These people don't get the picture. No one could do what might be called *good* if that person did not have an equal option for doing what might be called evil. The role of choice is essential for there to be any moral order in the universe at all. Your choosing to feed the hungry, or provide shelter for the homeless, or even give the thirsty little kid from next door a drink of water if he knocks on your door on a hot afternoon could not be described as "good" in any sense, unless you *also* had the freedom to ignore the needs of others and let them shift for themselves.

If people were like machines, they could do neither good nor evil, right nor wrong. The freedom to choose is what makes human behavior either moral or immoral. God is not pulling strings, not making us do this or that. We are not automatons. *We were created to make choices.*

The leper said to Jesus, "If you *choose*, you can make me clean." Almost every day, you and I are faced with moral choices: to do something good, or to do something evil; to act, or to do nothing. Almost every day, we could imagine a voice is saying to us, "If you choose, you can _____." (Fill in the blank.) We may not have the power to cure leprosy, but we *do* have power to choose to make a difference *for good* in the world around us—usually in small ways, but sometimes in big ways.

The ability to choose also entails the possibility of making mistakes. We can exercise our freedom of choice—intending only to do something worthwhile, something positive, something good—and later learn that what we did resulted in consequences quite different from the ones we had hoped for.—So, does that mean we should give up and remain inert because our well-intended actions might possibly turn out badly? . . . Or might not achieve all the good we'd hoped? Of course not. We do the right as God gives us grace to perceive the right, and then we trust God for the outcome.

Choice plays a crucial part in the life of faith. You may have heard me say this before, and you will hear it from me again: FAITH ITSELF IS A CHOSEN PERSPECTIVE. Faith, as I understand it, is not a "zap" from above. We don't say, "Yesterday I didn't have faith, but I got 'zapped' today, and now I do." Faith is not a zap; it's a *choice*. The Christian faith is a decision to look at ourselves, God, the world around us, and other people from a particular angle—from the perspective proposed by the gospel of Jesus Christ. Or we could choose the point of view, the perspective, of godlessness, or meaninglessness. There are philosophers who say that human existence has no meaning. We could buy into that. We're free to reject faith completely and choose to look at ourselves and other people if we were actors in a pointless play—characters in the theater of the absurd.

The life of faith is a life of repeatedly choosing to trust God. The choice has to be made again and again. The life of faith is a matter of putting ourselves in God's hands today and tomorrow and the day after, and choosing to behave in ways consistent with that chosen faith. Count on this: we're going to make mistakes. There are going to be times when—with all the best intentions—we'll decide to do something good only to see it turn out badly. But our faith tells us to trust God for the ultimate outcome and keep moving on. As Paul said: "In all things God is at work for good for those who love him, who are called according to his purposes." Those who trust him will come to see that God is at work for good "in all things," *even* our mistakes.

So, the next time you hear a voice—either out loud, from the lips of a fellow human being, or whispered by the Holy Spirit in the ear of your heart—saying, *"If you choose, you can* _____ *"* (do something to make a difference for good, for help, for hope . . . or for God), please answer by saying: "I choose to. I will." And then trust God for all that comes afterwards.

9. START LISTENING!

Matthew 17:1-9

I doubt there's anybody here this morning who has never been on top of a mountain. People *come* to Colorado for the mountains. Skiers get on a chair lift and go up our mountains all winter. In the summer, we hike in the mountains. Even if people don't ski or hike, they can come out here and drive their cars to a mountain top—at least in warm weather—since there's a road to the top of Mount Evans. Or they can ride the cog railway to the top of Pike's Peak. If you come to Colorado, we're going to make sure you can get to a mountain top.

Wouldn't it be strange to live in a place like Aspen or Snowmass and never go up the mountains? But the truth is that for most of human history, people who lived near mountains didn't climb them unless they had to get somewhere and going over the mountain was the only way. Either they were afraid—because mountains were thought to be the dwelling place of the gods and common people might be risking their lives to trespass on sacred territory—or they simply weren't interested.

Until modern times, everyone except a handful of aristocrats were so busy doing back-breaking work every day from sun-up to sundown that the idea of climbing a mountain during a lone afternoon off every few weeks didn't sound like fun. If *you* chopped at the hard earth with a hoe all day every day, or spent the whole day swinging a sickle the way they did, you probably wouldn't want to climb a mountain on your time off either. You'd probably want to take a nap. (Or hang out in the tavern.)

I did a little research and discovered that the history of mountaineering only goes back to the late 18th century. Except in the few places where civilizations developed in mountainous places, human beings stuck to the lowlands and avoided the mountain heights.—After all, you couldn't grow crops on mountain tops. You couldn't graze cattle or sheep on mountain tops. So, why go up there? That seems to be the way people thought. Besides, something scary might happen.

When Jesus invited Peter and James and John to climb a real mountain—not just a hill—with him, it must have seemed like a very odd request, even frightening. These men were Jews, and they remembered that God had spoken to Moses on the top of Mount Sinai. Joshua had gone with him part of the way, but Moses climbed to the top of Sinai by himself. In fact, God had given Moses strict instructions to keep everybody else far away from even the base of the mountain. If they got too close, if they even touched the mountain, they would die. So the Israelites just watched from a distance, and from far off they heard the thunder and saw the cloud and fire on the mountain as Moses was meeting with God.

So I imagine that when Peter and James and John went up the high mountain with Jesus, they were probably nervous, probably a little scared. The fact that they were climbing with Jesus was a source of comfort, but they were still uneasy. They felt what theologians call holy dread, the feeling that something awesome, something *supernatural* could happen any minute.—And, of course, it did.

Up on the high mountain, where they had never been before, they saw a vision. They saw Jesus "transfigured." That means he didn't look the way he ordinarily looked. Light was coming from his body and his face, light that was almost blinding. And he was talking to two men, men they somehow knew were Moses and Elijah—the great Lawgiver and the great Prophet. Suddenly a bright cloud came over the whole mountaintop and out of it came the Voice of God, which said, "This is my beloved Son, with whom I am well pleased. Listen to him."

Peter, James and John fell to the ground, hiding their faces, scared to death. After a while they felt a touch on the shoulder, and heard Jesus saying, *"Get up. Don't be afraid."* When they looked up, they only saw Jesus there—and he wasn't glowing any more. He looked like his usual self.

The moment of encounter, the revelation, the epiphany, was over. They went back down the mountain.

The Voice had said, *"This is my beloved Son . . . Listen to him."* I wonder what the three disciples on the mountain thought that meant. Jesus was their Teacher, their Master. They'd been following him since the day more than a year earlier when he'd called them from their nets and fishing boats to come along with him and learn how to fish for people. They'd been hearing his teaching, now, for months. So what did the Voice mean, *"Listen to him"*? They had been listening, hadn't they?—Maybe that's the issue.

Most of us have been Christians all our lives. We've been going to church all our lives. We've been hearing the words of Christ read from the Gospel since we were little children. Some of us read the Bible every day. What does it mean to us to hear God say, "Listen to him"?

Maybe we've just been *hearing* the Words of Jesus, but not *listening*. There's a big difference. We can hear somebody talking, but not be paying them very much attention. Maybe it's a person who talks a lot, and we're in the habit of tuning them out. God rest her soul, my mother was like that. She was a dear woman, but she talked all the time—about nothing in particular. So I tended to tune her out. She'd chatter away and occasionally I'd say, "Uh-huh," or "Really? You don't say," or "How about that?" But I wasn't honestly listening to her.

Or maybe the other person is talking to us while we're trying to do something else—like read the newspaper or watch TV or write something. Maybe we're thinking really hard about a problem or a project and our minds are focused on that, so we hear the other person speaking, but we're not paying attention. Husbands and wives do this to each other all the time. (Well, husbands do it to wives, anyway.) And parents do it to their children. We don't catch the other person's words because we're not really listening to them, we're just "hearing." If we suddenly realize the other person has said something important, something that demands a response, we're startled and reply, "What was that? What did you say? Please say that again?"

Maybe after they came down from the Mount of the Transfiguration, Peter and James and John had a fresh respect for Jesus. Maybe they started to listen to him more closely and think more deeply about what he was saying. These men had been with Jesus for months by that time, so perhaps they'd begun to take him for granted and felt as if they'd already learned everything important he had to teach.—You know, that's what happens to people after one year of seminary. We finish one year of theological education, and we feel ready to be ordained. We know it all. We're ready to be rectors, maybe even bishops. (I've been a priest for 35 years now, and I know so much less than I did after 10 years.)

In ancient times, people lived among the mountains, but rarely ever climbed them. They stayed in the valleys. People who live here can take the beauty of the mountains for granted because we see them year-round. We can go to a mountain top every day, if we want to—sometimes even in our cars. My question is: *Do we take our opportunities to listen to Jesus for granted too?*

The Voice of God spoke to Peter and James and John on the mountain top and said, "This is my beloved Son, with whom I am well pleased. *Listen to him.*" God is saying something like that to us right now: "You 'church people,' you who call yourselves Christians! Jesus is my beloved Son. Quit just hearing him and start listening. Don't take his words for granted. Don't imagine you've already understood everything he might have to say to you. Don't fool yourselves into thinking you have him all figured out. You have a lot more to learn, *if you're willing to listen.*"

Lent begins on Wednesday. Sometime during these forty days before Easter, Jesus is going to invite you to climb a mountain with him. When that happens, expect a mountain like none you've been on before. While you're up there, listen to him.—When you come back down, the valley won't look the same.

10. IT'S TIME FOR A MORAL INVENTORY.

Ash Wednesday
Matthew 6:1-6,16-21

"Remember that you are dust, and to dust you shall return." You'll hear these words as the cross of ashes is marked on your forehead today. They're meant to remind us of our mortality, of the words the priest says at a graveside: "Ashes to ashes, dust to dust."

No matter how rich we are, or how poor; no matter how important, or how insignificant; no matter whether we are wise or foolish—nothing can alter our common mortal end. We are all going to face death, sooner or later.

But Lent is a season of preparation and hope, not a time for gloom and despair. It begins with today's reminder of the grave, but it will end on Easter Eve with the glad shout *"Alleluia! Christ is risen!"* and the gospel affirmation that "because he lives, we too shall live."

Lent reminds us that were it not for Christ, the return of our mortal flesh to the dust would be The End. The Finish. Death would have the last word. Without the hope of resurrection, there would be no reason to examine our lives, repent and ask forgiveness for our sins, and strive to imitate Christ. There would be no point.

But Jesus has delivered us from the power of death. He has saved us from a meaningless existence. And he has invited us to live right now—in this mortal life—according to the standards of the Age to Come, that is, according to the norms of the Kingdom of Heaven.

We keep the season of Lent every year. It comes to us over and over *because none of us is perfect.* We are all frail, weak creatures of flesh, subject to temptation. Although we may truly be sorry for our sins and earnestly seek God's forgiveness and the grace to change our lives, the probability that we will need to do it again next year is 100%.

My prayer is that between this Lent and the next I will make *some* moral progress. I will make *some* changes that will stick. But I know that—come next year on Ash Wednesday—I will embrace Lent once more as an opportunity to grow.

Lent is the time to take a good look at ourselves and decide whether we professing Christians are living by the standards of the Kingdom of God to which we have repeatedly committed ourselves, or not. It's a time for what Alcoholics Anonymous calls a "fearless moral inventory"—a time to look in the mirror of spiritual and moral objectivity and be honest with ourselves and with God. We need to look at our lives and make note of *what needs changing.*

So, how do we go about this? Where do we begin? Ash Wednesday is the best of all days to develop a plan, and I'm going to offer you one.

First off, let me say that it's vital to be balanced, objective, honest, and as fair as possible in our self-examination. Neither excusing our sin nor beating ourselves up is o.k. You and I are unlikely to be either the best of people or the worst. Most of us fall somewhere in the middle. But all of us are people who "have left undone those things which we ought to have done, and have done those things which we ought not to have done."

The gospel that the Church gives us to contemplate on Ash Wednesday offers us some guidelines on how to examine our lives. Here, in the Sermon on the Mount, Jesus discusses the three traditional acts of righteousness that were prescribed by Jewish law: almsgiving, prayer, and fasting. These suggest three categories we can use for organizing our moral inventory.

THE FIRST CATEGORY IS ALMSGIVING — OR WE MIGHT LABEL IT "CHARITY." This demands that we think about our relationships with other people, particularly the poor. Ask yourself: *Am I a generous giver?* Do I have compassion for those who are suffering from poverty? Do I give happily to help others, or do I give regretfully and out of guilt, dreaming about what I *could* have done with the money? Am I instinctively sensitive to others' needs, or do I require someone to remind me? Do I count my personal resources—both money and talent—as something entrusted to me by God to be used for God's purposes in the world? When I start to buy something expensive for myself or my family, do I ever pray first and ask, "Jesus, is there something *else* you would rather I did with this money?"

THE SECOND CATEGORY IS PRAYER. Thinking about prayer calls for us to examine our relationship with God. Ask yourself: *How much do I truly want to be close to God?* Is my relationship with God all I would like it to be? Do I know how to pray in any way other than by using the formal prayers in the Prayer Book? Do I pray every day? Or just on Sundays? Or just when I need help? When I pray, do I remember to say "thank you" to God as well as "help me"? Do I spend time listening to God, or do I do all the talking? If someone asked me to describe a moment in the last week when I felt really close to God, would I be able to do that, or would I have a hard time with the question?

THE THIRD CATEGORY IS *FASTING*. That category is not just about food. It should lead us to think about how we deal with our personal desires and appetites. Ask yourself: *Am I self-indulgent, or am I self-disciplined?* Am I able to deny myself anything unless I'm on a diet or under doctor's orders? (When was the last time I simply told myself "No" when there was something I craved, something that wasn't bad and wouldn't hurt me, but that I just didn't need?) What am I hungry for? Money? Clothes? Toys? Security? Good things to eat and drink? Do I have a hunger for God? Do I have a desire for holiness? Does my spirit rule over my flesh, or is it the other way around?

When we've examined our lives in the light of these three Scriptural categories, then we arrive at the point of decision. Can we see the need to make some changes? Or do we find ourselves able to rationalize away all of our failures? Are we brave enough to make the changes, pay the price, take the steps, and do the work? Do we understand that God will help us do that work, if we only turn to him and ask him? (But, remember, it will still be *work*. It will still require effort and willpower.)

In the gospels it's clear that Jesus isn't hard on many people, even immoral people. The people he *is* hard on are the hypocrites, the play-actors, the people whose lives are organized around putting on an act, creating the appearance of holiness, rather than seeking the real thing. A religious hypocrite will do most anything it takes to *appear* spiritual, or generous, or self-disciplined—while remaining secretly wrapped up in his own ego—cut off from God, heedless of other people, and at the mercy of his appetites. In Lent, we're called to "be real," to put away all pretenses and let the Spirit of Christ help us become our true selves.

We have a Lenten Self-Denial Offering Project every year in our church. The project always benefits the poor or the hungry in some way, usually those in far off lands. And the project is always generously supported by everyone.—But I wonder how many of us actually deny ourselves something in order to support the Self-Denial project. Do we do without—in some sense—in order to help others, or do we just dig into our surplus and make a gift? The gift benefits the poor, no matter where it comes from; that much is certain. But the self-denial aspect of it might actually be good for *us*.

Many of us take on a spiritual project, like devotional reading during Lent or attending the annual Lenten study series. What matters is our authentic quest to hear God's Word and know God's will—our readiness to spend quality time with the Lord.

It isn't enough simply to skip meals on Ash Wednesday and Good Friday, the two fast days ordered by the Book of Common Prayer, and give up wine and desserts during Lent. It doesn't matter that we're hungry two days out of 365 and switch from cabernet sauvignon to cranberry juice from now 'til Easter. What *counts* is our really doing battle with the demons of our self-centered appetites and desires, until—by the power of Christ—they're defeated.

As Paul said to the people in Corinth, "Now is the acceptable time." This is the time. Lent is the season for a moral inventory, forty days for us to look into the mirror of conscience, analyze what we see there, and begin to do whatever is necessary in order to get moving on the journey—in the Spirit—from where we are to where Christ wants us to be.

Let us take the first steps on that journey now.

11. THREE TEMPTATIONS
OF THE CHURCH.

Matthew 4:1-11

The only person who can escape ever being subject to temptation is a person who has no wants or desires whatsoever, no appetites of any kind, and no life goals, dreams or ambitions. Since all of us by nature have desires, hopes, dreams, appetites and ambitions, we're all vulnerable to temptation. Temptation is always an invitation to do what comes naturally.

The story of Adam and Eve in the Garden of Eden is the story of everybody who ever lived. The serpent's invitation to Eve to eat the forbidden fruit is an echo of our natural appetite for what appears beautiful, delicious, and desirable. The serpent himself is an ancient personification of wisdom—human wisdom. And, of course, there's always the inclination in us—literally from birth—to take a shot at anything that some authority figure has forbidden. (Every parent knows the truth of this. Just tell a three year old that she can't go out and play in the puddles, and see how long it takes before she comes in the house all wet.)

In the Biblical sense, temptations are situations where we feel a pull to behave in a way that goes against our prior knowledge of God's order for life. This pull usually happens inside our heads. It's hardly ever a spoken invitation from an obviously shady character, much less the Devil himself.

The thing that often helps temptation succeed—the thing that makes us yield to it—is that temptation can easily look like a brilliant new idea. An insight. A discovery. A solution to a problem. And it might not really be something that obviously violates the will of God. After all, we're quite capable of revising our understanding of the will of God, or—as we like to put it—reframing our understanding of the Bible, so as to accommodate the realization of our desires.

In the Gospel story of the temptations of Christ in the wilderness, that's what the Devil was suggesting to Jesus in the first two of the temptations. He wasn't proposing anything obviously evil there, just a couple of things that challenged Jesus to reframe his understanding of how to be faithful to the Father's will. The story of the temptations of Christ is not the snapshot of a one-time event in the life of Jesus. It's really a parable of the temptations Jesus had to face all through his life. Let's look at the three temptations one at a time.

Since the conventional wisdom about the Messiah in those days was that he would provide an endless supply of food for Israel, the temptation to turn stones into bread was simply *an invitation to fulfill popular expectations.* (That seems like a reasonable suggestion. Why not give people exactly what they want?)

Jesus' critics kept asking him for a sign. Healing sick people did not impress them; they could explain that away as easily as we can today. They wanted to see something truly unusual, something fantastic—like making the sun move backwards in the sky. The temptation to jump off the top of the Temple was *an invitation to get attention and silence criticism by creating a sensation.* (And why not? It wouldn't have hurt anybody. A little showmanship can be quite effective. According to the Devil's proof text, it was even authorized by the Bible. And it sure would have made those picky Pharisees hush their mouths.)

The Roman Empire was a great political success. People recognized that if you had imperial power—the biggest army and the biggest navy and hordes of flunkies to do your bidding—you could get your way all the time. The temptation to bow down to the Devil and receive all the power in the world was *an invitation to play by the world's rules*—to enforce the will of God with the sword. (Now there's an idea that later caught on big with emperors, kings, popes, the Puritans, and even a few Presidents of the United States.)

But—Jesus was so centered in the will and word of God that he saw through every one of the temptations and recognized the wrong track that each one would have put him on.

Just as each of us face temptations, and Christ himself struggled with temptations, so the church is exposed to temptations too. Unfortunately, the church has regularly yielded to the temptations that have come along. Unlike Jesus our Lord, the church often seems to be so poorly rooted in an understanding of God's word and will that we seize on the Tempter's proposals as great ideas that will help us be more successful. To match the three temptations of Christ in the wilderness, I want to identify three temptations of the church in the postmodern world.

THE FIRST IS THE TEMPTATION TO TREAT WORSHIP AS A COMMODITY. This is an invitation to Christians to regard themselves as shoppers, as consumers of spiritual goods and services. When clergy and other worship planners begin thinking most about how to appeal to the market, we turn worship into the service of human appetites rather than the service of the Lord.—Our clear focus in worship is meant to be on God—on making an offering to please God, not on pleasing ourselves.

I heard Dr. Marva Dawn, a Lutheran theologian and ethicist, once tell about a conversation she had with another woman following a worship service in their church. The other woman had not liked a new hymn that was sung during the service, and after church she had said to Marva, "I didn't like that new song at all. It didn't do a thing for me." Dr. Dawn replied, "Oh, I didn't know we were worshiping *you*. I thought we were worshiping God."—Treating worship as a commodity, as a product for the market, makes worship all about *me*, and not about God.

THE SECOND TEMPTATION OF THE CHURCH IS TO UNDERSTAND SPIRITUAL SUCCESS IN MATERIAL TERMS. This is an invitation to practice spiritual secularism, to be focused on institutional goals instead of gospel goals. The church is tempted to fall for the magic of big numbers. There's a terrible temptation for priests and vestries and bishops, too, to look at the numbers (anything we can count or measure)—Sunday attendance, members on the roll, money in the offering plate, dimensions of the church buildings—and equate big numbers with success as a church. Marva Dawn, whom I quoted earlier, said that she overheard a revealing slip of the tongue at a clergy luncheon where one pastor, chatting with another, asked, "Well, how many are you worshiping on Sunday these days?"—The mission Christ gave us was to deny ourselves, take up the cross and follow him, not build an ecclesiastical empire.

THE THIRD TEMPTATION OF THE CHURCH IS TO SPEND ALMOST ALL OF ITS ENERGY AND RESOURCES IN SELF-SERVING. This is an invitation to selfishness, to treat the church the way we would a civic club, a voluntary association of like-minded people who have banded together to build an effective community organization. Like the temptation to treat worship as a commodity, the temptation to selfishness and clubbiness makes satisfying our personal appetites and felt needs the main work of the church. It puts us squarely on the throne and leaves God's agenda out of serious consideration.

William Temple, the great archbishop of Canterbury during World War II, said, "The church is the only organization in the world that exists exclusively for the benefit of those who are not its members." Yet in most congregations of every Christian denomination 90% or more of the church's total energy and resources is focused inward, not outward, not on those who are outside the church family. The typical church works hardest at pleasing itself and making its own house more comfortable.——The Great Commandments, however, are to "Love God with all your heart and soul and mind and strength" and to "Love your neighbor as you love yourself"—not just *"Love God"* and *"Love yourself."*

It's Lent. This is the time we're given every year for confessing our sins and changing our lives. This is a time for repentance, for choosing a new path. I have to confess to you that, as a priest and pastor, during three decades in the ministry I have personally yielded frequently to all of these temptations of the church that I described this morning. I repent. And I beg God's forgiveness. I pray that beginning this Lent (and continuing hereafter) I—and we who are the church—will:

- Make God alone, and not our personal taste, the focus of our worship.
- Identify success as a church with faithfulness to the Gospel of Christ, and not with bigness or wealth.
- And, remember that our mission is not to take care of ourselves, but to serve the world our Savior died to save.

12. BORN AGAIN? . . . WHO, *ME*?

John 3:1-17

Nicodemus was a first century Jewish big shot. I'm not sure what kind of person might be a 21ˢᵗ century parallel to Nicodemus—maybe a U.S. Senator with a distinguished pedigree, like a Rockefeller. When Nicodemus decided to pay a call on Jesus, he was taking a risk. He wanted to keep his visit a secret because the people from whom he wanted respect all despised Jesus—a man with no family, no learning, and no status, a village tradesman who'd become a street preacher. If his friends discovered he'd been visiting Jesus, they'd laugh at Nicodemus. His reputation might not be ruined, but it would surely be tarnished.

Nevertheless, Nicodemus took the risk because he felt that he *had* to have a face-to-face talk with Jesus. When they met, he greeted Jesus respectfully, without patronizing, and called him *"Rabbi."* He said, "Rabbi, we know that you are a teacher who has come from God; for no one can do these signs that you do apart from the presence of God." Although he was a colleague of the most prominent religious leaders of Israel, Nicodemus would not have described any of *them* as having "come from God." He knew them all too well. He knew where *they* came from.

Have you ever gone someplace you wouldn't want your peers to know you'd visited? When I was a young graduate student in the early 70's, living in a London suburb, I started attending a little Pentecostal house-church on Wednesday nights—maybe twenty people jammed into the living room of a modest, semi-detached house. They danced in the spirit and prayed in tongues and shook tambourines. They baptized people by immersion in the bathtub. I would not have been happy if members of the very proper Anglican congregation where I served on Sundays had seen me there. Or if some of the other graduate students I associated with on weekdays had learned about it and asked me questions. It was not intellectually respectable for a pretentious young academic like me to be doing something like that.

Maybe one or two of you here this morning might like to keep it quiet that you're coming to church. If they heard about it, some of your friends might raise an eyebrow, might gossip to one another about you: "You have to start being careful how you talk to her. She's 'got religion' now, y'know."

Jesus didn't respond to Nicodemus' flattering salutation. Instead he said, "Very truly, I tell you, no one can see the kingdom of God without being born from above." "Born again" is what this verse says in our older Bibles. People make jokes about born-again Christians. They mock, in the same way Nicodemus' friends in the Sanhedrin would have teased him and made jokes about his visit to the prophet from Nazareth. You've seen the bumper stickers that say "Being born once is enough." You've heard the jokes—maybe you've even told a few. Despite the jokes people tell, I think everybody really understands a little bit about what it means to be "born again."

I was actually brought into this world in Arkansas, by accident of that being the location of the hospital where my mother gave birth. But my parents lived in Texas, and that's where I was taken directly from the hospital and brought up. I left Texas when I was 21, though, and never moved back. This is now the eighteenth year I've lived in Colorado, and I consider myself a "born again" Coloradoan. This is my state, my home. I love it; I identify with it. No joke.

Joan and I moved from Denver to Bangkok in 1995, but when in church there we'd sing the part of "How Great Thou Art" that says, *"When I look down from lofty mountain grandeur, and hear the brook and feel the gentle breeze,"* we'd both get teary—eyed. We were missing Colorado. You may have only lived here a few years, but you might already have become a "born again" Coloradoan, too. It has to do with something that happens in your heart, your way of understanding your identity and sense of belonging.

I'm here to tell you from personal experience that what Jesus said to Nicodemus is the truth. It's nothing to laugh about. "No one can see the kingdom of God without being *born again*" or "*born from above.*" "Born from above" really is a better translation of the Greek. In fact, "*begotten from above*" would be even better, since the word translated "born" also applies to the role of the father in the birth of a child. But, however we read it, to be "born again" or "born from above" or "begotten from above" all mean one thing: *to have a new birth from God.*

And it's not something *we* can make happen.—Did you choose to be born? Did you choose your parents? Of course not. By the same token, to be "begotten from above" is not something you can make happen either. It's the work of God. Jesus told Nicodemus that without this new birth, no one could "see the kingdom of God." We might be life-long church members, but until God brings us to a new birth, to a new relationship with him, to a new sense of our own identity and sense of belonging, we simply do not have the capacity to perceive what God is doing. We don't have the ability to look at other people and see them as our brothers and sisters until we've been "born again"—"begotten from above."

Nicodemus believed that Jesus had come from God, but he had trouble understanding what Jesus said. That poor man was locked into a completely worldly, utterly mundane set of presuppositions about life. Jesus tried to help him understand. He said, "The wind blows where it chooses, and you hear the sound of it, but you don't know where it comes from or where it goes. So it is with everyone who's born of the Spirit." You have to know that the word for "wind" and the word for "spirit" were identical. Nicodemus could not hear Jesus say "wind" without also hearing him say "spirit." To be begotten above is to be born of the spirit.

There are scientists who can explain how much wind we're going to have and from what direction it will be blowing this morning and later on. However, most of us are as ignorant about these things as Nicodemus was. We have no idea where the wind is likely to come from, or how hard it's going to blow. We just feel it on our skin and see tree limbs bending and swaying—or sometimes breaking in a storm.

But we do know this: the wind *is* going to blow. There may be long hours of calm, but the wind *is* going to blow every day, either in soft breezes or a gale.

Nicodemus had a hard time with metaphors, but I hope we're prepared for them. Jesus says that the wind of God, the Spirit of God, is *always* blowing—first over here and then over there, sometimes like a tornado and sometimes like a zephyr. One day the Spirit comes and suddenly pushes a person to a new place, a new life, a new birth, a new way of understanding God as Father and other people as sisters and brothers.

When that happens to you, you will understand about being "born again." The world won't be changed, but your way of looking at the world, yourself, God, and the rest of us will be modified decisively, transformed. It happened to me. It has happened to many of you. It's not an experience only for a few specially chosen people. It's what God has in store for everyone who loves him and seeks him.

Furthermore, I believe the new birth that the Spirit brings usually happens more than once. Yes, you can be "born again" again! Jesus says, "The wind blows where it chooses." Maybe we should think of "wind" beginning with a capital letter, because what Jesus is talking about here is the Spirit of God. I doubt that I'm the only person here who can look back on his life and see more than a single occasion of God bringing me amazing new life, fresh insight, altered perspective, and transformed understanding. The Wind blows when and where the Spirit chooses.

But here's the thing: *We can't feel that Wind if we lock ourselves away from God.* If we put up windbreaks to insulate ourselves from the Spirit, we're hiding from exactly what God wants to give us.

Let Lent be a season to stand in the Wind, and let that Wind take you wherever God chooses.

13. OUR FAILURES TO BE GOOD HAVE NOT MADE US *BAD*.

Romans 7:13-8:2

The Ten Commandments are very popular in America. There are about 4,000 public displays of them in various places around the country, including the Supreme Court building and the Library of Congress. There's one here in Aspen, in Conner Park. Zeal for the Commandments runs high among us, but our zeal is diluted by ignorance. Two years ago a poll showed that nearly 80% of Americans oppose removing displays of the Ten Commandments from government buildings, even though a later survey showed that fewer than 10% can name more than four of them.—I wonder which four commandments people know? The poll didn't say. Apparently it's more important to post them in public places than to try to remember them.

Most people say that the function of the Ten Commandments is to provide moral guidance, to help us know the difference between right and wrong. They say the Commandments show us what behavior to punish and what behavior to reward. They say the Commandments cause us to have a better, more moral society. Those are modern answers, not Biblical answers, since they ignore God. The Biblical answer is different: the Commandments revealed the will of God to Israel. They identified the kind of behavior that was meant to set Israel apart from the nations around them and mark them as God's own people. The Commandments were about *holiness*—about being holy as God is holy. To keep God's law is to belong to God.

But even if, for the moment, we go with a modern interpretation of the function of the Commandments, we're confronted with a problem. Laws won't make society good because laws can't make us good. Being told the difference between right and wrong won't necessarily lead us to make more choices for good than for evil, though fear of punishment might keep us from blatant evils like murder and robbery. Knowledge of the law will, however, make us conscious that we're mired in moral failure. It's one thing to know the law, but something else to keep it.

St. Paul was a great example of somebody who tried really hard to keep the law—not just the Ten Commandments, but every one of the six hundred-odd precepts of God's law that the Pharisees counted. Paul tried and failed.

We heard this from him a few minutes ago: "I don't understand my own actions," he wrote. "For I do not do what I *want*, but I do the very thing I *hate*. . . . I can *will* what is right, but I can't *do* it. For I do not do the good I want, but the evil I do not want is what I do. . . . I find it to be a law that when I want to do good, evil lies close at hand." Then he talked about a war that was going on inside him. He said, "I delight in the law of God in my mind, but I see in myself another law at war with the law of my mind, making me captive to the law of sin." Paul knew his mind to be a battlefield between the "law of God" and the "law of sin"—between the principles of good and the power of evil. And it appeared that the law of sin was winning most of the battles. Paul felt like a moral failure, and it left him depressed.

We're not too different from Paul. All of us can tell some version of the same story. This operates on every moral level. To choose a very soft example, the sort I can talk about from the pulpit, have you ever decided that you were going to control your temper and always give a mild answer when someone provokes you?—I've made that resolution repeatedly, but every time I do, someone manages to get to me, and I lose it. My temper returns with an embarrassing vengeance, and I angrily blurt out something I shouldn't say. Especially to a parishioner.

It's impossible for us to single-handedly overcome the inclination to make bad choices: the inclination to vengefulness, the inclination to make other people do things our way, the inclination to grab as much as we can for ourselves, and to heck with the other guys.

Christians don't take their spiritual and moral standards from the latest public opinion polls, but from what God has revealed to us. We aim at a higher standard than the wisdom of the world. The world won't accept our standards, because our standards are impractical and politically unwise.

Take just the last of the Ten Commandments as an example: "You shall not covet." How can we follow that commandment and cheerfully promote a global culture based on consumerism? Consumerism utilizes greed and envy. It works by persuading people to covet products and services they don't need.

The values of Jesus take us even further than the Ten Commandments. He sets the bar higher. He says, "If anyone strikes you on the right cheek, turn the other also. Love your enemies, and pray for those who persecute you, so that you may be children of your Father in heaven."

The world tells us that Jesus' standards are utopian and unworkable. Maybe so. Jesus also says "if anyone wants to sue you and take your coat, give your cloak as well; and if anyone forces you to go one mile, go also the second mile. Give to everyone who begs from you, and do not refuse anyone who wants to borrow from you."—What does he mean, "Don't refuse a loan to anyone who wants to borrow from you"? Who could run a bank (or any business) like that? Jesus was *so* unrealistic.—But the question is: *How many Christians have the courage to say that the world is wrong and Jesus is right?*

Within all humanity, there's a tendency to evil. I don't think we're naturally depraved (John Calvin's opinion to the contrary notwithstanding). We're God's good creation, formed with potential for holiness. But what we might call *the option for evil* has become a habit for our species. We can recognize the highest good. We can set fine moral standards for ourselves and name the right things to do; but we can't make ourselves do them.—So, like Paul, we find a war going on within ourselves: "The good that I want to do I do not do, but the evil that I do not want to do is what I do." Then Paul adds, "Wretched man that I am, who will deliver me from this?" He knew he needed help. And we need help too.

The message of Jesus is not law but grace, not punishment for rule-breaking but forgiveness and hope. The two verses from Romans that follow the part we have in today's Second Lesson are crucial ones for us to hear. I can't imagine why they were omitted except that they're the first two verses of the next chapter. Why don't you take out your bulletin and let's read out loud together the last few lines of the passage from Romans, beginning with "Wretched man that I am . . ." and then I'll read what comes next.—"[But] there is therefore now no condemnation for those who are in Christ Jesus. For the law of the Spirit, the law of life in Christ Jesus, has set me free from the law of sin and death." [Rom. 8:1-2]

The Ten Commandments, the Golden Rule, the Sermon on the Mount—all of these show us right from wrong. And all of them convict us of failure and sin. We can recognize good, but we can't do it. The Good News, the authentic Good News, is that *our failures to be good have not made us bad.*

Lent, the season for self-examination and repentance, for cleansing our consciences the way Jesus cleansed the Temple, can sometimes leave us feeling like losers if we take the process seriously. We haven't lived up to our own highest standards. But in Christ we find forgiveness for our failures, mercy when we need it, and hope in times when our own guilty consciences might tell us we're not entitled to it.

God's holiness is what it has always been, and the law is there to show us when we've gone astray. But for those of us who've learned, as we said in the collect for today, *"that we have no power within ourselves to help ourselves,"* our guilt is swallowed up in God's mercy, through Jesus

    . . . whose love saves us from self-condemnation,
    . . . whose death on the cross has atoned for our sin,
    . . . and whose Spirit sets us free.

14. THE WISDOM OF THE CROSS.

1 Corinthians 1:18-25

Anywhere you go in the world, the cross is the symbol of Christianity. Atop the great lantern at the summit of the dome of St. Paul's Cathedral in London, there's a beautiful golden cross. On the side of a little, plain teakwood hall in the Thai hilltop village called Mae Salit Kee which we used to visit, near the Burma border, there's a simple painted cross. On the stone façade of our new building here in Aspen there will be a tall, back-lit cross.

More than a year ago, when the church was still in the planning stage, I heard this over and over: "The new church is going to have a cross on it, isn't it?" Wherever in the world you are, if you see a cross you say, "that's a church." The cross is the symbol of the church, of the Christian religion.

But there's a problem with a symbol that becomes so familiar. It can easily become nothing more than a marker, something like the familiar Interstate Highway sign.

It can even become just a piece of jewelry. In this post-Christian era, you see people wearing crosses around their necks, or strung on charm bracelets along with miniature tennis rackets, four-leaf clovers and their children's birthstones. Such wearers are people for whom the cross is no longer even a marker. It's just a casual item of personal adornment.

In one of his videos for the Alpha Course, Nicky Gumbel told about two young London women whom he overheard talking in a shop. They were looking at jewelry, and one of them said to the other something like, "Oh, look at the different crosses. Aren't they lovely?" And her friend said, "Oh, yes. The gold one with the ruby is very pretty. And look at that one! It has a little *man* on it."

"It has a little man on it." *Jesus.*

During the season of Lent, it's a tradition in the Episcopal Church that we put a purple veil over the cross, as you see here. For years I have been telling people that the veil is there to remind us that sin creates a separation between ourselves and the Lord, and Lent is a time to turn from our sin so we can draw close to Christ. But I am beginning to think that I should start saying something different. I should say that the veil is put there as a sign that we don't yet understand the meaning of the cross. The meaning of the cross and the power of the cross are veiled to us, obscure to us, until we have been raised to a new life in Christ.

In the Episcopal marriage rite, the most solemn moment comes at the very end, after the bride and groom have exchanged their vows and rings and have been pronounced husband and wife.

The very last thing in the ceremony is the Blessing of the Marriage. The couple kneel in front of the priest, and the priest pronounces over them a blessing which begins with these words: "Most gracious God, we give you thanks for your tender love in sending Jesus Christ to come among us, to be born of a human mother, and to make the way of the cross to be the way of life."

Jesus made the way of the cross to be the Way of Life. (Capital "W," capital "L.")

We Christians have crosses over the altars in our churches, and in stained glass windows, and on the top of steeples. We wear them around our necks or on our lapels. We stamp them on the covers of Bibles and prayer books and hymnals. Roman Catholic churches and some Episcopal and Lutheran churches have a large crucifix over the altar—a cross with the body of Christ fixed to it, a reminder that the cross is more than just an abstract symbol. It was an instrument of real suffering and real death—a humiliating death, a public embarrassment.

Holy Week is coming in three weeks, and during Holy Week many of us will spend time meditating on the Way of the Cross. We will look at Christ on the cross and ponder the mystery of it. But what is most important is the thing we're least likely to do.

When Holy Week comes there's a tendency among church people to let ourselves be absorbed in sentimental emotion about Jesus' physical suffering. A great deal of Christian art and hymnody does that: *"Ah, holy Jesus, how hast thou offended, that man to scorn thee hath in hate pretended? By foes derided, by thine own rejected, O, most afflicted!"* I can understand such emotions, and I feel them too when Good Friday comes around, because what the Son of God experienced for us was truly bitter, painful, and awful. He prayed in the Garden of Gethsemane, "Father, please let this cup pass from me. Nevertheless, let not what I want, but what you want be done." He went to the cross out of obedience, but also out of love. His love for us put him there.

But there is spiritual danger in sentimentalizing the cross and the suffering of Jesus. Because such sentimental emotion holds the suffering Savior "out *there,*" separate from us, detached from us—unattainably holy and distant—to be adored from afar. We are here on our knees, and Christ is "up there" on his cross. But what God wants is for us to put our knowledge of the crucified Lord deep in our own souls, fused with our own identity, and let it motivate our orientation to the world. God wants us to claim Jesus' cross for ourselves, to make the way of the cross our *own* Way of Life. Jesus said, "Take up your own cross and follow me."

Jesus of Nazareth started walking the way of the cross a long time before his arrest in the Garden of Gethsemane, a long time before his life was actually on the line in the Roman governor's courtroom. He started walking the way of the cross when he aggravated everybody by running the money changers and animal sellers out of the Temple and accusing the priests of turning God's House into a marketplace. (What a dangerous, foolish gesture. They were probably all back doing business as usual the next day.) Jesus was walking the way of the cross when he irritated the fraternity of Pharisees by telling a paralyzed man that his sins were forgiven, then proving it by saying, "rise, take up your bed and go home." In addition, he did all this on the Sabbath day, when carrying a sleeping mat was not permitted.

When Jesus did such things, he put to death any possible future for himself as a respectable rabbi. He was too unconventional, too outspoken, and clearly too threatening to the religious establishment. Saying "Destroy this Temple, and in three days I will raise it up," did not earn him the respect of the High Priest; it made him a marked man.—*How ready are we to be marked men and women?*

To Christians in Corinth who had a high opinion of their own sophistication (like many of us here in Aspen), Paul wrote "The message about the cross is foolishness to those who are perishing, but to us who are being saved it is the power of God." Letting himself be crucified was not a strategy for success in the eyes of the general public. It was a foolish mistake. It made him a messianic failure. Even his friends thought that—until Easter evening when he came to them in the Upper Room and showed them his nail-scarred hands and wounded side.

"The message about the cross is foolishness to those who are perishing, but to us who are being saved it is the power of God." Notice the verbs. The message of the cross sounds like foolishness to good, law-abiding religious people who "are perishing." But it sounds like "the power of God" to us sinners who "are being saved."

We're all on the way. We're in process—as we have been for some time. Either spiritual decay has already set in and we're perishing or redemptive transformation has begun, and we're being saved. But in either case, God isn't finished with us yet. There is still hope for the dying, and there are potential pitfalls ahead for the rest of us. In "fear and trembling," as Paul was to say a few years later, "we must work out our own salvation"—the movement from brokenness to wholeness and from double-mindedness to purity of heart—which is the process of being saved: becoming like Christ.

If you and I want to follow the Master, we must be willing to appear foolish in the eyes of the religious and the secular intelligentsia, the crowd, and even our old friends. To plant the cross deep in our own souls, to recognize that the cross is not just his, but ours too, may make us fools for Christ's sake.—Very well. So be it.

"Most gracious God, we give you thanks for your tender love in sending Jesus Christ to come among us, to be born of a human mother, and to make the way of the cross to be the Way of Life."

15. WILL YOU TRUST THIS GOD?

Genesis 22:1-14

We religious professionals, pastors and theologians, preachers and teachers, speak so glibly of God and God's ways, as if we understood everything. As if we *knew*. We put forward our creeds and catechisms, and publish books to convince each other that we've unraveled the secrets of the eternal and figured God out. We love our dogmas and definitions. We say "This is what God is doing. And this is what God is going to do."—We behave as if our doctrines limit God's options and God must conform to the dictates of our reason.

We should be embarrassed at such presumption. Our God is too small. God's name, revealed to Moses at the burning bush in the wilderness, is "I am that I am." Another way of reading that is, "I will be what I will be." All we can ever know is what God himself has revealed—nothing more. Beyond God's revelation there is only holy mystery. And the wisest posture for mortals in the face of holy mystery is what the Bible calls "the fear of the Lord"—deep humility. On our knees. Or better, prostrate, with our faces in the dust.

I've been talking about professional religious types, people like me. There's another group, though, and that's people like you: the faithful, the church members, the community that sits in the pews every week and listens to the religious professionals. Shaped by what we have said, most church folks have come to believe in a small, manageable God. A convenient God. A God whose role in the universe is to make us comfortable and happy. (Our religion is, after all, mostly about us.) We behave as if God's role is

79

to serve our needs and facilitate our getting what we think we should have. We figure that if we play by the rules laid down by religious professionals, God surely will provide what we want.

The common imagination—at least in America—is that there's a divine-human contract which goes like this: If people go to church as often as they're able (given the requirements of our business and social lives), and if they donate some money (more than a token amount, but it doesn't have to be a fortune) and if they don't engage in any truly wicked behavior (petty sins of the flesh are forgivable), God promises to deal gently with them. If we hold up our end of this contract, God should hold up his.

Now let's think about Abraham and Isaac, and the terrible story of the sacrifice.

First, I want to remind you of the background of this story—part of God's ancient revelation of himself, a part we know about but few of us ponder. Long, long ago—when the country we now know only too well as Iraq was the cradle of civilization—God spoke to an elderly man named Abraham, maybe in a dream. We don't know.

For his own inscrutable purposes, God chose Abraham and made a covenant with him, and the terms of the covenant went something like this: if Abraham would leave his family and his home and go to a far-off land that God promised to show him, then God would give Abraham and his descendants that land to be theirs forever. And as part of this covenant, he promised that Abraham and his wife Sarah—old as they were—would, indeed, become parents and their eventual offspring would be as numerous as the stars of the sky. Through Abraham all the people of the earth would be blessed. He would be "blessed to be a blessing."

Abraham did not take this visionary experience lightly. He didn't wake up the next morning and say to himself, "Wow. I wonder what *that* was all about," and keep right on worshiping the Moon Goddess. Abraham believed what this as yet unknown God told him, and he acted on it.—And everything worked out according to God's promise. Abraham was led far from home, to Canaan where he received a rich land to be his own. He acquired flocks and herds and servants and all the trappings of a Mesopotamian potentate. Finally, he and Sarah became parents when they were close to a hundred years old. You probably all learned this story as children. Abraham was The Man of Faith—with capital letters. God spoke; Abe believed and acted.

Can you imagine the joy of those two when Isaac was born? Here was the Child of the Promise, the seal on the covenant God had made with Abraham, the fulfillment of all their prayers and hopes and dreams. Don't you know young Isaac had everything a boy could want? He probably had his own camel when he was eight. This son of their old age was *everything* to Abraham and Sarah. If they lived in our day, Abraham would be the kind of father who has a camera in his hands all the time and who fills the hard drive of his new Mac with nothing but pictures of his precious boy.—400 gigabytes of Isaac. All Isaac all the time!

Then, after Isaac had grown to be 15 or maybe a bit older, the Bible says God decided to test Abraham. But God didn't tell Abraham it was "only a test." Abraham just knew what God told him—the God whose every word he had always trusted and obeyed. God said "Take your son, your only son Isaac, whom you love, and go to the land of Moriah, and offer him there as a burnt offering on one of the mountains that I shall show you." Abraham chose to obey God, awful as God's will seemed.

We're doing a study of the Lord's Prayer on Thursday nights this Lent. In a few weeks we'll come to the part of the Lord's Prayer that says: "Lead us not into temptation." Another way of saying that is: "Do not bring us to the test." In that model for our prayer, Jesus is saying *It happened to me. Pray that it doesn't happen to you, too."* But the Biblical record of God's dealing with human beings is that there are times when God DOES bring us to the test.—He tested Abraham. He tested his own Son. And it's possible—even likely—that God will also test you and me.

What will we do if we're put to the test? Let's hope that, if such a testing comes, we'll have learned from Abraham and we'll have learned from Jesus: No matter what happens—no matter what—*keep trusting God.*

Abraham took his only son, the delight of his life, his source of joy and the only assurance that his name would be remembered on earth, and he set out to go to the place of sacrifice. Genesis doesn't tell us, can't tell us, what Abraham was feeling. But we can guess. What was he thinking?

We can't know that for sure either, but we're told what he answered when Isaac—who knew exactly what sacrifices called for—said, "Father, here is the fire, the wood, and the knife, but where is the lamb for the burnt offering?" Abraham answered, "God himself will provide the lamb, my son."

"GOD HIMSELF WILL PROVIDE THE LAMB." That's the message of this story, perhaps the message of Scripture itself: *God will provide*. Abraham trusted God, but God tested that trust. There's something else in this story that might be easy to miss: Isaac trusted God, too, and his trust was also tested.

Nobody else was up on Mount Moriah except frail, one hundred-and-fifteen year-old Abraham and strapping, fifteen year-old Isaac. But young Isaac yields himself for the sacrifice. He could easily have pushed his old father down on the ground without harming him and run away. But he didn't try to escape. Instead, he probably helped build the altar and put the wood on it. Then he climbed up on it and let himself be bound. He watched as Abraham picked up the knife.—Then God stopped the test and said, "Do not lay your hand on the boy or do anything to him; for now I know that you fear God, since you have not withheld your son, your only son, from me."

"God himself will provide the lamb." Jesus told his disciples more than once, "The Son of Man must undergo great suffering, and be rejected by the elders, the chief priests, and the scribes, and be killed, and after three days rise again." But in the Garden of Gethsemane, he prayed, "Father, if it might be your will, let this cup pass from me. Nevertheless, not my will but yours be done."

As we walk on towards Good Friday and Easter, please consider Isaac, Abraham's only son—carrying the wood for his sacrifice, stretched out on the altar on Mount Moriah (an altar of his own obedient making), ready to accept the will of God, 'til God stopped the test, and said: "Now I KNOW that you fear God, since you have not withheld your son, your only son, from me."

Then consider Jesus, "the only Son of the Father, full of grace and truth," carrying his heavy cross to the hill of Golgotha—only a short walk from where Abraham and Isaac had built their altar so long before. But nobody stopped this test, because on Golgotha MAN was, in Christ, putting GOD to the test.—And God passed the test. God did not withhold his only Son, but gave him up for us. God kept faith with Abraham. He provided the Lamb, the Lamb who has taken away the sin of the world.

How big is *your* God? What claim does God have on your *life?* . . . on your *trust?*

If God brings you to the test—as he brought Abraham, as he brought Jesus—will you put your faith in this God and trust him, no matter what happens? . . . *no matter what?*

16. BELIEVING IS SEEING.

John 9:1-41

Think about what it feels like to be in the dark, in a place with absolutely no light. Have you ever been in a cave, underground, or in a windowless basement when the lights went out? People step on each other, push each other down, and poke their fingers in one another's eyes.

And if it's not totally dark, but nearly so, we still get confused about what we're seeing. Shapes are hard to make out. An overcoat on a peg looks like a person. Color is impossible to discern. Everything is some shade of gray. Smiles and frowns alike are indistinguishable. Forget about reading anything. Our depth perception is thrown off, and we can't tell how steep a flight of steps may be. Dim light is only a slight improvement over darkness.

Jesus said, "As long as I am in the world, I am the light of the world."

In the story of Jesus healing a man born blind we have the fascinating description of a situation where an assortment of people see the same person, but their perceptions of him are all different. Everybody in the story—except for Jesus—sees the blind beggar as a one-dimensional man.

Jesus' own disciples look at the blind beggar and they see him simply as living proof of someone's sin. Either he sinned or his parents sinned. There's no compassion for him. The poor man is merely fodder for a theological debate.—If nobody sinned, why would he be blind? Misfortune in this life, they think, has to be the result of *somebody's* sin. So the interesting question is: whose sin was it?

People in the neighborhood who are accustomed to seeing the blind man daily on the street only see a beggar. Seeing him is the same as seeing a tree or a vegetable stall. He's part of the local scenery, scarcely even human. They don't really know him, even though some of them walk past him every day and have even tossed a coin onto his blanket a few times. They've just treated him the way they'd have treated any other object that was blocking their path—as merely an obstacle, a thing. So, when Jesus has given him sight and he is able to move around freely, these people aren't sure who he is.

The man has been defined exclusively *by the role he has played in relationship to them.* That is: he has been a blind beggar, immobile in the road, and they have been—at best—at least potentially, donors.

The Pharisees see the blind man in two ways: as a problem to be dealt with and as an ignorant, sinful person beneath their contempt. He has obviously been Jesus' partner in violating God's commandment concerning the Sabbath and, therefore—as far as they're concerned—when the beggar refuses to parrot their judgment on Jesus, he and Jesus are both to be condemned as law-breakers, outside the pale—people with whom good, law-abiding people such as they are must refuse to have fellowship.

His parents, from whom the man might have expected some compassion, who should have been filled with gratitude that their son has received his sight, instead see him only as a kind of threat to their own status. He's in trouble with the Pharisees; and they're afraid that somehow they might be implicated in his problems. If anyone is going to be expelled from the synagogue, they don't want it to be them.

Finally, there is the perspective of Jesus. He sees the blind beggar quite differently from the way his disciples or the bystanders or the Pharisees do. He sees him as full of wonderful potential. He says that the man's blindness is simply a dimension of his existence which will allow the work of God to be done, the glory of God to be revealed in him. And he proceeds to deal with the man in a way that finally releases the man's potential.

Jesus demonstrates to anyone who has eyes to see (that is, to *us*) that the true work of God is not hair-splitting about what's legal or deciding about who are the sinners according to this or that Biblical precept, but rather about being *agents of new creation.* And that's the symbolism behind his spitting and making mud from the dust of the earth to put on the blind man's eyes. Remember the Genesis creation story? God forms Adam from the earth. Jesus uses a mud-pack to give the blind man sight, and the man becomes a new creation.

This raises for us the question of how *we* see other people and their situations and how we respond to them. To what extent are we "in the light" and to what extent are we "in the dark"? To what extent are we able to be agents of God's new creation?—How quickly and glibly we take one look at them and pronounce a hasty judgment on other people. For example:

- We might see a Latino shoveling snow at a big house here in the West End this morning and say to ourselves, "Oh, there's another illegal alien. We need to do something about 'those people.' They're everywhere." If we really knew the man who's shoveling snow as a *person,* we'd know that his parents came from Mexico in the '60s and live in Alamosa, where he was born and raised. The man has lived in Colorado all his life. His children go to kindergarten with some of our grandchildren.

- We might hear about a friend who has lost a lot of money because he invested heavily in a company that just went bankrupt, and we say to our spouse "It serves him right. He didn't do careful research, and he didn't even take the time to ask my opinion. I know about companies in that field, and I would have steered him away from that one." Of course, if we had talked at length with the man, we'd have learned that his brother is president of the company into which he sank all his money, and he felt obligated out of love for his brother to take a big risk—which later proved unfortunate in a financial sense, because the company ultimately went under. But in another sense his risky investment was brilliant, because it forged a bond with his brother that will endure for a lifetime.

- We might hear about a couple who are divorcing and say immediately, "I've seen him in Starbucks with another woman. He

has probably been cheating on his wife, and she got wise to it."
If we knew the truth, we'd have known that the couple had been
undergoing marriage counseling for more than two years—trying
hard to keep their relationship together. And the woman we saw
in the coffee shop with him was their therapist.

Don't *you* grow weary of the labels that we hang on people? I do. Once
we've labeled someone, we've put them in a box and we don't have to think
about them anymore. We don't have to listen to them. We don't really have
to *know* them. They've stopped being three-dimensional, multi-faceted,
richly interesting individuals and have become pigeon-holed. We do it with
partisan labels like "conservative" and "liberal" in politics or "traditionalist"
and "revisionist" in the church.

The last verses of today's gospel are the spiritual heart of the story of Jesus
healing the man who was born blind. I want to read them to you:

> After the healed blind man said, "Lord, I believe," and worshiped
> him, Jesus said: "I came into this world for judgment, so that
> those who do not see may see, and those who do see may become
> blind." Some of the Pharisees nearby heard this and they said to
> him, "Surely, we are not blind are we?" And Jesus replied, "If you
> were blind, you would not have sin. But now that you say, 'We see,'
> your sin remains."

The message here is clear: BELIEVING IS SEEING.

When we walk in the light of Christ, when we live in a world illuminated
by the One who is the light of the world, then we have insight and the
capacity to perceive a level of reality that is more than merely superficial.
We are in a position to be God's agents of new creation.

There's an old English proverb that goes back to the mid-sixteenth
century: "None are so blind as those who will not see."

The question for us to ponder is this: *By what light are we making* OUR *way
in the world?*

17. THE HEART OF GOD.

Genesis 9:8-17

Guess what most children's favorite Bible story is. It's the story of Noah and the ark. If you go to department stores—even in this secular age—looking for things like sheets and bedspreads, or curtains and wallpaper for a little child's bedroom you'll run into the Noah's ark motif again and again. You'll see Noah with his big boat full of animals and a rainbow in the background.—Noah is right up there with Spiderman. That's amazing.

Little kids who've never been to Sunday School are probably clueless about the story, but they like the pictures of the big boat with all the animals in it and the rainbow. Noah's ark gives us the Biblical image for our Lenten Self-denial Offering this year: the Heifer Project. We're aiming to raise money in Lent to provide an "ark" full of animals, not two of every kind of animal, but an assortment of different useful farm animals that can benefit poor and hungry people around the world.—Read the brochure that you'll find in your bulletin and pick up an ark and other materials from the display in the narthex.

I want to talk about the story of Noah this morning, but I don't want to concentrate on the aspect of it that fascinates the children—the stuff about the big boat and all the animals. Instead, I want us to think about a dimension of the story of Noah and the great flood that we rarely consider: that is, what it tells us about the nature of God, what we might call the heart of God, as revealed in the Hebrew Scriptures.

This is important for Christians, because if we reflect on what this old, old story from the first book in the Bible tells us about the heart of God, it helps us understand why God sent his Son Jesus to share our humanity and give himself for the world's redemption. John 3:16 says *"God so loved the world that he gave his only Son."* In an amazing way, that verse links right back to Noah. It really does.—So let's see how that works.

Genesis starts with the creation story. Without getting into the current flap about creationism versus evolution, let's just agree that the Genesis creation story gives us a *theological* picture—not a biological picture—of the essential connection between the human and the divine. The Biblical story says that human beings were formed in God's likeness, particularly in the sense that the Man and the Woman had freedom to make choices: to love, to create, and to live in intimacy with God and the rest of creation. This freedom made them like God.

To compress the first six chapters of Genesis into one sentence I'll simply say this: the Man and the Woman and their descendants used their god-like freedom to choose evil much more often than good. They chose to hate, to destroy, and to reject intimacy with God and the rest of creation. Their bad choices turned into ingrained attitudes and evil habits. It became so bad that human evil even tainted the rest of the living creatures in the world—a world that the Creator had looked at, in all its freshness at the beginning, and lovingly said "It's good. It's very good."

The Book of Genesis doesn't give the details about humanity's degradation, it just tells us that "the LORD saw that the wickedness of humankind was great in the earth, and that every inclination of the thoughts of their hearts was only evil continually. And the LORD was sorry that he had made humankind on the earth, and it grieved him to his heart." [Gen. 6:5-6] There is nothing in the Old Testament to suggest that God knows the future in an absolute way. We have to assume from the story that God had not expected things would turn out like this. It was a tragic disappointment. So God decided to blot out the human beings that he had created and, along with them, all of the other creatures that shared God's gift of breath, because human wickedness had even corrupted them.—All were sullied, tainted, ruined—except for one man, Noah. He was "a *righteous* man," the only *blameless* man on earth.

Now, let's not start to argue with the story and ask, "How could aardvarks and emus, polar bears and partridges, all be 'corrupted'—no matter how wicked the human beings were?" This is a STORY. And its point is not to give scientific facts about natural history but to communicate spiritual truth about the heart of God. And that truth is this: it grieved the heart of God to send the great flood to wipe out the creatures into whom he had breathed his own life, and to whom he had given the gift of his own freedom. He looked at his creation and said, "I am so sorry."

The nature of God is revealed here—as Israel understood God—and theirs was a unique understanding: namely, that God is open to and affected by his world. God isn't detached from the realm of matter and utterly beyond emotion, the way the Greeks insisted God had to be—cold and passionless. Rather, Israel saw God as intimately connected with the material world and affected by it. Israel never hesitated to ascribe human feelings to God. In fact, the very capacity to feel was a divine gift to humankind, along with the gift of freedom.

The story of Noah and the flood is about God's covenant love—his pledge and bond with his creation. God determined to renew the world with Noah and his family and with pairs of all the living creatures. He didn't abandon the whole project, even though it had gone terribly awry. We might say God's heart was broken by the evil in humanity that had tainted the world, and God determined to purify the world—to wash it clean—but *not* to reject it, even though he regretted what it had become.

The pain in the heart of God that we see in the Noah story reminds us of the pain that has to be in the hearts of human parents who watch one or more of their beloved children go wrong and become enmeshed in a life of crime. These parents love their child, but cannot excuse or justify their crimes.

Righteous Noah and his offspring, preserved by the ark that God commanded Noah to build, become (in a sense) the bearers of God's hope for the renewal of his world. Noah, like Abraham in the next part of the book of Genesis, *believes* God. He believes, and he *obeys*.—"Trust and obey." Isn't this a major theme in Scripture?—Because he believes God and is obedient, Noah and his wife and their family are saved—along with pairs of all other living things. As we look at the long story of salvation history that we're given in the Bible, this is one of the essential stages in God's work to save and redeem his creation.

Here we see the heart of God as the wisdom of Israel knew it. We see the suffering of God, the grief of God, as he watches the flood erase all his beloved creatures not kept safe in the ark with obedient Noah. God's grief brings about, as Genesis tells the story, a *change in God*. And the change in God is greater than the change wrought in the world by the flood.

When the flood waters subside and Noah and his family and the animals come out of the ark, God sees that they are still inclined to evil and still able to corrupt the created order, but God has decided that he loves the world so much that he will never deal with its sin again in such a way. He makes a covenant with Noah and with every living creature, promising that there will never again be a flood to destroy all life. Then God hangs his bow in the clouds as a sign of his covenant promise. God will see the bow, and mortals will see it, and both God and mortals will *remember the promise*. God has made a covenant with all flesh. He will deal with our sin and its consequences hereafter in a new way.

As I said before, there's a long straight line from the story of Noah in the Old Testament to "God so loved the world that he gave his only Son"—from the rainbow to the cross. Instead of preparing some future comprehensive punishment for human sin, God decides—after the flood—to endure the wickedness of the world while opening his own heart to that world. God decides to carry its pain himself, so that the world might have a future. This is the message of Christ, the message that's at the heart of Lent, Holy Week and—especially—Easter.

Our Lenten journey has begun. Let's pray that it includes a growing consciousness of the heart of God, a patient seeking for the signs of God's covenant love in the world around us, and an overflowing gratitude that God keeps his promises. Remember: *we can still see rainbows.*

18. ME AND MY SHADOW.

Romans 5:6-11

*G*od *proves his love for us in that while we still were sinners Christ died for us.*

A couple of weeks ago we went to see the new movie, *Crash,* at the Isis. Maybe some of you have seen it. If you haven't, you should. But now it's only on down in Carbondale at the Crystal. I'm not about to give a movie review, but this film about racial and ethnic conflict demonstrates one significant truth about human beings: the best of us always have a dark side, and the worst of us have at least a glimmer of light in us.

"So what?" you might say. "We already knew that." And you probably already know this too: that our ability to get beyond our personal darkness (our *shadow* as the psychologists call it)—the ability to transcend it rather than be destroyed by it—depends entirely on our willingness to confront it. But often we refuse to do that.

Lots of us live year after year—well into maturity—denying that we *have* a shadow side at all. We simply won't look at it. The shadow is a potent metaphor, because everyone who stands in sunlight casts a shadow. And anyone who ventures into that light (which is, of course, another metaphor) can see his shadow, if he has the courage to look. This is a subject of both Greek and Shakespearean tragedies. It's a standard theme because it's a universal truth. You and I are dealing with it today, each in our own personal way.

My shadow is not an illusion. It's real. So is yours. The darkness in us is not simply a matter of misperception. A biblical rather than psychological way of putting it is to say that we all must contend with the reality of *sin* in our life. The Bible says that "God is light, and in him there is no darkness at all." We've known people whose lives seem to be all sunshine, haven't we? They appear golden. Everything always goes their way; they never have a bad day; they come out of every situation looking good.—Well, let me tell you, even these golden people struggle in secret with their own personal blends of sin, guilt, failure, and self-rejection. There's darkness there, too, under the gold—though it may be well hidden.

Today we heard a few key verses from Paul's Letter to the Romans. I haven't run into very many people who feel much fondness for old Paul, but I like him. I have an icon of Paul hanging on the wall beside my desk. It's a pity more people don't have warmer feelings for him, because I think Paul is somebody any Christian can identify with, if we just get to know him through reading and re-reading his letters. We call him "Saint" Paul, but he's not wearing a halo. He's a very normal human being: imperfect, impulsive, hot-tempered, and vain—but at the same time dedicated, selfless, compassionate, and tender-hearted.

Read Galatians or Romans and you see a man who's obviously wrestling with his shadow. In other letters he alternates between being embarrassingly arrogant and self-deprecatingly humble. He's so brilliant his intellect sometimes carries him beyond our comprehension. We just don't get what he's driving at. At other times he can be as direct, full of feeling, and down-home in his language as my dear old East Texas grandma used to be.

The key insight into Paul—the one that can unlock the power of his letters—is that he had been bowled over by the unimaginable grace God had shown him, personally. And I mean *grace* in the theological sense: unmerited favor. Paul, then known only as Saul, had been a dedicated young persecutor of Christians. He was building himself a career as an agent of the High Priest, seeking out disciples of the crucified Messiah and dragging them off to prison, when suddenly and without any preliminaries at all Jesus himself confronted him on a Syrian road in a blinding noonday light.

Instead of thundering in a terrifying voice, saying "Leave my people alone, or your doom is sealed," Jesus called Paul to be his own special ambassador. His conversion experience was so vivid, and his amazement at being chosen as a witness for Jesus, despite his own personal evil, was so great that it shaped his message—his gospel—for the rest of his life. Paul was a new man after the Damascus Road event, but he always had to struggle with his shadows: the constant need to prove himself, recurrent bouts of legalism, and occasional displays of self-righteousness. You can find all this in his letters.

Romans is Paul's self-introduction to a little community of disciples who had never met him. The letter was sent on ahead of him by a messenger in order to give the Christians in Rome a sense of who Paul was and what he stood for before he arrived there for a visit. In the part of Romans we heard this morning, he tells how Christ made it possible for him to face his own shadow—which he goes on to describe later in these agonized words, where he tells how, although he is trying hard to do good things, his personal weaknesses keep causing him to fail. He writes,

> "I obviously need help. I realize that I don't have what it takes. I can will it, but I can't do it. I decide to do good, but I don't really do it; I decide not to do bad, but then I do it anyway. My decisions, such as they are, don't result in actions. Something has gone wrong deep within me and gets the better of me every time. It happens so regularly that it's predictable. The moment I decide to do good, sin is there to trip me up. I truly delight in God's commands, but it's pretty obvious that not all of me joins in that delight. Parts of me covertly rebel, and just when I least expect it, they take charge. I've tried everything and nothing helps. I'm at the end of my rope. Is there no one who can do anything for me?—Isn't that the real question?—The answer, thank God, is that Jesus Christ can and does."

Maybe I like Paul because I can hear myself in his words. I was brought up in a Bible-centered household and spent much of my life—starting in childhood—trying hard always to do the right thing, obey the Law, and keep all the rules. I was a kind of Christian Pharisee. And sometimes those old reflexes kick in, even now. When that happens, I feel like I ought to have been a hero for Jesus—but I haven't been, and I'm not, and so I figure I've somehow let God down. I've failed him.

When I start thinking like that it's clear that what I want is to *deserve* God's favor and achieve some imaginary spiritual success through my own efforts or virtue. Pride is what that's called, and vanity. Then I get over it, and I'm ashamed of myself, and I try to get back on track.—Let me assure you, if you stand in the pulpit and presume to preach the gospel to other people, you put yourself squarely in the brightest light that shines—the light of God's Son—and that brilliance makes your shadow so dark you can't miss it.

The comfort for me, and I pray the comfort for you too, as we face our own sin, our personal shadows—whether they're pride, or vanity, or greed, or anger or something else—is expressed perfectly in the words of Paul we heard this morning: While we were still weak, at the right time Christ died for the ungodly. God proves his love for us in that while we still were sinners Christ died for us. If while we were enemies, we were reconciled to God through the death of his Son, much more surely, having been reconciled, will we be saved by his life.

Accepting these words of Paul as insight into the work of Christ, not just for Paul but *for me*, is what brings me back to my senses again and again. I'm a mixed creature, just like the characters in the movie *Crash.* I have some good qualities, sure, but I also cast a dark shadow. I'm not golden. I'm weak, not strong.

If my salvation depends entirely on my virtues and spiritual successes, I'm in serious trouble. But the Son of God gave himself for me, and for every single soul that ever *has* lived and ever *will* live.—That's *grace!* The Son of God loved us in advance of our birth. His love was not, is not, and never will be conditioned on our being spiritual heroes or good people or even on our being sorry for our sins.

In his ministry among ordinary mortals in Judea and Galilee, Jesus made friends with unrepentant sinners. He did good to them. He healed them. He had supper with them and laughed at their jokes. He didn't hold himself aloof until they got religion, or made a perfect act of contrition, or answered an altar call. While we still were sinners, Christ died for us. All we have to do is believe this and behave as if it's the truth. Because it is.

What a relief! What a joy! Still casting our long shadows, we are already reconciled to the God who is pure light, in whom there is no darkness at all. And this blissful end to the separation from God that comes from our ego-bound willfulness is accomplished entirely from God's side, not from ours.

Efforts at earning God's favor can't succeed. But we've been given that favor as a love-gift. God proves his love for us in that while we still were sinners Christ died for us. Deliverance from the destructive power of our own personal darkness has been worked in gentleness and love by the costly sacrifice of God who was, in Christ, reconciling the world to himself.

Ponder the power of what we're about to *do* in our worship this morning. Don't let the significance of these acts be lost because they're so familiar. The Peace of Christ we'll exchange in a few minutes is a simple reminder that we've been reconciled to God and each other through his Son. The body of Christ and the blood of Christ which we'll share after that is a constant assurance that we mixed creatures—full of aspirations to goodness but equally aware of our own darkness—have been accepted into the Eternal Light.

19. LAZARUS, COME OUT!

John 11

When do we feel the most alive? Lots of people here in Aspen might say they feel the most vital and physically vigorous after a great day of skiing or hiking in the mountains, or doing something else in the great outdoors. But, surely, life is more than simply getting our heart-rate up—healthy as that might be. The right question is: When does life have the most *meaning?*

For me, life has the most meaning when I feel secure and fulfilled in my relationships with God and other people—my family, my friends, and *you.* Belonging, and feeling good about that. Loving and being loved. Giving and receiving. Learning and growing. Working and sharing.—Truly to *live* is to have the energy and freedom to take spontaneous action, to have a sense of purpose and a vision that sees beyond our selves. To *live* means to have dreams for the future at the same time we're grateful for the past. To *live* means to have the capacity for authentic joy, no matter what our present circumstances might be.

Today we hear about the raising of Lazarus. After Lazarus had sickened and died and been in his tomb four days, Jesus called him *out* of that tomb *into* a new life. The raising of Lazarus is a miracle story, sure, but it was also meant as a *sign*—not just for the family and friends of Lazarus, but for you and me.

Look at some of the details. Mary and Martha and Lazarus were among the inner circle of Jesus' closest friends. One time the two sisters sent a messenger to look for Jesus, to tell him that their brother Lazarus was sick. They didn't say, "Lazarus is dying," but they didn't have to. People didn't send messengers across country in those days just to say, "Lazarus has the flu."

If you or I received a message like that from one of our dearest friends, we'd be on the next plane to Atlanta, or Houston, or wherever. But instead of dropping everything and going straight to them, Jesus deliberately dawdled 'til Lazarus died. Mary and Martha and Lazarus were probably thinking, "Soon, the Master will come; he will lay his hands on Lazarus and he will recover. Then this nightmare will be over." But that didn't happen. Jesus left the sisters to suffer through their brother's fatal illness and death—left them wondering why their friend Jesus didn't come in time to save his life.

How many times have we asked God for some great thing—some help, some healing, or some intervention in the negative course of events—and felt that we received no help? I've felt that way before. You probably have too. There have been times in my life when I sent urgent messages to the Lord, and had no results of the kind I was looking for.

To make a point, Jesus allowed Lazarus to die. He allowed nature to take its course. The man was dead and in his tomb four days before Jesus even got there. In the midst of the sisters' and neighbors' grief and pain—when their hope was finally gone—then, at last, Jesus showed up.

In itself, that raises some awkward questions. But one inescapable point is this: no matter how close we are to God, no matter how long we pray, simply delivering us from suffering, even from death, is not necessarily THE most important thing God wants to do for us. One of the most poignant verses in the Bible is this one in the Letter to the Hebrews, where it says concerning Jesus: "It was fitting that God, for whom and through whom all things exist, in bringing many children to glory should make the pioneer of their salvation complete through sufferings." [Heb. 2:10]

If the New Testament has a central message, the message is that God loves us. But God's love for us doesn't compel him to protect us from pain. God knows—and we know, too—that there are some things we can never learn *except* through pain, *except* through distress, *except* through failure.

Jesus wanted to help Lazarus and his sisters—but his help required the three of them to go through an ordeal first.

And what did Jesus *do* when he finally arrived in the midst of their suffering? One of the first things he did was join them in their grief. He wept with them. You know, it's a fact that sometimes the most comforting thing a friend can do for us is to join us in our tears—to share our pain in so deep a way that it becomes their own.

Then, after having delayed until Lazarus was dead, and even after joining the sisters in their grief, Jesus called their brother out of the tomb. When the sisters had given up, when there seemed to be no more room for hope, when all that was apparently left were pious thoughts and painful tears, Jesus ordered the stone removed from the opening to Lazarus' tomb.

Practical Martha, who expected not to see her brother again until the Last Day, said "Oh, no, Lord. He's been in the tomb four days. The smell will be disgusting." (Or, as the King James Version put it, *"He stinketh!"*) Jesus answered her with words that I'd like to see inscribed over the door of every church: "Did I not tell you that if you believed, you would see the glory of God?"

Here's the way it is: *The Lord comes to us when our hope has died.* He comes to us when the stench of our loss has become the only reality we can perceive and then—contrary to our natural expectations—if we trust him, he gives us life again. If you only believe, you will see the glory of God.

Ignoring Martha's resistance, Jesus asked that the tomb be unsealed and then he issued a command to the lifeless ears of a man who'd been dead four days, "Lazarus, come out!"—The bystanders held their breath. Then they heard sounds from inside the tomb, and Lazarus came shuffling out, with his feet and hands and head still tied with burial clothes. Jesus said, "Unbind him, and let him go!"

The story of Lazarus is for people who're spiritually tied up in the burial clothes of a tepid, diluted Christianity whose Jesus is merely a wise man and whose faith—if we can call it faith—is little more than a hopeful lack of certainty. The Lazarus Experience brings us to a new place in our relationship with God. It gives us what Jesus told Martha about. It gives us, not the sense that there's a way to get whatever we want from God whenever we ask, and not confidence that there is spiritual insurance against pain and heartbreak, but *the capacity to see the glory of God,* the nature of God revealed in action.

The world is filled with people who, in a spiritual sense, are the walking dead. They're lifeless.—We may even be among them.—But the voice of the Son of God has power to call us out of our figurative tombs into a bigger life than we ever imagined—one rich with meaning, energy, purpose, vision, and joy. Not just a pale existence, but what Paul described to Timothy as "the life that really *is* Life."

When we hear the word of Christ and come out of our tombs, we can see, as never before, the breadth and beauty of the life God has for us. We're also able to see other lives where they're most vulnerable, most threatened, and most in need of what we can offer as agents of God's new creation.

Jesus is asking us to have confidence that no matter how bad things stink right now, no matter how many times we've felt beaten down by misfortune, disease, prejudice or any other circumstances, the Life-giver is still among us. He gives life to the dead—and I mean "dead" in every way we want to use the word, metaphorically or otherwise. He calls forth new life in circumstances where our reflexes and our education make us want to scream, "No, don't open the tomb. There'll be a stench."

Right now Christ is calling the dead to "Come out!"

- Come out from the tomb of your self-sufficiency, where you can't admit that you need either God or other people.

- Come out from the tomb of self-absorption, and open your eyes to the needs of others.

- Come out from the tomb of your obsession with things that don't matter, and reach out for the things that are essential to *real* life.

- Come out from the tomb of worry and anxiety, and trust your future to the One whose love for you is boundless, and whose ability to help you is infinite.

- Come out from the tomb of knee-jerk skepticism, and choose the perspective of faith. (And it *is* a choice.)

The last thing Jesus said was to the bystanders, family and friends of the man who'd been dead, but was alive again: "Unbind him and let him go!" When Christ calls people out of their "tombs" into a new life, a new hope, a new relationship with God, it's up to us who care about them—us who are standing (you might say) at the doorways of their tombs—to "unbind them and let them go." That's something only *we* can do for them. We have to tear off the "tomb wrappings" with which we ourselves once bound them, hand and foot—our *own* old perceptions, habitual assumptions, and negative characterizations of them and our *own* indifferent, lukewarm faith. It's our job to unbind them and set them free to be new people, new creations, able to enter the new life God has for them, uninhibited.

Christ is sending us to be agents of his new creation, midwives for souls new-born into eternal life.—*Unbind them, and let them go!*

20. I AM BARABBAS.

Good Friday
The Passion according to John (18:1-19:37)

The worship of the church during Holy Week involves a lot of role play, a lot of dramatic re-enactment. It's a way of getting us out of our heads and into our hearts, our feelings, which is an important thing to do. We've just played out the parts of the Passion, the suffering of God in Christ, as recorded in John's gospel. This drama portrays a conflict of wills, a conflict of good versus evil.

The part of the story we re-enacted just now leaves the impression that evil seems to have won the day. But the mysterious truth is that in these apparently tragic events the will of God was done. For that reason we call this Friday "Good," not "Dark" or "Sad." Appearances can be deceiving.

The drama of Good Friday is about the overcoming of evil through the willing death of the Son of God. As in every great drama, we who witness the play are invited to make some personal, emotional connection with one of the characters. As we reflect on what we've just read and participated in, with whom do we connect?

There is no hero in the story except Jesus and no strong characters other than the Beloved Disciple, the Lord's Mother and her female companions. So, unless we're spiritually vain, we'll have to look for ourselves among the weaklings or the villains.

So let's begin with the arch-villain, Judas. He was one of Jesus' closest friends, but he betrayed his friend into the hands of his worst enemies. Judas may have engineered the events that led to Jesus' death. At the very least he cooperated with those who did. Judas' name has become a curse. Nobody wants to be called "a Judas."—But there must have been at least some potential good in him, otherwise why would Christ have called him to be one of his disciples? What good might Judas have done, had he made different choices?

He handed Jesus over to his enemies. But why did he do that? It seems highly unlikely that he did it for the money, since thirty silver pieces wasn't really much money. Maybe he was frustrated by Jesus' lack of aggressiveness. It could be that in his frustration with Jesus, Judas decided to force a confrontation between the Messiah and his enemies, hopeful that Jesus would summon angels from heaven to defend him. Let's give Judas the benefit of the doubt.

Maybe he was a well-intentioned, behind-the-scenes schemer, trying to push history in the right direction, but his scheme backfired. Maybe Judas thought he could provoke Jesus into seizing political power through the use of miracles instead of weapons. We can believe this about Judas: he put his faith in power. And the only kind of power he really believed in was power that could compel others to do what *he* wanted.

Judas was sure that he knew what was best. And he lived for power.—Is there a piece of us that's like Judas?

Next we turn to Peter, the Rock. Peter looks like an attractive guy: a John Wayne type—big, strong, and forceful—but humble, too. He was ready for anything. He was Jesus' strong right arm and spokesman for the Twelve, never afraid to speak his mind. In fact, old "Rock" seems to have been used to speaking first and thinking later. He wore his heart on his sleeve. During the scuffle with the soldiers in Gethsemane, Peter began bravely—swinging his sword around and managing to wound an attacker. But big, bold Peter ended up running away, leaving Jesus behind.

Earlier, he had loudly proclaimed his loyalty to Jesus and said "Though everyone else should abandon you, Lord, I will never leave you."—But he did. He abandoned Jesus, just as the others did. We were there with Peter just now at the house of the High Priest. We saw what happened: Jesus stood up to his accusers and denied nothing. Peter cringed and denied everything. Some friend. Some "rock".

Lots of bold talk from Peter, but it's all just hot air.—Are we ever like that? Brave talk, but cowardly behavior?

Let's not leave out Caiaphas, the ruling High Priest, and his father-in-law, old Annas, the retired High Priest. For Jews, the High Priest was God's supreme representative. High Priests were entrusted with holy things, but they were never what we'd call spiritual men. They were more like Renaissance popes. They had political matters on their minds all the time, because their nation was a tinderbox, full of crazy Zealots burning with rage against Rome. A High Priest had to be smart, and these two—Annas and his son-in-law and protégé, Caiaphas—certainly were that.

They knew that if Jesus were not put down, some of his followers might start a war with Rome—and then all that was precious to them would be destroyed. Caiaphas was tuned-in to political reality. He knew that if a war with Rome came, the Jews would lose. He was right. When war came, 34 years later, Jerusalem was leveled. The Temple demolished. The High Priest killed. And all the survivors enslaved.

Caiaphas thought, "Yes, this Galilean preacher is probably harmless, but he can become a figure around whom the fanatics rally. Anyway, he is a heretic, talking about 'destroying the Temple and building it again in three days.' Maybe he's insane. Madmen are everywhere, and a madman leading a mob could destroy us all." So Caiaphas said to the Elders, "It's better that one man should die than that the People be destroyed."

Annas and Caiaphas were nominally religious, totally pragmatic, and utterly cunning.—Do we admire any of those qualities? Have we ever laid a clever trap for someone?

What, now, about Pontius Pilate? In the drama we just read, Pilate is the key protagonist. Pilate was the official representative of the greatest power the world had known 'til then. Though he was sophisticated by certain standards, Pilate was known to be ruthless, cruel, and impulsive. His hands were already stained with Jewish blood. The only reason he was up in Jerusalem, rather than in his official residence on the coast, was because of the risk of riots at Passover. At the end of every Passover meal, there was a prayer that God would drive unbelievers out of the land of Israel. Pilate knew which unbelievers that prayer was aimed at.

Though he was cruel, Pontius Pilate was an experienced judge. He could tell the difference between a dangerous revolutionary and a mild-tempered preacher. He was able to distinguish between the innocent and the guilty. Roman justice was the best the world had yet seen.

The fact is that Pilate might even have been biased a bit in Jesus' favor because the High Priest was the Roman governor's nemesis. Pilate might have let Jesus go free, just to twist the noses of Caiaphas and Annas.

But Pilate was ambitious, and his career was under the control of one person: Tiberius Caesar.
Pilate's entire noble Roman demeanor vanished when he heard the chief priests yell: "If you release this man, you're no friend of Caesar." Woe to the governor who fell afoul of paranoid old Tiberius, who in his palace on the Isle of Capri heard every whisper in every office of every governor of every province in the Roman Empire.—So, Pilate the Judge reasoned to himself, "What's one more crucified Jew, after all?"

Pilate was building his career. He was ambitious.—Are we ambitious too? Have we ever compromised our values for the sake of our careers?

OK. Have we found a character with whom to identify so far? Maybe we have seen something of ourselves in all of them.—No? Well, there is ONE more. He just has a tiny part, but we mustn't overlook him. He's the one I identify with. Maybe you will too. *Barabbas.* Barabbas was guilty of everything Jesus had been falsely accused of. John calls Barabbas a "bandit," but he was really a revolutionary, an assassin, a dedicated enemy of Rome. We would call him a convicted terrorist. Barabbas had already been tried by Pilate and found guilty. Everyone knew it. Barabbas was slated to occupy one of the three crosses that were set to go up on Skull Hill that Friday. Yet Jesus died on that cross, not Barabbas—who, if he knew of Jesus at all, probably despised him as a weakling.

The gentle, humble carpenter from Nazareth, whose touch had healed the crippled, given sight to the blind, cleansed lepers of their sores, soothed the demon-tormented and raised the dead to life stretched out his innocent arms and died on the cross where the blood-stained hands of Barabbas were meant to be.

By popular demand the guilty man was excused and the innocent man was executed in his place. How ironic—and appropriate too—that the One who obeyed his heavenly Father faithfully all through his life should be tortured and crucified in the place of one whose name in Hebrew literally means "Son of the Father."

"Son of the Father." Yes, that's me. I am Barabbas. No doubt about it. The crowd calls out in sympathy for me. They identify with me because they're guilty too. And I fear death, now that it has come so close. But I'm spared. Jesus is guiltless, brave, and unafraid to die. And so he does.—For *me*.

Now, because Jesus hangs there in my place with his blood trickling down the wood of the cross that was made for me, I'm free to go. I am Barabbas, "Son of the Father." And so are you, my sisters and brothers. We are Children of the Father, and because of that, there's still hope for us.

Our brother, the Father's first-born, has died in our place, and so now we're free to go. Our lives can begin again today.

21. WE'RE DEFINED BY OUR EXPERIENCE OF THE RESURRECTION.

Easter

Acts 10:34-43

In the years after the resurrection of Jesus, his followers spread out from Jerusalem. As they went, they shared their memory of the things their Master had said and done. But what impelled them to talk the most was their experience of his Resurrection.

A dear lady down in Florida, a member of my first parish who is now in her 90's, told me something long ago that I've never forgotten. She said, *"A person with an experience is never at the mercy of somebody who just has an argument."* I've come to know that this is true. And that's what this sermon is about.

The first followers of Jesus were all Jews. Their fellow Jews ultimately came to despise them as blasphemers and expelled them from their synagogues. Gentile enemies either mocked them or flogged them. Sometimes they stoned them and left them for dead.—Just read the Book of Acts for details.

Some people—more of them gentiles than Jews—became Christians but later fell away because the personal cost of being a follower of Jesus was too great. Nevertheless, the number of Christians grew steadily, in spite of hostility from the synagogue, rejection by family members, persecution by the Roman government, and harassment by pagan neighbors who thought the Christians were just too different.

It's logical to ask the question *"Why?"* What made Christianity grow in popularity when it was so risky to be a Christian? And the answer to that question is the *same* reason that brings millions of people to churches all around the world on Easter Day. You can find it in the portions of the New Testament we just read this morning. The answer is this: it's their experience of the Risen Christ.

Their experience of meeting the Risen Christ made Peter and the other apostles bold and fearless. It transformed them. Encounter with the Lord after he had risen from the dead became the foundation of their lives. The changed lives of people like Peter and Paul and their willingness to die rather than deny their faith in Jesus is one of the primary pieces of evidence for the credibility of the resurrection. There is simply no evidence of people ever accepting death or persecution for the sake of something they *knew* to be false. If Jesus had not died and risen again, there would be no Christianity today.

I ask you: Do you believe in the resurrection of Christ? And, if you do, has that belief made a difference in your life? I do. And it has.

Today we heard about Peter speaking of Christ to some gentiles. He told them that God had chosen him to be one of the witnesses who met Jesus after he was raised from the dead. I'm a witness too, and on this Resurrection Day I want to tell you my story.

When I left grad school and went to seminary, I had my sights set on being a church history professor. I was career-focused. I had a plan for my life, and I was working my plan. The priesthood might turn out to be part of that plan, but only as an adjunct to my academic profession. I didn't want to work in a parish. Not ever. And I had no interest whatsoever in preaching. I was comfortable in a lecture room, but uneasy in a pulpit—mostly (I know now) because I had nothing to preach.

I was a philosophical rationalist. Though I had studied Greek in college and had focused my seminary studies on the New Testament, the Bible was mainly a subject of academic interest for me. I was a historian, and I was on the quest for the historical Jesus. I entertained serious doubt about whether the gospel stories of Jesus' resurrection were anything more than that—just stories.

In November of 1972 came the time for my ordination as a priest. I saw that as just another step on the way to the fulfillment of my ivory-tower career plan. During the ordination service, as I was kneeling on the floor of the seminary chapel with the hands of the Bishop and priests on my head, I suddenly heard a Voice speaking to me. I'd always mocked people who claimed to "hear the Lord," so this was a shocking and unexpected experience. The Voice that was speaking in my head drowned out the voice of the Bishop. The Voice said, "Until now you have done what you wanted to do. Hereafter, you shall do what I want you to do."—This experience made the hair stand up on the back of my neck. Nothing remotely like this had ever happened to me.

I was stunned. The experience shook my intellectual foundations. I didn't believe in things like that. I thought people who "heard voices" were schizophrenic. But I was quite mentally sound, and I was having an experience I could not explain.—After that day, my life changed. I began to read the Bible differently. Instead of reading Scripture in order to have grist for academic debates, I began to read in order to hear God.

Six weeks later, I was back in Texas visiting my family for Christmas and attending my home parish. The rector there had the flu, so he asked if I wanted to fill in for him at services on the Sunday after Christmas. I jumped at the chance.

Preaching wasn't comfortable for me, so I worked extra hard on my sermon—just the second one since my ordination. I don't know if what I said made much sense to the sparse congregation in church that Sunday after Christmas, but I can remember how deeply the assigned gospel spoke to me. It was the prologue to John. You know the passage. It begins, "In the beginning was the Word, and the Word was with God and the Word was God." And it goes on to say ". . . He came to his own people, and his own people received him not. But to those who received him, who believed on his name, he gave power to become the children of God."

As I drove back to my parents' house after church, I was still thinking about that gospel, about how much it resonated with my recent experience. I was sitting in the car at a red light, just feeling happy and peaceful, when suddenly it happened—I heard the Voice again. Only this time it was laughing, like someone suppressing a chuckle as he spoke. He said, "Yes. It's true. My gospel is true. And behold, I am alive forever more!"

Tears began to run down my cheeks. And I sat there at the traffic light, crying, as the signal changed from red to green and cars honked and drove around me. I collected myself and drove on towards my parents' house. But I hadn't gone half a mile before I had rationalized the whole thing. I said to myself: "I've just had an emotional experience, nothing more. These were merely echoes of my own thoughts." I went home and said nothing about this episode to anyone for about five years.

But the experience changed me immediately in two ways. The first was that, after hearing that Voice while I was in the car, I couldn't even make myself doubt the resurrection. All the contrary arguments now seemed shallow or silly. *I had had an experience. I had heard the Lord, and I knew he was alive.* The second was that I began to want to preach. Though I was back at the university, working on a dissertation (which I later discarded) and teaching undergraduates, the pulpit became more interesting than the lecture hall. It still is.

That's my experience. Because of it, I can say that I'm a witness to the resurrection. And, believe me, there are other people around you right now—in this church today—who are witnesses to the resurrection in similar or even more dramatic ways. They just don't happen to be giving the sermon today.—But maybe some Sunday one of them will.

"A person with an experience is never at the mercy of somebody who just has an argument."

We've had an encounter with Jesus Christ. Our experience of the Risen Christ defines us.—And nothing can change that.

Sure, witnesses to the resurrection have bad days, just like everybody else. I can lose my temper and get mad, or grumble, or feel depressed. I sometimes fuss about trivial things. But since that Sunday after Christmas in 1972 I have never been without hope, never doubted the future, and never feared death—because I know that my Redeemer lives.

Like many other people in the past twenty centuries, I have met the Lord. He spoke to me and changed my life.

I've had an experience, and my experience has made all the difference.

22. WHAT ABOUT "DOUBTING" THOMAS?

John 20:19-31

Thomas—the hard-nosed realist—is frequently portrayed by preachers as typical of modern people: skeptical (maybe even a little bit cynical), stubborn, scientific, serious-minded, a very contemporary kind of person.

I wonder where he was on the day Jesus rose from the dead. How did Thomas happen to be the only one of the inner circle absent when the Lord first appeared to his fearful disciples as they trembled behind locked doors—afraid that their Master's fate would soon be their own?

We *don't* know why Thomas was missing. But we can see from the gospel record that Thomas was an independent thinker.

Mary Magdalene had seen the risen Jesus on Sunday morning. She told her story. Peter and James and John and the rest had all seen the risen Jesus that same Sunday evening—when Thomas had been absent. They told him their story. Did Thomas believe his friends? No. Thomas had to see for himself. No number of eyewitness reports from friends would convince Thomas. He had to see for himself.—And demanded not only to see, but also to touch. There were not going to be any tricks or illusions for Thomas.

Thomas was serious. If he was going to believe—really believe—and commit himself to a resurrected Jesus with the same intensity that he had committed himself to the flesh-and-blood Jesus of Nazareth who had called him from his trade to be a disciple, then Thomas would require truly convincing evidence. For him, that meant a first-person, eye-witness experience of his very own.

And so Jesus returned, on the Sunday following the Day of the Resurrection, and he showed himself to Thomas. He put that skeptic's doubts to rest. Thomas was convinced. He saw. He believed. He worshiped.

How can Thomas teach a lesson to Third Millennium skeptics? We don't anticipate any more post-resurrection appearances of the Risen Christ—at least not of the sort that we can tell contemporary skeptics to *expect*. So what can we say? I think the gospel permits us to say this: that the Lord in his love for us, in his gracious compassion for us, will provide whatever is needed to overcome the doubts of any serious seeker who truly *wants* to believe—no matter how skeptical that person might be.

Thomas loved Jesus, and he *wanted* to believe that his Master had been raised from the dead. He really *wanted* to believe that the grave could not hold him. But before he could believe, he needed to *have an experience* on which to ground his faith. He had loved Jesus too much and had been too committed as a disciple to accept anything less than an authentic meeting with the risen Lord. The gospel shows us that Jesus honored Thomas' honest doubt and gave him the experience he needed in order to move from doubt to faith.

I say this to sincere seekers after truth: Doubt is not a bad thing. Asking hard questions is not a bad thing. But skeptical or questioning seekers—if they're truly looking for the Lord—are willing to be convinced. They're *willing* to believe, *IF* given good grounds for that belief. There is a way of distinguishing between serious seekers and those people who just want to mock and belittle Christians. Serious seekers are willing to believe, willing to let faith change their lives—*if they have the personal experience they need.*

Jesus once healed the son of a man who said to him, "Lord, I believe. Help my unbelief." *That's* where many people today find themselves. Such people are saying, in effect, *"Lord, I do believe—at least a little. Anyway, I want to believe. Please do something to help my unbelief."*

If you are in that category, or if you know other people who are, I make this pledge to you: If you want to believe in Jesus, but need to have a personal experience to sustain your faith, God will give you the kind of experience you need. Just ask him.—But keep this in mind: *the faith-building experience you ultimately have may well turn out to be very different from the sort you originally demanded.*

It's important for the modern seeker (and for us) that when Jesus showed himself to serious, disbelieving Thomas on that first Sunday after the Day of Resurrection, he did not do so on a lonely road where Thomas was sitting all alone, or in another place where Thomas might have been in solitude. We need to take notice that Jesus came to Thomas when Thomas was right in the middle of the group of disciples who had already seen the Risen Lord and believed in him. Thomas met the Lord when he was surrounded by believers.

I think this is where the serious, but questioning religious seeker is going to meet the living Christ today: *in the midst of a believing community of Christian people.* This raises for our church—and for every church—a painful but necessary question: do *we* as a community of Christians possess the kind of faith that provides the setting where a doubter might meet the risen Lord?

In the gospel accounts of Jesus' appearances to the Ten Disciples on the evening of the first Easter and his appearance to the Ten plus Thomas exactly a week later, we notice one very special thing: Jesus was identified by the Ten and by Thomas *only* by the physical marks of his sacrificial death—the nail wounds in his hands and the spear wound in his side.

They had spent three years as his disciples, but they didn't identify him by his familiar face or his hair color, or his height and weight. The Bible says that when he first appeared in the locked room and spoke to them, they were afraid. But when he showed them his hands and his side, they knew him, and they were glad. The signs of his having suffered were the assurance of his true identity.

This is the message that the Risen Lord has for the Church in our time. This is his word for those who believe in him and especially for a community of believers who would like to be able to help skeptics and doubters find faith. Jesus wants to say, "He who has seen me has seen the Father. He who sees you must see me. *And I am going to be identified only by the signs of self-sacrificing love.*"

One of the characteristics of Pope John Paul II that reporters commented on during the last few days of his life was that he didn't try to hide his personal suffering or accommodate his own physical needs. Though he was crippled by Parkinson's disease, he pushed himself to serve and give of himself to the limits of his capacity to the very end. His example touched a countless number of people.

A church that reveals Christ to the world is going to be a church that is willing to pay the price of self-sacrificing love. The church that reveals Christ to the world is going to be a church that has some wounds to show.

Our postmodern world is filled with doubters like Thomas who demand to see the Lord before they will believe that he is alive. They demand to have a personal experience of Christ before they will believe in him. And they know how to identify him, just as Thomas did. *They will recognize that Christ is really present when they can see his wounds*—the marks of his self-sacrifice. Nothing else is a sure sign of his identity.

The question left for us to answer is this: *Will they find him here?*

23. FOUNDATIONS.

Matthew 7:21-27

A few years ago, the church where I was then the rector had a big building project. We demolished an older building and built a new ministry center adjacent to the church and parish hall. The contractors put up a safety fence around the site, but there was one window in the older part of the building where people could go to look down on the work. I'd go there every day to see what was happening.

One thing that amazed me in the beginning was how deep the hole was that the contractors started with . . . how far down they excavated to lay the foundations for the building. Though they were working every day, it was months before there was anything to see from outside at ground level. All the work was happening down in that big hole. Putting in foundations and footings was the most time consuming part of the project. But it had to be done right, because our church was situated in a river valley. It had only been five or six years since the lower level of the church had been flooded.

Once a building is completed, it's very difficult to go back and replace the foundations. It *can* be done, but it's a complicated, costly, and time-consuming operation.—Just ask the engineers who put new foundations under the Leaning Tower of Pisa. That job took hundreds of years to get done right. Lots of smart people took a stab at it and failed—until now. And the tower still leans; it's just not going to fall down.

Today we heard the conclusion to Jesus' Sermon on the Mount, which you can find in chapters five, six and seven of Matthew. We don't have time to review everything in those three chapters, but we can say this about it: the Sermon on the Mount is a collection of Jesus' precepts for godly living. Jesus said, "Not everyone who says to me, 'Lord, Lord'"—which is to say, "Not everyone who just spouts off correct doctrine"—"will enter the kingdom of heaven, but only the one who does the will of my Father who is in heaven." The precepts found in the Sermon on the Mount reveal the will of God.

I'm sure you're familiar with these few excerpts from the Sermon: "Be reconciled to your brother or sister who has anything against you. . . . Forgive, and you will be forgiven. . . . If anyone strikes you on the right cheek, turn the other also. . . . Love your enemies. . . . Do good to those who hate you. Pray for those who despitefully use you and persecute you. . . . Give to one who begs from you, and do not refuse one who would borrow from you. . . . Do not lay up treasures for yourselves on earth, but lay up treasures in heaven. . . . Do not judge and you will not be judged, for the measure you give will be the measure you get back. . . . You cannot serve God and money. . . . Do not be anxious about tomorrow. . . . In everything, do to others as you would have them do to you."

Jesus wanted his disciples to understand that he was calling them not just to a new way of thinking about the old, familiar Law of Moses, but to a completely new way of living. This new way of living was a lifestyle of radical obedience to God, who had said to the Old Testament prophets things like, "I desire mercy and not sacrifice," and "I reject your festivals; take away from me the noise of your songs; but rather let justice roll down like waters and righteousness like an ever-flowing stream." To put it simply, Jesus tells us that his heavenly Father is far more concerned with how we treat one another than with any other aspect of our religion.

One of my all-time favorite quotations is from *The Promise of Paradox* by Parker Palmer, a Quaker philosopher and educator. I put it on the message board outside this week. Palmer wrote, *"You don't think your way into a new kind of living; you live your way into a new kind of thinking."* What that means is: the way we choose to act ultimately re-shapes our attitudes—not the other way around. How you choose to behave will—in time—change the way you think. That's the point Jesus makes in the Sermon on the Mount: this is the will of God for you; *live this way and you will come to see the world differently.* This way of living is wisdom, the foundation for ultimate happiness.

The task of the disciple of Jesus is to apply what we learn from him—not just be able to quote him correctly. That's the difference between knowing things and being wise. We're not preparing for a final exam; we're preparing for eternity in the kingdom of God. Our work is to hear and obey. Jesus said, "Everyone who hears these words of mine and acts on them will be like a wise man who built his house on rock."

It's graduation season. Lots of us know someone who's graduating from high school or college. These graduates have been—in various ways—laying foundations for their lives. They've been learning facts, concepts, principles, and methods (and they'll learn more of these as time goes on). But the quality of the foundations they've been laying isn't going to be measured by how many facts, concepts, principles and methods they've put into their heads—how much information they have—but rather by the way they live out those facts, concepts and so forth, day by day and year by year over the remainder of their lives—how much *wisdom* they've acquired. The quality of their educational foundation will be tested by the degree to which these young men and women ultimately *apply what they've learned.*

If you know the truth, but don't live the truth, you've failed—no matter how high a grade you might score on an examination that tests how much truth is in your head. The test of the foundation of a building is in how well that building endures the winds and floods that are sure to come against it. To what extent do we put our faith into practice? To what extent do we not only remember the words of Jesus, but *obey* them?

I want to try a slightly different angle on my "foundations" analogy. We might say that, in reality, our lives are really more complicated than I've portrayed so far. It's more accurate to say that—for most of us—our lives are like houses which are partly built on solid foundations and partly on no foundations at all. Sometimes we both remember and apply the teachings of Jesus (like the ones in the Sermon on the Mount), and sometimes we don't. In some cases, we may not even be clear about what God expects of us.

Most of us—and I mean us who are well beyond the age of our grads—are people who are willing to remodel our houses from time to time, if that project seems called for. We're prepared to make really big changes, if we can be convinced that they're necessary. And that includes tearing down a part of our house that we've learned has dangerously weak foundations in order to rebuild that part on solid footings.

Spiritually-speaking, you and I are always works in progress. We're always under construction. We may be living in two or three rooms while the rest of our house (by which I mean our life) is being completely rebuilt on new foundations. We may even need to move out and stay with friends until the reconstruction work is done.

God does his reconstruction work in our lives through the community of his people, the Church. We're here to help each other the way good neighbors help when there's been a flood or a tornado, the way the pioneers helped one another in the days of the Old West. When a house or a barn needed to be built, folks came from miles around and pitched in to help. That's what happens in a healthy church. We help each other lay firm foundations. We help each other build on those foundations. And we stand ready to help again if somebody needs to rebuild.

People whose lives have solid foundations are wise people who've learned to implement faithfully the will of God in their lives. Such people have learned that lives like that are only possible in a *community* of faith. We can't manage it all alone. We can't grow wise in a vacuum. *We need each other if we're to build lives of obedience to Christ.*

If you're concerned about the strength of the foundations under part of *your* house—part of your life—don't worry. God has a construction crew right here to help you get things set right and maybe even build a new addition, founded on the Rock.—Just let us know when you're ready to start.

24. PLANTING SEEDS.

Matthew 13:1-9, 18-23

Jesus told parables often to answer a question and in order to make a point—usually just a single point, not to offer a long, complex lesson. In his parables Jesus used the kind of illustrations that would work best for the people he was talking to, who were living in an agricultural society. In the same way, a typical American preacher today might try to make a point using an illustration drawn from a popular TV show or from baseball. Preachers' illustrations are analogies that we hope will help our congregations understand the point we want to make.

We're not a church full of farmers here, but Jesus' parable of the seed and the soils connects even with our experience. I'll use the McNabs as an example. At our place I am the yard man and Joan is the flower lady. Before we moved to Aspen, we lived in a house in Midland, Michigan, on a lot where a veritable forest grew. There were 53 trees around the house, to be exact. Because the place was so shady and so many of the trees were maples (whose roots are shallow), there were always big bare patches in our lawn.

For the first three years we lived in that house, I thought that watering and fertilizing would make the existing grass spread over the bare spots. But it didn't. The next year the garden center people told me to plant grass seed, the kind that's supposed to thrive in shade. However, I never got around to preparing the soil. (O.K., to be truthful, I was both lazy and optimistic. I think those qualities often go together.) What I did was to throw a few handfuls of grass seed on one big bare patch on the west side of the house, water it a lot, and hope for the best.—As intelligent gardeners might have warned me, nothing good happened. I don't know if the birds ate the seeds, but they didn't grow. The bare spot remained bare . . . and muddy.

The following spring I bought more top quality, shade-loving grass seed and decided to buckle down to doing the hard work of preparing the soil so that the seed would actually germinate and take root. I hoed and raked the bare patches and mixed in the fertilizer that was recommended by the experts. I did everything I could to get the soil ready. Then I scattered the grass seed and went back with the rake and did my best to cover it up with the required one-eighth inch of soil. (By the way, have you ever tried to plant anything just *one-eighth* of an inch deep? When I was finished, some of the seeds were visible on top of the cultivated, fertilized soil, not buried at all; and some must have been buried under at least three-quarters of an inch or more.—But some seeds were buried just right.)

Then I did the next thing I was supposed to do: I misted the newly planted areas very gently a couple of times a day to keep them moist so the seed would sprout.—And guess what? In the places where I actually planted the seed at about the right depth, we ultimately had new grass. And it was gorgeous.—But where the seed was planted too deeply or not buried at all, there remained bare patches.

Jesus' very familiar parable of the seed and the soils is about the revelation of God's truth, God's living Word in Christ, and about what happens to people in whom that truth flourishes. In Matthew's version of Jesus' parable we can talk about the seed and the soils a couple of different ways. There are some well-known, classic interpretations. I used one of them in the Children's Sermon at the beginning of this service. But for you adults I want to propose a new interpretation of the parable, one that's uniquely my own.

I want you to think about the seeds that the farmer scatters on the land as *people*, people who have been told the truth of God's love for them in Christ and who have really listened to the gospel. They may not have totally accepted it yet, but they haven't rejected it either. These seeds represent, therefore, what I call potential disciples.

The four kinds of soil in Jesus' parable represent four different sets of circumstances that have an effect on these "seeds," these potential disciples. They stand for life situations or intellectual environments that affect whether these potential disciples are going to believe the gospel and mature to the point where they experience its fruit in their lives, or not.

The first kind of soil Jesus mentioned was the hard-packed soil of the path between the fields, where the seed just lay on the surface until the birds came and ate it. To me, this stands for the situation of people who hear the gospel, but whose minds, hearts and affections are so hardened that the gospel revelation is rejected pretty quickly by them.

These folks are totally sure of themselves. They have the world figured out and their lives under control. They're firmly in the driver's seat, and feel no need for God. They have no need of salvation, since they feel pretty good about things in their lives just as they are. Their spiritual hearts are hardened. Their spiritual ears are stopped up. They don't imagine that Christianity could possibly have any truth to communicate to them that they haven't already mastered some other way. These people never become disciples.

The next kind of soil that Jesus described is the rocky ground. The layer of soil is thin there. Seed will germinate and sprout, but when there isn't much rain, it will wither and die because there isn't any depth to the soil and nobody has done any cultivating. There's no way roots can grow and keep on growing.

This is the situation of people who have listened to the gospel, but find their environment to be only mildly nurturing. Their position is rather like that of the grass seed that I scattered on the bare spots in my Michigan yard and watered a lot, just hoping for the best. They perceive something of God's truth in the gospel, but nothing is done to help them understand what to do about it.

Such people may have a month or a year of mild interest in Christianity, but nobody really encourages their interest, guides them, or befriends them. They get no help. Before long, church services begin to feel boring and they decide to put Christianity on the shelf. These people do not become disciples.

Then there's the seed that gets planted in a fertile place, but that place hasn't been prepared for these seeds to be planted. It's a place where too many other things are already growing—like the thorns in Jesus' parable. These are the people whose life situations are full of interests and distractions of all kinds. They're just too busy, too pulled this way and that. They don't really have room in their hearts for the new thing that God wants to do in them through Christ.

These are not necessarily bad people, and their many concerns and interests are not necessarily bad either. A person in this situation might be volunteering at the hospital, working to raise money for several charities, running a business, raising a family of four, looking after a sick parent, learning to fly an airplane, and trying to write a book—all at the same time. Their concerns and interests are time and energy consuming. And there are way too many of them.

Such people have listened to the gospel, and perhaps their hearts have been drawn to Christ. They might even have said to themselves, "I ought to get involved more in the Church. I ought to read the Bible. I ought to cultivate my faith."—But they're tired. Their lives are choked by everything else they're doing. These are the people whom I believe often become "admirers of Jesus," but never really become disciples.

The last category is that of the seed that was sown on good soil. Jesus says, "this is the one who hears the word and understands it, who indeed bears fruit and yields, in one case a hundredfold, in another sixty, and in another thirty." This is like the grass seed that I planted in Michigan in soil that I had cultivated and fertilized, seed that was buried at just the proper depth and that was misted gently with water until it sprouted.

What kind of people who have listened to the gospel are represented by these last seeds? Surely, these are the people who find their way quickly—once they have heard the gospel—into a church where they're welcomed, loved and cared for, a church where they're offered appropriate spiritual direction and nurturing, tailored to their needs, a church where somebody in addition to the pastor takes a true interest in helping their faith to grow.

These are the people who develop in faith and grow in an understanding of what the gospel means in their lives. Such development is a process;

nothing happens overnight. All seeds have to be allowed to grow to maturity. But these are the *potential* disciples who are properly cared for and cultivated until they become *mature* disciples of Christ, ready to reproduce the life of the Master. And these are the ones who will be fruitful: in some cases a hundred-fold, some sixty, some thirty.

The parable leaves us with this question: *are we the kind of soil—the kind of church—where such seeds can grow, mature, and bear fruit?* And if the answer to that question is "No," then are we willing to do the hard work that it will take in order to become that kind of soil, that kind of church?

25. THE "BAD BOY" AND THE "IDEAL CHILD."

Luke 15:11-32

I f you spent much time with Jesus, you got to hear lots of stories. Jesus didn't give dry theological lectures; he mainly just told stories—the best kind of stories, the kind that pull you in and make you feel as if, though the story is being told to a crowd, it's really meant just for you. And if you listened often to Jesus, you learned that he was always pointing to God, telling stories that gave people a picture of what God is really like.

Jesus realized that most people are either confused about God, or scared of God, or have exceedingly peculiar ideas about God. Even religious people. (I should have said, "*Especially* religious people.") That makes Jesus' stories particularly good for us to hear again and again, because according to polls 79% of the people in America believe in God and 58% are absolutely sure. For the majority of us, *God is there*, beyond a doubt. But we still have the same confusion and distortion in our thinking about God that people had 2,000 years ago.

The story we just heard is the best loved of all the ones Jesus told. We usually call it "the Parable of the Prodigal Son." A more accurate title would be "the Story of the Loving Father," because the father in this story clearly stands for God. But I have my own name for it. I call it "The Story of the Bad Boy and the Ideal Child." It could easily be a piece of theater.

A prosperous Jewish farmer had two sons. Lots of Jesus' stories feature two sons who illustrate opposite moral types. (I wonder why it's never two daughters. Maybe daughters in those days were always assumed to be "good.") The elder of the rich farmer's two sons was an Ideal Child, obedient, hard-working, perseverant, and thrifty. In contrast, the younger one was a Bad Boy—a rascal—flippant, fun-loving, and irresponsible, chafing under authority, cocky and shallow, but clever in a certain way. No doubt, he mocked his self-righteous older brother, and even teased his father—who just laughed and indulged him.

The Bad Boy was bored on the family farm. He was ambitious. He was sure that if he just had some capital, a little stake, he could amount to something *big* elsewhere—away from these country yokels. All he needed was for daddy to give him right now his share of what would ultimately come to him anyway once the old man died. He asked for his inheritance and his dad gave it to him. This deed was amazing in itself. It never occurred to the young man that such a request showed the world that he really wouldn't mind if the old man died. It said to the neighbors that his dad was only a source of money for this boy and nothing more. It was disrespectful, but the boy was too thick-headed to understand that.

As Jesus' tale went, things didn't work out well for the pushy Bad Boy. He had a blast as long as he had a bankroll, but pretty soon that was all gone. It wasn't so much that he indulged in debauchery as that he was just foolish. He was what folks down South would call a natural-born loser—self-indulgent, impulsive, un-teachable, and stubborn. He thought he was really smart, but he was mistaken about that.

This Jewish boy ended up in a gentile country, reduced to a job lower than any he could ever have imagined: feeding pigs. And nobody in that region knew either him or his rich daddy back in Judea. Nobody way out there cared about him at all. As far as his boss and everybody else cared, he could just eat the hog slop.—Our smart-alecky Bad Boy never had expected his life would turn out like this. His dreams were gone. His fantasies of success had been swept away. He felt worthless. He was scum.

It was then, Jesus said, that he "came to himself." That's the pivotal moment in the story: *"He came to himself."* That means he remembered who he was. He was his father's child. Sitting in the pig-sty, the foolish young man realized how rebellious and insulting he'd been to his dad, but he also recalled that good man's kind nature—slow to get angry, patient, gentle, and generous. So he said to himself, "I will get up from here and I'll go home to my father." What a momentous decision.

Millions of people in this world have deliberately cut themselves off from God and thumbed their noses at him. How wonderful if every one of them found themselves in a situation like the one the Bad Boy in Jesus' story came to, circumstances that would bring them to say: "I will get up from here and I'll go home to my father."

And so the Bad Boy went home, rehearsing every step of the way a humble speech of apology that he planned to offer his dad as soon as he saw him. He knew his father's field-hands had a decent, though humble life. Maybe, since his father was a compassionate man, he'd let him be a field-hand on the farm. His inheritance was gone, but at least he'd have a roof over his head and decent food.

Now the father comes to center stage, and we see him shading his eyes, peering down the road. We get the feeling that he's probably gone out and looked down the road every day since his younger son left home. Therefore, when the young man is still a very long way off, his dad sees him coming. He recognizes his son's silhouette, or his gait, or something. The father knows: "*That's* my boy!" And he goes running out to meet him.

See? *Jesus is telling us what God is like.* You might not know it, but prosperous gentlemen in that era never ran. Never. Not even for sport. They walked—slowly and with great dignity. Underlings, flunkies, servants, and children could run. But rich, important men had too much class to run. Nevertheless, in Jesus' story this father ran down the road to welcome his foolish, lost, younger son home—the Bad Boy.

When the two met, the Bad Boy launched into his memorized speech: "Father, I've sinned against heaven and against you, and I no longer deserve to be called your son . . ." But dad wouldn't let him finish. The son didn't get a chance to say "just let me be a field hand." His father hugged and kissed him. He snapped his fingers and a servant came running with sandals for the wanderer's bare feet, a robe to replace his rags, and a ring for his finger. Though the boy knew he had forfeited any right to be called a son, his sonship was restored. Then the father ordered a feast: "Let's have a celebration. Music! Dancing! He who was lost is found. He who was dead is alive again." So the party began, and it was a wing-ding. People could hear the racket over in the next valley.

The older son, the Ideal Child, who was out working hard in the field as always, sunrise to sunset, heard the zydeco music, the fiddles and the accordions playing in the middle of the day. When somebody told him what was going on, he was not one bit happy. In fact, he was in a rage. The Ideal Child would not join the party even when his dad came out to him and—with great tact and gentleness—begged him to come in. Big Brother had always been obedient, frugal, hard-working, respectful of authority, sensible, and pious: A Perfect Son. His father trusted and relied on him without reservation. This is a story about the Bad Boy and the Ideal Child. And the Ideal Child's resentment boiled over.

He told his father off for not ever showing him adequate recognition for his obedience and hard work, and he scolded the old man for putting on such a big welcome for the Bad Boy. The Perfect Son felt like he had a legitimate gripe: "This is *not* fair. This loser gets a big party and what do I get? Nothing!" Even when his father gently pointed out that the whole estate would one day belong to him, that didn't soften him up. He was mad at dad, and he detested his worthless, coddled little brother.

Consider the possible symbolism here. If the wandering Bad Boy who came home stands for people who once fell for the myth of self-sufficiency, thumbed their noses at God, and nearly died trying to manufacture happiness for themselves without God in their lives—who, then, does the Ideal Child stand for? Why, he stands for good religious people in every age who always work hard and do the right thing: *us!* He stands for us who practice self-discipline, responsibility, and piety and attend church every Sunday, while our neighbors go in for self-indulgence, irresponsibility, and godless egotism and maybe—*maybe*—go to church on Christmas.

Jesus' story still pulls us in, even if we've heard it a thousand times. We have sympathy with the wastrel who came to his senses and went home.—But we're "religious people" here, and chances are good that we're likely to share more character traits with the Ideal Child than with the Bad Boy.

What will we do with this drama? Jesus told the story to show what God is like. And what is Jesus' picture of God? It's the portrayal of a lavishly loving, forgiving Father *who takes the initiative* in being reconciled with the most rebellious, willful, errant bad boys in the family, and who yearns for his ideal children to be just as forgiving of them as he is.

Jesus leaves this little bit of theater tantalizingly without an ending. The final curtain has not come down.—What will happen next? Will the resentful Ideal Child decide to go to the party, realizing that *he* has been just as self-centered as little brother ever was? Will the Bad Boy be transformed by his father's mercy? You get to write the next scene.

26. IF YOU LOVE ME, YOU WILL KEEP MY COMMANDMENTS.

John 14:15-21

Jesus said to his disciples, *"If you love me you will keep my commandments."* One time quite a few years ago—when I still had little kids at home—I went on a men's retreat with a group of guys from another parish. They put us in small groups and, to start things off, we were asked to share with one another the words we remembered hearing most often from our fathers when we were under the age of twelve.

The words most of the men remembered hearing from dad were these: "Sit down. Be quiet. And do what I say." We all laughed about that. And we admitted—since nearly all of us were parents—that we seemed to be passing along the same message to our kids, at least the *"do what I say"* part.

I have to say that the dads I observe in action these days—and the moms, too—seem a lot more patient with their children, better listeners to their tales about school and friends, and much more likely than those of my own generation to leave them with a better parental message to remember from childhood than "Sit down. Be quiet. And do what I say."

In one respect, though, parents now are still pretty much like parents of earlier generations. They expect their children to listen to what they tell them and be guided by that. But today's parents are more patient than *I* ever was in explaining just *why* their advice is worth following.

Jesus didn't have any children. But a rabbi with his disciples was considered to be in the role of a father with his children. It was a patriarchal culture, and the traditional duty of the Jewish father was to teach the wisdom and will of God to his children—to instruct them, train them, discipline them, correct them, guide them and reward them.

It was well known that a rabbi's teaching had to be conveyed in more than just memorable *words*. It had to be passed along through memorable *deeds*—in the conduct of his life. The effectiveness of a rabbi's teaching depended largely on the quality of his example.

Disciples would almost inevitably develop affection for their rabbi. That was natural. But if the disciples failed to obey their master's commandments, their liking or feeling friendly for him was of no value. *Behavior* is what counted, not feelings.

Jesus said to his disciples, "If you love me, you will keep my commandments." People get confused about love these days. Most of the confusion comes from the fact that we who speak English as our mother tongue have only a single word to use for a wide range of human behavior and emotions.

June is just around the corner, and that means it's almost wedding season. We pastors have various techniques for helping young couples discern whether they're just having great emotional chemistry together (often called being in love) or they're actually ready to make a commitment of body, mind and spirit to each other—"for better, for worse; for richer, for poorer; in sickness and in health," for the rest of their lives. Some couples get married on the basis of great emotional chemistry, but when the hormonal high wears off one or the other says "I'm not sure I'm in love with you anymore." Or, "Things are just not the way they used to be between us."

When Jesus said, "If you love me you will keep my commandments," he was making the essential point that authentic love is a choice not a neuro-chemical reflex. Loving Jesus isn't about, as we might say, "liking Jesus," but about choosing to pattern our lives according to his word and example.

When Jesus told the disciples to keep his commandments, he wasn't referring to a law code either. Actually, his commandment was this: "Love one another as I have loved you." So, in other words he was telling them "If you love me, then you will love one another the way I have loved you." People who've learned that love is a choice, not an emotional reflex, know that the love Jesus commanded is demonstrated by *deeds*—simple acts that can be repeated if we choose. Jesus told his disciples to treat each other (and by extension, everyone else) just the way he had treated them. That's pretty simple, isn't it?

Jesus didn't just give his disciples, his spiritual children, a lot of rules to follow. He just told them to love one another, and then he demonstrated what that meant. And he did so in obedience to his Father. As the epistle this morning put it, "We know love by this, that he laid down his life for us. And we ought to lay down our lives for one another."

Jesus demonstrated his obedience to the Father by care-giving love. He washed the disciples' feet—an act of great humility. After he did that for them, he said, "I have given you an example, that you should do for one another what I have done for you."

If love is about emotions, about affectionate feelings, it can't be commanded. I can't feel a certain way about someone else just because I'm told to. That's impossible. Nobody can tell you how to feel. Feelings come in response to experiences. Feelings just are. Even God can't dictate them, because God made us the way we are.

But I *can* treat another person with justice and dignity because I'm told to do so. I *can* give my money to help a poor person because I'm told to. I *can* shelter the homeless out of obedience to Christ. I *can* feed the hungry because I'm told to. I *can* work for the welfare of another person because I've been commanded to. I can do these things out of obedience, no matter how I may feel about the people in question.

Frederick Buechner said, "When Jesus tells us to love our neighbors . . . he is telling us to love them in the sense of working for their well-being, even if it means sacrificing our own well-being, our own interests, to do that." This means that, in Jesus' terms, we can *love* other people even if we don't *like* them. Buechner also said, "Liking them may get in the way of loving them by making us overprotective sentimentalists instead of reasonably honest friends."

It's not easy to love one another this way. It's hard to obey Jesus' commandment. That's why Jesus goes on to say that he will give us "another Counselor," the Spirit of Truth, the Holy Spirit, to be with us forever. The Spirit helps us in our weakness. The Spirit—and only the Spirit—enables us to get free of our self-interest and our egos enough to develop a sacrificial love that might resemble that of Jesus.

When in obedience we're able to love others the way Jesus has loved us, it's because of his Spirit working in our hearts. Our new life and our unselfish love depend on the One who fills us with his empowering presence. When we reveal the love of Jesus in our treatment of one another, our neighbors, and even our enemies, we show the world that Jesus is alive. As his words that have been on our outside signboard since Easter (and are part of today's gospel) say, "Because I live you too will live."

"We know that we have passed from death to life because we love one another."

27. CALL YOUR FIRST WITNESS.

Mothers' Day
Acts 1:8

There was a children's Easter program at a big downtown church. A young fellow of about five or six was chosen to play the part of Jesus. He was so excited. He had a white robe to wear and just a few lines to say. He practiced them at home with his mother—over and over. When the time came for the program, mom was in the front pew, ready to prompt him in case he forgot anything. Well, the little guy hadn't appeared in front of a crowd before, and this was a very big church. He came out front and suddenly had stage fright. He went blank. There was a long awkward silence, during which his mother was silently mouthing his first line, to get him started: "I-am-the-light-of-the-world." She did it slowly several times.—He didn't get it.—Finally she resorted to a whisper, "I am the light of the world." He got it. His face broke into a grin, and he said in a big voice, *"My mom is the light of the world!"*

Today is Mother's Day, but in the Church calendar it's a Sunday of anticipation—a day of waiting. Thursday was Ascension Day, the day when Jesus spoke the words we heard in the second lesson this morning from the Book of Acts. For forty days after the Resurrection, Jesus appeared again and again to his disciples. They saw him, touched him, ate with him, talked and walked with him. At the end of those forty days they were convinced beyond any shadow of a doubt that Jesus had, indeed, risen from the dead. Then came the day when he departed from them to return to God. But before he ascended, Jesus told his friends to stay where they were—in Jerusalem—until they were filled with the Holy Spirit, whom

Jesus called "the Promise of the Father." He said, You will receive power when the Holy Spirit has come upon you, and you will be my witnesses in Jerusalem, in all Judea, in Samaria, and to the ends of the earth.

The Holy Spirit is the breath of God. The New Testament Greek word for *spirit* is the same as the word for *breath*. The Breath of God is what makes it possible for us to speak about Jesus, to be his witnesses. Without that Breath, we'd be as scared as the little boy in the Easter program I told about, and we wouldn't be able to say a thing. To be a witness is to "give testimony"—out of our own experience. It's an act of communication. To be Jesus' witness doesn't mean telling other people about *what* we know—like a lot of catechism answers that we've memorized—but rather talking to them about *whom* we know: Jesus, our Master and our friend. It's easy and it makes us happy to tell somebody else about a person that we love—about our wife or husband, or our children, or (considering what day it is) about our mom.

From experience we understand that it's possible to know and love and have a deep, meaningful, intimate relationship with a person and not have all the facts about that person's life history, or perhaps even to think we have some of the facts, but actually to have them wrong. The quality of the relationship doesn't depend on the amount of data we have about the other person. Instead, it depends on the depth of the spiritual bond between us. Take, for example, the relationship between a child and that child's mother. A little child doesn't necessarily know about mom's early life, or where she went to school, or what kind of work she used to do. A child might not know much about mom's personal history. But the child *knows* mom: *"That's my mom! She loves me."* The child knows how mom treats him, how she communicates approval and disapproval, how she teaches the right way to act. That's the way it is with us and Jesus. We don't need to be expert Bible students or theologians before we can talk about the Jesus who loves us and who has come in the power of his Spirit to live in our hearts forever.

I enjoy lawyer novels—like the ones by John Grisham and Scott Turow. I enjoy the tense court room scenes and the clever arguments from the underdog lawyer. In those scenes, when the rival attorneys' opening presentations to the jury are finished and the trial is really getting under way, one of the first things the judge says is "Call your first witness."

"Call your first witness." Let's think about that in the context of our own lives. Who was the first person you can remember who talked to you about God? Who first told you about the love of Jesus? Who first gave you a personal, real-life example of how to be like Jesus?

I know who my first witness was. It was my mom. She taught me to pray before I went to sleep at night, and she sat on the bed and listened to what I was saying to God. (As I recall, she never stopped me from saying whatever was on my mind, but sometimes she suggested additions.) She read Bible stories to me and helped me learn to read the Bible for myself—creating a habit that has remained with me ever since. Sometimes mom would ask me, particularly if I had engaged in some clearly out-of-bounds behavior, "Do you think the Lord likes it when you do things like that?"

Mom wasn't perfect—she could nag and complain and had a gift for using guilt to manipulate me—but she wasn't bashful about telling me about the Lord she loved and knew. And she didn't hesitate to speak on his behalf, either, if she felt I wasn't listening closely enough to him for myself. Mom was my first witness. But her testimony was in more than words. Her actions spoke just as loudly as her words, maybe more so. I'll give you just one example.

When I was a kid, mom was a clerk in a single-window postal substation downtown. Now, back in the 50's, before suburban shopping malls were built, downtown was lively—even in towns like the one I grew up in. All the banks, businesses, shops and most of the restaurants were there. A little developmentally disabled fellow named Jerry used to come into mom's sub-post office a lot because he ran errands for a downtown store—like taking parcels to be mailed. Jerry wore funny clothes and didn't talk like an adult, even though he must have been middle aged. And he didn't bathe as often as he should. He would hang around for a long time and talk to mom after he'd mailed his packages. (Jerry was the kind of person that people called "retarded" back in those days.) Mom was patient with him and laughed with him, and sometimes she would take him down to Otto's drugstore on the corner and buy him an ice cream at the soda fountain. My dad used to tease her about her "boyfriend." He'd say, "Did you take your smelly boyfriend to Otto's for ice cream this afternoon?"

I can remember Mom's simple answer: "Jerry's o.k. He needs a friend. Jesus wants us to care about people like him." Mom was my first witness, and her testimony lingers in my heart. The Breath of God gave her words and gave her energy to live out her faith.

Jesus said, You will receive power when the Holy Spirit has come upon you, and you will be my witnesses. There's a word I wish I could rescue from the oblivion to which most Episcopalians assign it: that's the word *evangelism*. To evangelize means "to tell the good news." That's what we do when we communicate—in words or in actions—the truth that Jesus is alive and at work in the world. *Witnesses* are people who have a relationship with God and an experience with God that we can't keep quiet about, an experience that has re-shaped our lives.—But we can't be an evangelizing, Good News-telling, witnessing Church until we are collectively filled with the "Breath of God," the Holy Spirit.

Jesus says that this filling with the Spirit is a *promise from God*. It's a promise, and God keeps his promises. What we need to do is believe that Jesus is raised from the dead, stay united, be patient, and pray. I believe that God wants our little Episcopal Church here in the heart of faith-resistant Aspen to be an effective witnessing body of Christians whose words and works demonstrate the amazing love of God. I believe God wants us to be a church where people who haven't known any of us before can come into our gatherings—for worship, or work, or even for play—and say, "God is truly here. We meet God among you."

The Holy Spirit will come to the church that wants him.
The Holy Spirit will come to the church that is waiting for him.
The Holy Spirit will come to the church that is praying for him.

28. WE NEED CPR OF THE SPIRIT.

The Day of Pentecost
Luke 24:48-49

How many of you have had CPR training? Wow, that's great, because the Red Cross would like everybody to learn how to perform simple CPR—cardio-pulmonary resuscitation. You never know when you might be able to save another person's life. Even the few of us here who haven't taken a CPR course know something about how it works. It involves mouth-to-mouth resuscitation. The person who is giving CPR puts his or her mouth over the mouth of the traumatized person, pinches the victims nostrils shut, and *blows* the breath of life into that person's lungs. This powerful breath gets the other person's lungs working again, and stimulation of the heart gets the heart beating again.

I'm not here to get you signed up for CPR training—though it's a fine thing—but rather to remind you of something you already know: Breath gives life; in fact, breath *is* life. That's the important thing to remember; because this is the day the Church celebrates the life-giving Breath of God, the Holy Spirit. And I believe the Holy Spirit wants to "give CPR" to the Church in our time. Maybe even to us. (Imagine that.)

In the second chapter of Genesis, we read the familiar old story about God forming the first human being from the earth itself. The Bible says, "the Lord God formed man from the dust of the ground, and breathed into his nostrils the breath of life; and man became a living being." The Book of Acts tells us that fifty days after Jesus' Resurrection, a group of a hundred and twenty disciples were gathered in a room in Jerusalem, staying together, waiting patiently, and praying. They were doing what Jesus had told them to do. He told them to stay there in the city of Jerusalem until they received what he called "The promise of the Father." He said "John baptized with water, but you will be baptized with the Holy Spirit not many days from now . . . You will receive power when the Holy Spirit has come upon you; and you will be my witnesses in Jerusalem, in all Judea and Samaria, and to the ends of the earth."

These disciples didn't really know what to expect while they were waiting and praying. They'd read that the Spirit of God filled Israel's prophets, priests, and kings long ago. But they *didn't* know exactly what Jesus had meant when he said, *"You will be baptized with the Holy Spirit not many days from now."* For them, baptism meant "washing." It implied cleansing. But to be baptized could mean more than just a quick scrub. It also meant to be *soaked,* to be *saturated,* to be *filled up.* When the Day of Pentecost came, with the sound of rushing wind and visible tongues of fire, the Breath of God came into them, cleansed them, and filled them with new life.—But until that happened, they hadn't known what was coming.

When a priest like me talks to his congregation about the possibility of experiencing a new Pentecost, it tends to make proper Episcopalians nervous. (And proper Presbyterians and Lutherans and other main line Protestants, too.) We more low-key, reserved Christians, we who like Bach and Handel and prefer the hymns of Ralph Vaughn Williams, get scared that if we have a new Pentecost and get filled with the new life of the Spirit, then we'll *lose our self-control* and maybe start behaving in embarrassing ways—doing things we don't really *want* to do. We don't want to be like those disciples in Jerusalem whose neighbors wondered whether they'd been drinking at nine o'clock in the morning.

Those of you who have been in the Alpha Course may remember a story Nicky Gumbel tells about an American woman who attended a Sunday service at a very traditional, rather stiff and staid English village church. As I recall his story, there were not many people in the church and it was a rather stiff and formal service. Suddenly, right in the middle of things, the American woman shouted out, *"Hallelujah! Praise God!"*

One of the sidesmen, as they called ushers in Britain, came over to her right away and said, "Madam, you must not shout during the service."

She replied, "Why not? I've got the Spirit!"

And he answered, "Well, you certainly didn't get it here."

I'd like for you to have the Spirit, and I'd like for you to get it here.

I like to remind people that in his Letter to the Galatians Paul wrote that the "fruit of the Spirit" is: "love, joy, peace, patience, kindness, goodness, faithfulness, gentleness and self-control." Please make a note of the last item in the list: self-control. The Holy Spirit is NOT going to make us lose control of ourselves.—But the Spirit will lead us to live our lives in a new way.—How would we like new ways of experiencing love, joy, peace, patience, kindness, goodness, faithfulness, and gentleness along with the self-control? (Do you already manifest all the patience, kindness, and goodness you'd like to? You tell me.)

OK. So if we in our little church here in Aspen are seeking the Spirit of God, earnestly, prayerfully, and faithfully, what might we expect when the Spirit comes?—Are we likely to rush out into North Street and run down to the Music Tent, speaking in unknown tongues? I would say probably not. (But, then. you never know.)—If not speaking in unknown tongues, then will there be some other sign? How will we *know* for sure that God's Spirit has really come to us and a new life has begun in us? How will we know that the Holy Spirit has come "to give us CPR"?

I want to stick with the CPR analogy, because what CPR does is to get the victim breathing and his heart beating. The Holy Spirit does his biggest work in the human heart. Long before the time of Christ, when the Jews were still in captivity in Babylon, the prophet Ezekiel told them what God was going to do—and it's one of the best descriptions of the work of the Holy Spirit there is. I want to read it to you from *The Message*, Eugene Peterson's translation of the Bible into colloquial American English. God says, "I'll pour pure water over you and scrub you clean. I'll give you a new heart, put a new spirit in you. I'll remove the stone heart from your body and replace it with a heart that's God-willed, not self-willed. I'll put my Spirit in you and make it possible for you to do what I tell you and live by my commands."

What will the Spirit do when he gives us CPR? Here's the main thing: He'll give us a new heart—a heart for God. If you remember, a few weeks ago I warned you about the risk we face of slipping into "functional atheism." The risk is very apparent in our modern world, because the culture we live in teaches us—even us professing Christians—to live day-by-day without reference to God, to live as if there were *no* God or as if God were indifferent to *our* existence.

When the new life of the Spirit begins in people, they make a basic change. They start *choosing* to center their lives on God. Their hearts become God-willed, not self-willed. They look around at the world and they begin for the first time to see that God is active. Before the Spirit came, they didn't consider that God might be doing anything at all. But once the Spirit has come and their hearts are changed, people discern that God is doing things in their lives and in the world around them all the time.

Along with the new heart that the Spirit gives, there is a new heart knowledge of who we are in God's eyes. If you want to read a chapter in the Bible that will tell you a lot about the work of the Holy Spirit, I recommend the eighth chapter of Romans. It's my favorite. We read a little bit of it this morning: "All who are led by the Spirit of God are children of God. For you did not receive a spirit of slavery to fall back into fear, but you have received a spirit of adoption. When we cry, 'Abba! Father!' it is that very Spirit bearing witness with our spirit that we are children of God"

The heart knowledge that the Spirit gives us is the assurance that we (yes, *we*) are truly God's own beloved children. We may have been told that all our lives, since we were little kids in Sunday School, but when the Spirit comes and fills us, he makes us *feel* the truth of that relationship. He makes us *feel* a kind of heart assurance that God is our own loving Father. "*Abba*" was a Jewish child's familiar name for Daddy. As a little child, Jesus learned to call Joseph *Abba*. And I think that when the Spirit came upon Jesus at the Jordan, when he was baptized by John, he began calling God *Abba*. When the Spirit fills us and gives us a new life, a new heart, we begin to *feel* as well as *believe* that God, the Creator and Lord of the Universe, is also our *Abba*.

When we have that kind of assurance about our relationship with God, it changes the way we pray. When people ask me to give them one thing to look for that will be a sure sign that the Spirit of God is doing his work in their life this is the one I propose. I say: If you know, when you pray, that the One to whom you are praying is your own dear *Abba,* the Father who unconditionally loves you, and you're addressing him out of the heart knowledge of that relationship, then you can rest assured that the Spirit has done his greatest possible work in your heart. "When we cry, 'Abba! Father!' it is that very Spirit bearing witness with our spirit that we are children of God."

Now, here's a warning. The Holy Spirit is not going to make us perfect. Not right now, not in this life. We will make moral progress under the Spirit's guidance and we will be more aware of when we're going down a wrong path, but we won't become finished products in this earthly life. We'll continue to be works in progress. We'll do things we shouldn't do, and we'll fail to do some things we should have done. We'll keep needing God's forgiveness as much as God's guidance. But we won't be overcome by guilt and misery, the way we used to be, and start imagining that we're worthless and unlovable. We'll be able to accept God's forgiveness and trust that in all things—even instances of our own sin—God is able to bring about something that will ultimately be good.

If you feel like you need the CPR of the Holy Spirit, the simplest thing to do is ask. So, bow your heads and let's ask together: *Breathe on us, Breath of God; fill us with life anew. We need you. We want you. We await your coming. Give us new life, dear Abba. We ask this in Jesus' name.*

Hallelujah. Praise God!

29. DO WE HAVE FEAR OR FAITH?

Fathers' Day
Mark 4:35-41

There was a little boy of about four or five who was scared of thunderstorms. Every time there was a big storm, the kid would wake up and cry, and his mother would have to come into his room and calm him down. Sometimes she'd lie down on the bed beside him until he finally fell asleep. One night there was a big storm with lots of thunder and lightning, and the boy started crying. After his mom came in and sat beside him for a while, he settled back down—even though the thunder was still rumbling. So, she stood up to go back to her own bed. Then the little boy said, "Mommy, aren't you going to *(sniff)* stay with me?" She answered, "No, I have to go and be with Daddy." The boy responded, *"(sniff, sniff)* . . . The big sissy!"

When I was a kindergartener, I was the exact opposite of the kid in my story. I didn't like thunderstorms either, and I was scared to death of lightning. (I still am.) But if my dad were there—even if he was just in the house, not even in the room with me—I was fine. When Daddy was in the house, or the car, or the boat, I felt as if nothing could hurt me. Nothing bad could happen to us. We were sure to be o.k. I had never seen my dad command a storm to cease, but somehow—if he was with us in the storm—I knew we'd all be o.k. Such is the faith of a little child in his daddy—and such must be the faith in God possessed by all who want to share God's kingdom.

When Jesus asked his disciples to take him across to the other side of the lake, he'd had a very full few weeks of intense ministry. Earlier that very day he'd been speaking down on the lakeside, and the crowd had grown so large that he'd had to get into a boat and push out from the shore in order to be heard. Then other boats came up, and their owners sat in them to listen to him.

When Jesus was finished speaking it was late afternoon, and he asked the disciples just to row the boat on across the lake to the opposite side—a distance of about eight miles. He was certainly exhausted, and probably wanted to take a break, escape the attention of the crowd for a while. Eight miles is a long way, but most of his disciples were big, strong fishermen who'd spent their lives on this particular body of water. Rowing that distance presented no challenge to them. And if the wind was fair, they could put up the sail.

You know how it went. Jesus, worn out by many days of non-stop ministry—preaching, counseling, healing, answering questions—fell asleep on a cushion in the stern, entrusting himself to the boating skills of his friends. They were in their element, doing what they knew best how to do. So Jesus could relax and take a nap while they crossed the lake. But a sudden storm kicked up, and the situation got so scary that the fishermen—who had faced many other storms on this lake before—woke Jesus up and said, *"Master, don't you care that we're about to die!?"*

The gospel says that Jesus woke up and commanded the wind and waves to be still, *"and there was a great calm."* Then he asked his friends, the terrified fishermen, *"Why are you afraid? Have you still no faith?"*

The last bit of teaching that Jesus had given to the crowds before he and the twelve headed across the lake was a pair of simple parables about seeds. (That was our gospel reading last Sunday). The basic message of these parables was that everything has to start small—especially faith—but in time it will grow and grow and finally be fruitful. Jesus might have assumed that if his disciples had even "a mustard seed" of faith—if they were even just *beginning* to trust what God was obviously doing in him—they would not have been afraid in the storm.

When Jesus had called these twelve people to follow him, he knew they had no faith yet. But they were attracted to him and had enough interest in what he was saying and doing that they were willing to follow at least for a while and see what would happen. Now he said to them, in effect, *"Has* nothing *you've seen or heard over the last six months weeks with Me given you* ANY *faith?—What's it going to take?"*

Then they turned to one another and asked, *"Who* IS *this man, that even the wind and waves obey him?"* "Who is this," indeed! They didn't really know who he was. Of course, that's the crucial question, for them and for us: *"Who is this man?"*—Why, this is the Lord of the storm! This is the One who answered Job out of the whirlwind and asked, "Where were you when I laid the foundations of the world?" . . . the One at whose decree all things were made. This man in the storm-tossed fishing boat was none other than God-Himself-Here-With-Us.

Last week we learned that when Paul was trying to explain what the new life of faith in Christ felt like, he described it this way, "If anyone is in Christ, there is a new creation: everything old has passed away. See, everything has become new." People who have put their trust in Jesus see the world differently from the way other people do.

Believers must sometimes sail into storms—and I'm not mainly talking about bad weather. There are the far worse storms of anxiety and doubt that can come upon us when we face the death of our spouse, or a child, or the approach of our own life's end. And in these times of economic uncertainty many believing people also have to cope with the loss of their jobs, or the failure of their businesses, or the possibility that everything they own might become worthless. At our men's group on Wednesday morning we went around the room and all of us named something that scares us. Not a man there said, "I fear nothing," because that would not have been true. We're all scared of something. A few had phobias, like I do. (I'm still terrified of lightning.) Some were afraid of failure. Others were afraid of economic catastrophe.—How about YOU? What's *your* biggest fear? Go inside yourself and think about this for a minute. (And don't tell me that you have no fear. I won't believe you.) I invited the men on Wednesday morning, and I invite each of you right now to ponder this: *How can you muster your faith to overcome your fear?*

In addition to our personal fears, there are also storms of panic that come when some human institution which we have relied on shows itself to be frighteningly frail, when a boat in which we expected to ride out the hurricane springs some serious leaks.

Speaking of leaky boats, next month the Episcopal Church will hold its once-every-three-years General Convention. Many Episcopalians are hoping this huge assembly of bishops and clergy and lay people—the largest deliberative body on earth—will bring an end to the long series of storms our denomination has been through and usher in a new, sweet era of calm. That would be wonderful, but frankly I'm not holding my breath.

It's not that I don't have hope for the Church, though. I have *great* hope for the Church. It is the Lord's chosen instrument to do his work in the world. But I'm referring to that universal, Spirit-filled community of love and grace which cannot be identified with any single denomination. My hope is for the worldwide community of souls who have given their hearts to the Lord Jesus Christ and put their trust in him.

As I have said before, for those of us who are in Christ, there's a new world. The old world has gone and everything has changed. That means we no longer see either the storms of this mortal life or the storms of ecclesiastical politics through our old eyes of fear. Now we look *beyond* the storms, with eyes of faith.

What can move people from fear to faith, from living in the old order of things to living in a new creation? I can't give an absolute answer to that question, but I can tell you this much from personal experience: *fear is contagious.* One or two scared people can persuade a boatload of others that the end is near. One or two can infect a multitude with terror. But *faith is contagious too.* One or two people with a simple, child-like faith, can rescue a fearful multitude that has no faith.

What the disciples in their little boat on Galilee needed on that stormy afternoon was for just *one* to say to the others, "Don't be scared, men. We're going to get through this thing. Just take a look at Jesus there. See how peacefully he's sleeping? He *told* us to cross over to the other side, and—by golly—I believe that if we're doing what HE told us to do, then we can forget about the storm. We *will* get to the other side." First one man and then another would have grabbed his oar and pulled harder.—And

Jesus could have finished his nap. What the Lord asks you and me to do, he always gives us the power to accomplish. All things are possible through him.

So, whatever the future might hold, don't let your fears own you. God Himself is with us. The Lord of the storm is in our boat.

30. YOU REAP WHATEVER YOU SOW.

Galatians 6:7-10

If you haven't noticed, there's an amazing profusion of flowers right now out in the front garden of the rectory. Joan, the deacon-gardener, could tell us what each plant is called. I can't. I just know that we have lots of pretty yellow flowers, as well as blue ones; quite a few purple ones, some red ones, and clumps of little-bitty white ones. Many of these are pansies; even I know that much. We have pinkish-red coral bells and cobalt-blue lobelia. There are tall, spiky lupines. (I like those.) We have columbines, too, of course, and some kind of sage. (Maybe it's not sage. Whatever it is, the bees like it.) There are also delphiniums nearly ready to bloom—and, last but not least, geraniums. Joan has been known as "the Geranium Lady" everywhere we've lived.

Once, not too many years back, the place where these flowers are growing was just grass and dirt. Three summers ago, ladies in the church paid for landscaping professionals to come and turn that grass and dirt into a real garden. The landscapers planted a few things and Joan added some more things, both then and afterwards. And she fertilized, weeded, watered and loved the garden. Today there's an exhibition of color and beauty where there was nothing but grass four years ago. Grass is o.k., I guess, especially on a golf course or in the outfield at a ballpark, but lots of different pretty flowers growing together in a complementary display is much more enjoyable to see in front of a home. Many of you have magnificent gardens, and you know what I mean.

Gardens—whether the practical, vegetable-sort or the purely ornamental, flowery-sort—take time. They don't just happen overnight. And they don't come together without a plan. Somebody has to have a *dream* of a garden, a vision of what might be possible on that particular plot of earth. Then somebody must do the hard work of breaking up the sod and establishing a suitable place for planting. Preparation is crucial. After that comes the time of planting. Whether gardeners plant seeds or seedlings, planting time is always a period of hope and expectation. Next comes the phase of waiting.—Will the seeds sprout? Will the seedlings survive and thrive? After the waiting, if our garden is blessed, comes the reward. For an ornamental garden, it's the time of blooming flowers and the joy we take in contemplating them; for vegetables, it's the harvest and the pleasure we derive from eating them.

One of the classic proverbs of Holy Scripture—a proverb so obvious that it's also found in the sacred texts just about every culture around the world—is one that St. Paul quoted to the Galatians in the epistle reading we heard this morning: "You reap whatever you sow," and "we will reap at harvest-time, if we don't give up."

To be specific, Paul says to the faction-ridden, indecisive new Christians in the churches of Galatia, "Do not be deceived; God is not mocked, for you reap whatever you sow." To put it in the gardening context that I've been using, you can't plant bull-thistles and expect geraniums—even if you're a fine Christian believer and you pray very hard for God to make those thistles into geraniums. No matter how devout you are, and no matter how faithful you have been in coming to church every Sunday, you shouldn't count on getting something beautiful and desirable in your garden if all you planted was giant ragweed and cockleburs. Regardless of your piety, the seed you plant, or the baby seedling you carefully put into a little hole in the soil—*that* determines what's going to grow in your garden

The principle that God built into the natural order will always hold. What you plant *will* be what you harvest, whether you're talking literally about gardens or metaphorically about life in relationship to God and other people.

You're probably wondering where I'm going with all this, and so I'll tell you plainly. For the past year or so, as we have pondered the possibility of a building project, we've been like people dreaming of a garden—expanding an old garden, we might say, by adding some new ground to it. We've talked about it, drawn pictures of it, revised our pictures, re-thought our plans, and today we've come to the time when we'll decide whether we're going to dig up the grass and get started, or not. And we're going to determine what we'll plant there, once we've broken the sod.

I've been involved in a variety of different church building projects, and I'll tell you one important thing up front: a building project is *not* a salvation experience. It's a lot of work. It's costly. And at the end of it, you just have a building—a material structure made of wood, stone, metal and glass—a *thing*. It's not going to get you or anybody else one inch closer to God all by itself. It is simply a means to an end.

By the same token, if you plant a flower garden or a vegetable garden, and you do all the work involved in bringing your dream of a garden to fruition, in the end you just have a bunch of plants—nothing more—*unless* you have a VISION that goes further than simply getting the seeds in the ground and seeing the plants come up, a vision that goes beyond the garden itself.

An ornamental garden is meant to be enjoyed. It's a thing of beauty. You want to sit in the shade of the trees and watch the bees buzzing around the flowers. Smell the roses. Clip some beautiful buds and put them in a vase so you can get pleasure from them indoors, too. If you've planted watercress and spinach, pole beans, squash, tomatoes and zucchini, you want to savor the fresh produce at your dinner table. You want to notice how much better these taste than veggies bought at the grocery store. And you want to bless your friends with them—especially the zucchini.

As we consider whether to remodel our church and put on a new addition, we need clarity of vision about the project. Like people dreaming of a garden, whose dream must go beyond simply seeing the plants come up, our dream of a renovated church has to extend further than just what the building will look like when the contractor's task is finished. I said that a church building is a means to an end. It's a *tool*, really, to help us accomplish work for which the Spirit of God has given us a vision.

The Vision Statement of Christ Church is printed on all our parish publications: CHRIST CHURCH: SHARING HIS LOVE. As I have said many times, our mission is not *mainly* to the people whose names are on the church roll; rather it's a mission *of* us who are members *to* those who are not—whether they're locals, part-timers, or weekend tourists. Our remodeled church, as we have pictured it, is a tool to help facilitate that mission.

Christ Church is a body of Christians who believe that God has gathered us here to serve our neighbors as well as the travelers, students, artists, music-lovers, scholars, skiers and other sojourners that come to Aspen every year from many far-off places. Our calling is to share the love of God that was incarnate in Jesus Christ, and to share that love in as many different ways as the Spirit gives us opportunity.

The most important ways we share his love are through worship, outreach, and the practice of hospitality. We welcome every stranger and seek to meet each one's needs—spiritual, social, or material, as the case may be. And we invite everyone, our friends and neighbors, area residents and visitors from far away, old and young, to join us on the journey to faithful Christian discipleship and spiritual transformation.

That's not a complicated vision; it's pretty simple to grasp. Being church is about serving *others,* not about serving ourselves. And as we serve them, we serve the Lord who has redeemed us and called us to follow him in the path of self-offering love.

"Do not be deceived; God is not mocked, for you reap whatever you sow." We trusted God for the dreaming; we trust him for the planting; and we will trust him for the harvest. We're planting faith, hope, and love, and we're looking for a harvest of souls. We're going forward with confidence that the same Lord who "planted "Christ Church back in the 19th century, when people from all over America were coming to Aspen to find the Mother Lode, intends that we carry his planting into the 21st century—a time when people from everywhere are coming to Aspen to find tranquility or spiritual and physical renewal, to learn more about music or physics or the environment, and to find joy on the slopes of our mountains.

A building project may not make large numbers of people become members of Christ Church, but it might make those who go past our church on their way to concerts or events at the Aspen Institute or to go skiing, running or mountain biking realize that the Episcopal Church in Aspen is "here for good."

We're here—*for good!*

31. WE'RE IN THE HOSPITALITY BUSINESS.

Hebrews 13:1-2

The church is in the hospitality business. Did you know that? It's not just hotels and restaurants in Aspen that are in the hospitality business, we are too. The second Bible reading for this morning, from the 13th chapter of the Letter to the Hebrews, begins with these words: "Let mutual love continue. Do not neglect to show hospitality to strangers, for by doing that some have entertained angels without knowing it."

Right up to modern times, the law of hospitality prevailed almost everywhere in the world. It was understood slightly differently in different cultures, but the basic idea was always the same: if somebody came to your home needing shelter, it was your moral and religious duty to take them in, provide them with a place to sleep, feed them, protect them from enemies who might be pursuing them, and treat them as members of your household. And it was their duty not to presume on your hospitality for longer than was reasonable. In due course, when it was safe to do so, they were expected to move on, not move in. But as long as they were under your roof, you were obligated to take care of them.

In our own country, back in frontier days, it was not uncommon for travelers to knock at a farmhouse door and ask for a place to sleep. Towns with hotels were few and far between, and settlers expected to extend hospitality to strangers on the road. Wayfarers—whether an individual or a whole family—might have to sleep in the hayloft, but they'd never be sent away. And they'd be offered a share of the family's supper, too, before being shown to the barn, where their animals would also be given shelter and fodder. When a solitary traveler on a horse or a family in a wagon continued their journey, the host family would always provide something for them to eat on the way—even if it was just a hunk of cornbread and some cold bacon.

"Do not neglect to show hospitality to strangers, for by doing that some have entertained angels without knowing it." In the Bible, angels always brought a message from God. That was their job; and it still is. In fact, the word "angel" means *messenger.* But sometimes those to whom a heavenly messenger came didn't recognize right off that they were dealing with anybody special, much less an angel, because the angel had arrived in disguise. Angels could look just like anybody else until there was a moment of revelation and their identity was disclosed. In fact, I'd say that there are people among us who are angels and don't even know it! The point is that the message from God which the angel speaks is what's really important, not the angel himself.—But if we fail to be hospitable, if we fail to take time to listen to the angels who come our way, we'll fail to hear the message they bring us from God.

"Do not neglect to show hospitality to strangers, for by doing that some have entertained angels without knowing it." Christ Church is in the hospitality business. When we had the exhibit of plans and drawings of the remodeled church on display in the library, you might have noticed that the new gathering space on the main floor, the space we're naming in honor of Peggy Rowland and Marian Davis, is labeled the "hospitality hall." That's a deliberate decision. We want to emphasize our church's ministry of hospitality to the stranger and welcome to the wayfarer. I hope that somewhere in that new room we'll have a plaque with this Bible verse inscribed on it.

All of us Episcopalians who've driven from town to town around America are familiar with the old red-white-and blue "The Episcopal Church Welcomes You" signs. You know the ones I mean, the ones with the church shield on them that you can see on street corners all over the country. We'd have one hanging on the lamp-post down at 5th and Main Street if the Aspen sign code would allow it.

Well intentioned critics within our church have said these old signs are boring and their message is trite. Maybe so. "The Episcopal Church Welcomes You" *is* a bit bland. It's not "with-it." It doesn't tell people that we're a "happening" church. We should probably have a more electrifying message, something really 21st century in orientation that will make passers-by want to come check us out on Sunday, such as: *"Guess what? The Episcopal Church is really cooler than you thought."* (On the other hand, I guess maybe that wouldn't be quite the right message either.)

It's true that the sign we've always used is old-fashioned. Its graphics aren't contemporary. A picture of the Episcopal Church shield is not particularly enticing. But there's another side to the argument. If the message on our signs is sincere rather than phony, then it is *very* up-to-the-moment, very relevant indeed.

At a time when American society feels terribly polarized, when people might *not* be welcome in certain churches if they have the wrong theology, or the wrong politics, or the wrong accent, or the wrong lifestyle, it's vital for us to proclaim the old message that "The Episcopal Church Welcomes You." For people who have felt *un*-welcome elsewhere, a church that announces, "We welcome you," and *means it*, will seem exceedingly attractive.

Some people may see this as a weakness in our church, but I see it as a virtue: We don't screen those who want to join us in order to eliminate any who don't fit some pre-established mold. You don't have to pass a doctrinal test. There's no Bible quiz, not even pass/fail. We won't pry into your personal history. We just do these simple things: We proclaim Jesus Christ as Savior and Lord. We express our theology concisely in the Nicene Creed. We share the sacrament of our Savior's Body and Blood every week. And we believe that we're sent into the world in Jesus' name to love other people—*all* other people—with Jesus' love. That's our life. If it's attractive to you and you want to share it, you're welcome. The Episcopal Church welcomes you.

The practice of authentic hospitality—a sincere, heartfelt, arms-open-wide welcome to everybody—is a ministry entrusted to us by Christ himself, who said "Anyone who comes to me I will never drive away." Authentic hospitality means more to most people who visit a church than a great sermon does, or music from a paid choir, or classes taught by brilliant teachers. Hospitality lies deep in the heart of the message of Jesus. Someone said that hospitality is like the seed sown in good soil which brings forth a hundred or thousand-fold harvest.

We expect that from April of 2008 until Easter, 2009, while our building is under construction, we're going to be holding our Sunday services somewhere else, and I don't yet know where that's going to be. But wherever it is, we're going to be a whole congregation of people needing hospitality. The very fact that we'll be wayfarers of a sort, needing to be welcomed by others, is going to be a significant learning experience for us.

And during the time next year that we're worshiping off campus we're going to be depending on one another in our congregation to demonstrate mutual love and hospitality in different ways. Some events that usually happen here in the church building will need to take place elsewhere. We'll want to plan for small groups to gather in homes for fellowship, study, prayer, and ministry formation. And if we're going to keep up our practice of hospitality to strangers, we'll need to make sure that we reach out to our guests and visitors from near and far and include them in all our home-based small group events. Sure, it's going to feel different next summer. Sure, it's going to be a challenge. But it's also going to be a time when God can teach us lessons we might never learn otherwise.

"Let mutual love continue. Do not neglect to show hospitality to strangers, for by doing that some have entertained angels without knowing it." Let's ask God for teachable hearts and readiness to welcome and heed the messages brought by all the angels that come our way.

32. LET YOUR LIGHT SHINE.

First Sunday in the New Church
Matthew 5:13-16

I've been thinking about this day and looking forward to it for a long time.—A *long* time! And so have a great many of you: our "Homecoming Day." Now it's here. *Hallelujah*! I hope you're as happy as I am.

Before I say anything else, I want to thank Steve DeClute, the superintendent for our project, and his boss, Bill Baker, and all the great people working with them who came early and stayed late, who worked often on Saturdays (and sometimes Sunday afternoon), who were unfailingly polite to the always-nosey rector and many curious church members who came wandering through the work site, and who did everything humanly possible to get us into this sacred space today.—I think some serious applause for this hard-working team of builders is fitting and proper, don't you?

It will be another week or more before everything is in place and the Baker Construction crew moves on to other projects, but it's wonderful to be here today and see how far we've come since that Sunday morning in February of 2007 when we gathered on this spot and voted to build.

As we sit in this magnificent remodeled church, our field of view is dominated by this dazzling, new altar window. Its focus is the cross of Christ, surrounded by rainbow rays of glory. The cross itself is big and bold and clear—open to the light of the sun and the blue of the sky. The beams of glory radiating from it pull our eyes back to the center, back to the cross—and draw our minds and hearts back to the Savior whose chief symbol it is. Our new window doesn't really have a name, but I think of it as "The Light of the World."

Jesus said, "I am the light of the world. Whoever follows me will never walk in darkness, but will have the light of life." Our church here in Aspen is dedicated to Christ. We are "Christ Church." He has called us to follow him and do his work in the world, and so I can't think of a better image for us to identify with than his shining cross. Jesus is the light of the world, the light that's always driving away this world's darkness.

Jesus said, "I am the light of the world." But it's interesting that when he gathered his disciples on the mountainside to teach them his precepts for living—the "constitution and bylaws of the Kingdom of God" which we know as the Sermon on the Mount—he told them that *they* were "the light of the world." Christ is indeed the light, but *so are we*. We are his "light" in exactly the same way that we're also his "body" in the world: his hands to serve others, his feet to go everywhere, his ears to listen to the hurts and needs of those around us, his smile to cheer, and his eyes to see people everywhere as our sisters and our brothers.

When the detail work on the building is finished, metal letters mounted on the wall beside the door leading out from the church into the world will spell out the words of Matthew 5:16, "Let your light shine before others so that they may see your good works and give glory to your Father in heaven." We've adopted the first four words of that verse as our new parish mission statement: LET YOUR LIGHT SHINE.

Does anybody remember reading Robert Fulghum's book, *All I Needed to Know I Learned in Kindergarten*? I see a few hands up. Well, in a later book he described attending a seminar on reconciliation years ago on the island of Crete, led by a Greek philosopher named Alexander Papaderos, many of whose family members and friends had been killed by the Nazis during the German invasion of Greece in World War II. At the end of his seminar, Dr. Papaderos asked the group, as seminar leaders often do, "Do you have any questions?" Bob Fulghum raised his hand and asked the biggest possible question of all, *"What is the meaning of life?"*

Papaderos didn't sidestep the question. Instead he said, "I'll answer that." Then he took out his billfold and fished around in it 'til he found a little round mirror, about the size of a quarter. He said:

"When I was a small child, during World War II, we were very poor and lived in a remote village in Greece. One day, on the road, I found the broken pieces of a mirror. I tried to find all the pieces and put them together, but that was not possible, so I only kept the largest piece. This one here. By scratching it on a stone, I made it round. I began to play with it as a toy and became fascinated that I could reflect light into dark places where the sun would never shine—into deep holes and crevices and dark closets. It became a game for me to reflect light into the most inaccessible places I could find.

"I kept the little mirror, and as I grew up I would continue to take it out in idle moments and play the game of shining the light into difficult places. As I became a man, I grew to understand that I am not the light or the source of the light. But the light is there, and it will only shine in many of these dark places *if I reflect it*. . . . This is what I'm about. This is the meaning of my life."

Those of us who have responded to Jesus are about the business of shining his light into all kinds of dark places, reflecting love and hope and forgiveness and peace. To change my metaphor a little bit (without changing the message), I might say that if the light we shine in the world comes only out of *us*, it will sooner or later grow dim and burn out, like a flashlight whose batteries have gone dead. To keep our light shining, we have to be connected to the unfailing power supply, and that power supply is Christ. He is the energy that gives us our light. Our light is *his* light, too.

Over the door leading out from the church there will be, in six-inch high letters, the words: "LET YOUR LIGHT SHINE." Turn around and look, the words are up there on a paper strip this morning, exactly where they will be in permanent letters in the future. We will look at those words every time we leave the church to go out into the world: *"Let your light shine."*

Don't sell YOUR light short. Let it shine! Don't minimize what YOUR light might accomplish. Let it shine! We all know the children's song, *"This little light of mine, I'm gonna let it shine."* Your light might seem quite small to you, but when you shine it in the right place or for the right person, your little light can make the deciding difference.

When Jesus was talking to his disciples, he didn't say, "Some of you—the exceptionally gifted and chosen ones—you are the light of the world." He didn't say, "You might be" or "With some hard work, you might have the potential to be" the light of the world. What he said was, "You *are* the light of the world."

If we have come to Christ, we have been lit as a lamp of the Lord. And as long as we stay plugged into the unfailing power supply, we'll keep shining.

This beautiful, sacred space, this new center for ministry which we begin to occupy this morning—as I have said so many times in the last couple of years—is merely a *tool*. It is not an end in itself. It is a means to an end. Its purpose is to help us, as a congregation, shine our light more brightly and more effectively for the benefit of those around us.

Joan and I lived in Michigan before we moved to Aspen, and there are many lighthouses all around the two peninsulas of Michigan. I think of this new building as being like the prismatic glass Fresnel lenses that were one of the greatest inventions of the first half of the 19th century. The Fresnel lens would narrow and concentrate the light of a kerosene flame so that it would shine twenty miles out to sea from a lighthouse, to keep sailing vessels from foundering on the rocks. This church is meant to be a kind of "lighthouse" for the Lord.

In the Sermon on the Mount, Jesus said that we were to let our light shine "so that others might see our good works" and give glory to our Father in heaven. We have work to do: God's work. This new building is intended to help us accomplish that work.

Inserted in each of the bulletin booklets this morning is a tan card with something printed on it. I want you to take that card out and look at it. Last Tuesday morning, as I was praying and writing in my prayer journal as I do almost every day, I had the sense that the Lord had something to say to me, for our church. For all of us. So I wrote it down, and it's printed on that card. The Lord said this to me:

"I will do a new thing in this place, if you are willing to cooperate with me and with one another. It will be a healing work. It will be a work of renewal. It will be a work of the Spirit, not the flesh.

"Offer this new building to Me with sincere hearts. Offer it to Me, and I will accept it. But offerings like this, sacrifices like this, must be unconditional. If you offer Me this edifice, I will accept it and I will use it in ways you might not yet imagine and of which you might not approve, for My ways are not your ways; My ways are higher than your ways.

"But more than this house of stone and metal and glass, I want you to offer Me your hearts. Give Me your hearts, and I will renew your life, your affections, your vocation, and your sense of purpose.

"Open your hearts and open your doors. Expect that I will do a new thing. When you see what I am doing, you will be glad, if you truly love Me."

It would be fair for you to ask me, "How can you say these words are 'God's word'? How do you know?" All I can tell you is this: I have heard the Lord before, and this *sounds* like him to me!

Therefore, I present the words that are printed on this card to you today as an invitation from God—an invitation *and* a warning. The Lord says that he will do a new thing among us, IF we're willing to cooperate with him and with each other . . . a work of healing and renewal, a work of the Spirit and not the flesh. *If* we offer this new building to him as a gift—with no strings attached—he will accept it, and he will use it for his own purposes, his own work—work which he warns could surprise or even shock us—since *God's* ways are not *our* ways, his ways are higher than our ways. God invites us to open our hearts and open the doors of this church and trust him to use it, if we love him. We DO love him; therefore, let's do what he asks of us, and do it right now. Please stand and join with me in offering our church to God.

Rector: We have built on the sure foundation, Jesus Christ our Lord.
Congregation: *Father, we give this house to you.*

We have been touched by your Spirit and summoned by your love.
Father, we give our hearts to you.

We have heard your call to serve others as Jesus, your Son, served us.
Father, we give our hands to you.

We have the Light of Christ kindled within us. We are lamps lit by the Lord.
Father, we give our lives to you. Make us shine with Christ's light in this place, to help your children find their way home to you. Amen.

33. THE GIFT AND BURDEN
OF FREEDOM.

Sunday nearest Independence Day
Galatians 5:1, 13-25

"*For freedom Christ has set us free.*" On this Sunday before the Fourth of July, *freedom* seems like a good subject for a preacher to tackle. In America we assume that freedom is desirable. It's an article of our American Creed that we believe all people *ought* to be free and independent. But freedom is a burden. Real freedom doesn't make us footloose and fancy free. It doesn't make us care-free. There are two very serious aspects to freedom, and they are closely related to one another:

First: THE ESSENCE OF FREEDOM IS THE LIBERTY TO MAKE CHOICES FOR OURSELVES. Nobody chooses for us. When we're free, *if we intend to stay free and not submit to another kind of slavery*, we must pray and think things through and then make choices. To be free is itself one choice we make. Free people don't just follow the crowd; they decide for themselves.

If we read the Bible with care we see that from the story of Adam and Eve in the Garden of Eden straight on through the Old Testament narrative of God's dealing with Israel to the New Testament and the coming of Christ into the world, God always appeals to human freedom. God places on us the burden of *choice*. The Creation Story in Genesis says that God made human beings in his "likeness." The ability to make free choices is the main way we are "like God." We were created to be free. We're meant to make decisions for ourselves. We can believe, or we can choose not to believe.

Second: IF WE'RE FREE, WE'RE ACCOUNTABLE. Slaves have to do what they're told. They don't get to choose. Slaves do what the master says; and the master assumes moral accountability for them. People who can't choose can't be held morally accountable, but free people are always morally accountable. One of the duties of free people is to refuse to submit to the immoral demands of tyrants. The Jewish Community Center recently sponsored a seminar here on the *Shoah*, the Holocaust. Those who cooperated in the Holocaust because they were under the heel of the Nazis and justified their complicity because they were afraid of punishment were morally accountable for their partnership in that evil because they *could* have refused to obey. Exercise of that freedom would almost certainly have cost them their lives, but some people believe freedom is worth that much.

If we're free, we carry a burden that unfree people don't have to carry: the burden of costly choice.

Freedom is preferable to slavery. But some kinds of slavery *masquerade* as "freedom," though they're really only captivity in camouflage. And it's easy to fall subject to these slaveries that pretend to be dimensions of our God-given liberty. I want to mention four: slavery to self, slavery to comfort, slavery to ideology, and slavery to legalism. There are others you might add to my list.

- First, there's SLAVERY TO *SELF*.—This is also called "selfism," and we find it hiding under many kinds of psychological camouflage in our society. Bondage to our own ego, whether it arises from feelings of inadequacy or a sense of grandiosity, channels all our energy toward self-interest, self-indulgence, self-promotion, self-satisfaction, and self-protection. The only thing involving the *self* that "selfism" doesn't permit is *self sacrifice!*

- Then there's SLAVERY TO *COMFORT*.—This one sneaks up on Americans. We quickly grow accustomed to having a pretty easy way of living; we take for granted our opportunity to enjoy relative luxury, compared to the privations endured by three-fifths of the world's people; and we assume there will always be somebody else we can pay to do our dirty work. Slavery to *comfort* can be an addiction we don't recognize until our comforts are temporarily taken away.

- There's SLAVERY TO *IDEOLOGY*.—Ideologies are the dogmas and idea systems of dominant social, political or religious movements. And, yes, there are *ideologies* in the Church. Ideologies give rise to the factionalism currently causing so much pain in our own Anglican Communion. Here is a fact: *ideologues* are never interested in *dialogue*. Ideologues are public figures that we allow to do our thinking for us. (And there are lots of people out there who'd like for you to let them do your thinking.) I mentioned the Holocaust a moment ago; Hitler was an ideologue before he became a dictator. Hitler was evil. There are other kinds of ideologues who don't seem wicked, but who *do* invite us to quit trying to figure things out for ourselves, climb up on their ideological bandwagons, and enjoy the ride. People enslaved to an ideology give up their freedom to think and make their own decisions. We can tell we're becoming slaves to an ideology if we get anxious because we're having doubts or ideas that conflict with the dogmas of "our group" or its official representatives.

Let me make this clear: the gospel of Jesus Christ offers us *freedom,* not bondage to dogma. Remember the Bible verse we started with this morning: *"For freedom Christ has set us free."*

- Finally, there's SLAVERY TO *LEGALISM*.—The "Rule of Law" is necessary if people are going to live together in relative harmony and cooperation whether it's in a town, or a country, or even on the planet. But legalism exalts the law above the law-giver, and turns mechanical obedience to the letter of the law into an excuse for behavior that, under other circumstances, would be deemed immoral. It's for good reason that the Bible says, *"The letter of the Law kills, but the Spirit gives life."* There's nothing sadder to me than seeing Christians beat each other up with Bible verses. That's an aspect of legalism.

Keep this in mind: *Faith in God—real FAITH—is manifested by freedom from fear of breaking the law.*

Earlier this morning we read these words that Paul wrote to Christians who were struggling to retain the authentic freedom that Christ came into the world to offer: *"For freedom Christ has set us free. Stand firm, therefore, and do not submit again to a yoke of slavery. For you were called to freedom, brothers and sisters; only do not use your freedom as an opportunity for self-indulgence, but through love become slaves to one another. For the whole law is summed up in a single commandment, 'You shall love your neighbor as yourself.'"*

The greatest of Christians have not been obsessed with doing right and avoiding wrong, with keeping the rules and avoiding heresy, but rather with loving others and trusting the future to a loving God.

Jesus said, *"Come to me, all you who labor and are heavy laden, and I will give you rest. Take my yoke upon you, and learn from me; for I am gentle and lowly in heart, and you will find rest for your souls. For my yoke is easy, and my burden is light."* This is an invitation to take up the "burden" of freedom, the "yoke" of Christ, an invitation to serve the Master whose service, according to the Apostle Paul, *"is perfect freedom."*

How does this work? How can we who are "heavy laden" with the slaveries that others have imposed or that we've unconsciously—or maybe deliberately—chosen for ourselves, find *rest* in shouldering any *other* "burden"? And how can one who chooses to follow Jesus as Master and Lord be, at the same time, gloriously *free*?

Let's think about this. What is our present heavy burden, if not the awareness of our own sin, our moral shortcomings, the things we have freely chosen to do or not to do? We're free, but many of us feel crushed by the recognition of our moral failures. The world and the law and our own meditations tell us that we must save ourselves by making amends for our mistakes, but *we can't really do it!* We can't ever be good enough to make up for our shortcomings. So they become an unbearable load, an impossible burden.

Jesus says that he wants to take that burden from us and give us a *different* load to carry, one that's *"easy and light."* What's the difference between the two? The difference is that the old burden is the impossible demand that I save myself, in spite of the knowledge that I can't ever fully make up for my past failures. In place of that crushing load, Jesus offers me the "light burden" of *faith working through love.* Love your God and love your neighbor, and follow the One who will lead you step by step and demonstrate how to do that.

We become *free* in "serving" Jesus because the service we give him is our free response to his gift of himself for us. Look at the gospels. You will see that Jesus never tried to control, dominate or manipulate anyone. He never pushed people around. And he doesn't do that to you and me. He just loves us unconditionally and wins our devotion and allegiance by that love. All Christ asks of us is that we come with him. And even that's an invitation, not an order. We're *invited* to follow. If we choose not to go, or if we start following and then drop out, he'll grieve for the choice we've made, but he'll never whip us back into line. It's always our decision, every day.

Voluntary and loving service (rather than obedience coerced by threats of punishment) and *heart-centered faith* (rather than fearful conformity to rules and dogma)—these are the marks of the freedom that is ours in Christ.

As we celebrate the 231st anniversary of the signing of the Declaration of Independence of these United States this week, we who are also by God's grace citizens of Heaven celebrate the charter of our true liberty: *the Gospel that sets us free.*

34. FAITH-FILLED FRIENDS.

Mark 2:1-12

Jesus may well have slept under the stars when he was on the road, preaching from village to village, but in Capernaum, the town where he had moved from Nazareth some years earlier, the Bible tells us he had a little house. It was probably his shop too. Mark says, "When Jesus returned to Capernaum, after some days it was reported that he was AT HOME." "*At home*" in Greek literally means, "at his house." A carpenter also worked on houses in those days—the Greek word means "builder"—so it seems logical to me that Jesus would have a house of his own. It was just good business. After all, would you want a carpenter to build a house for you who hadn't built one for himself?

So the local crowds gathered at Jesus' place to listen to what he was teaching. So many people came to listen that there wasn't enough room for all of them in the house, so the rest were standing outside, looking in through the single door and the single window, trying to hear as best they could. He was apparently just teaching; there's no mention of any healing going on. Some of the crowd were Scribes and Pharisees—people more likely to be critical of Jesus than friendly to him.

The roof of Jesus' house would have been flat, and there'd have been narrow steps outside, along one wall, leading up to the roof. In that area, where it gets very hot, people would sit on the roof in the evening to catch the cool breeze off the lake. The walls of the lower part of the house would be stone, the upper part of the walls wood, and the roof made of a thick layer of clay laid over a lattice of boards and sticks.

As Jesus sat in his house speaking to the neighbors who crowded inside and were standing around outside, some others arrived with a paralyzed man carried on a pallet by four of them. The dense crowd formed an impenetrable barrier for newcomers. So the four pallet-carriers took their paralyzed friend up on the roof—which must have been a very delicate operation, since the steps were usually very narrow. While they were slowly getting the sick man to the roof, others of their group took tools and went ahead of them to make a big hole in the roof so that when the pallet-carriers arrived they could lower their friend down on his pallet through the hole.

Let's observe something here: *This story begins with friendship.* Real friendship is more than just being able to go out on the town and enjoy a good time together. True friends feel one another's pain. They don't hesitate to share one another's burdens or troubles. They identify with one another. Our real friends don't just have warm feelings towards us; they don't just wish us well. They *do* things for us. They *act.* They help us. They make themselves useful. These people were focused on getting their paralyzed friend to Jesus, and the most important thing was to get around or over or through whatever barriers might be in the way. These people were *motivated.* Motivated by love.

So the question for us is: To what lengths will we go to bring a friend to Jesus? . . . a friend that needs help. . . . a friend that needs healing of body, mind or spirit? . . . a friend that needs to meet the Savior? When a friend of ours is in need, what's the first thought that occurs to us? . . . Do we ever think: *"Ed needs Jesus"? "Sally needs Jesus"?*

The man in the gospel story was paralyzed. Maybe he'd had a stroke. Maybe he'd been kicked in the head by a donkey. It's also possible that he was paralyzed by *guilt,* by pathological anxiety. (Psychosomatic paralysis happens.) Perhaps he couldn't even speak.—We don't know the details of his condition. But the friends who brought him to Jesus' house had *faith.* They trusted that God was working in an amazing way through their village carpenter. So they believed that if they could somehow just get him through to Jesus, their friend would be O.K. Jesus would know what he needed.

It's a proven fact that amazing things can happen when people *believe.* There's a big difference between being in a crowd of praying believers and being in a crowd of non-praying skeptics. You know what I'm talking about. When people of faith are present and praying, the power of God is there to heal and help.—*Where there is little or no faith, there is little or no power.* That rule particularly applies to churches.

Remember when Jesus went back to Nazareth, to the village where he'd been raised, and preached in the synagogue? The Bible says "he couldn't do any mighty works there, because of their unbelief." There was no atmosphere of faith, no community of expectation—even in Jesus' home-town.

The paralyzed man was brought to Jesus' house by *friends who had faith.* There were more than four of them. Four carried his pallet, but there were others who had come with them and believed just as strongly.

Imagine what it must have been like in the house. First they heard people tramping around on the roof. Then, pieces of plaster and roofing material started coming down on everyone packed into the room below. Somebody was digging through the roof.—Word was passed from those standing outside: "They're making a hole in the roof to pass a sick man down to Jesus."

Everybody probably got away from the falling sticks and ceiling plaster and waited to see what would happen. I don't think Jesus just kept preaching as if nothing strange was going on. First there was a little hole, and sunlight streamed into the dark room.—That was a powerful visual symbol right there.—Then the hole got bigger. Then down came a pallet, lowered by ropes tied to the corners, and on it was a man who couldn't move or talk.

Many faces looked in from the hole in the roof, faces full of hope and expectation. (How does a hopeful, expectant face look? Try making a hopeful, expectant expression right now.) Jesus looked up at them and smiled. Nobody said anything. There was what we'd call a pregnant silence. The gospel tells us that Jesus, *"seeing their faith,"* said to the man on the pallet, "My son, your sins are forgiven."

There's more to this passage, but I just want to focus on this part today. Let's think about sin for a minute. I know it's probably not your favorite subject. It's not mine either, but we need to spend some time on it.

There's a moralistic way of regarding sin as simply bad behavior, offenses (great or small) against the moral law. But there's a more accurate way to understand Sin—Sin with a capital "S"—that is as a state of being, of which wrong behavior may be only a symptom. The Bible teaches that the purpose and destiny of human existence is to be in union with God, to receive and share God's love. *Sin is the state of being separated from God, disconnected from God . . . in a situation where we can't fulfill our destiny.*

Forgiveness of sin brings us back into relationship with God. It breaks down the wall of separation that our self-centered behavior creates. In this story, the *barriers* between the paralyzed man and Jesus—the crowd and the roof, physical symbols of spiritual separation—are overcome by faith. And we are not necessarily talking about the faith of the paralyzed man—since we don't know if he had been paralyzed for days or weeks or even years, or whether he could even speak. But we're talking about the faith of *his friends.* How important it is to have faith-filled friends. And how important it is to *be* a faith-filled friend!

All of us have times of being at least partly paralyzed, don't we? Our paralysis may not be physical, but we can be paralyzed spiritually. We can be paralyzed emotionally. When people are emotionally numb and tell us they "just can't feel anything," we'd say they're emotionally paralyzed.—What can paralyze us?

It could be shame or humiliation. It could be fear or anxiety. It could be doubt. It could be guilt—legitimate guilt (arising from a healthy conscience that tells us we have done something wrong) or *false* guilt (produced by neurosis). Guilt of some kind was probably what led to the paralysis of the man in this gospel story.

When we're paralyzed, we need *friends.* We can't help ourselves. We're frozen. We need faith-filled friends, intermediaries who will bring us to God so we can be healed.—And when others are in need, we're called to be their faith-filled friends.

Don't forget: there are times when our own words of forgiveness can function as if they had been spoken by the Lord himself—when our forgiveness is addressed to someone paralyzed by guilt and shame because of an offense committed against *us.* Our choosing to forgive can set that person free from the paralysis of guilt. When we forgive them, they are released, because *when we forgive them, God forgives them.*

Faith-filled friends have courage to overcome every barrier, and bring us to the Lord. We need to have friends like that. And we need to be friends like that.

35. COMPASSION IS NOT JUST A FEELING. IT'S A DECISION TO GET INVOLVED.

Luke 7:11-17

It seems as if every time I turn on the TV or pick up a newspaper, I learn about another tragic disaster, another population left homeless and destitute, another ten thousand injured and thousands more dead. Every day we get requests to donate money to truly worthwhile causes: feeding the hungry, caring for orphans, curing terrible diseases, educating poor girls in backward regions of the Third World where girls don't get sent to school, housing the homeless, and so on.

Compassion is a moral imperative for all the world's great religions. But being constantly bombarded with news about the plight of poor, suffering people causes some of us to experience compassion fatigue. We don't want to hear about one more tragedy or one more disaster. We don't want to see one more picture of a starving child. The endless deluge of sad news can leave us numb. The needs of the world are so numerous and so great, and our personal resources are so obviously limited, that we can develop emotional detachment from further tragedies. We say, "There's another earthquake in China, and another flood in Bangladesh, and another civil war in central Africa.—What can I really DO about it? I'm sorry, but I have my own worries to deal with, so please leave me alone."

Let's consider Jesus. Wherever Jesus went, he drew a crowd. Some people adored him and wanted to be near him. Others despised him and wanted to heckle him. And there were many others who were just curious about him. But in addition to the devoted, the hostile, and the curious, there were the needy. Hundreds of sick, leprous, deaf, blind, or lame people flocked to him everywhere he went, begging him for healing. It was so exhausting, there were times he had to escape to the hills and be alone.

One day when Jesus and his entourage of disciples, admirers, critics and needy people came to the little town in southern Galilee called Nain, they were met by another crowd of people going the other way, heading out the town gate. This was a funeral procession.

Now, Jesus and the others might simply have stopped and stood quietly at the roadside to let the funeral procession go by, on its way out to the tomb—just the way we do on the highway when a hearse comes along, driving slowly, followed by a line of cars with their lights on. That's probably what most of the people around him did—but not Jesus.

Jesus watched the funeral procession. The body of the deceased was being carried out on a bier, as was the custom with the poor. There was no coffin; the corpse was wrapped in a shroud and laid on a wooden plank. Following the body there came a weeping woman—dressed in the customary garb of a widow. Burials always took place on the day of the death, so the woman was in the anguish of fresh grief. She was leaning on a couple of other women and surrounded by sympathetic friends. Jesus saw no young people or children with her, and so he knew right away that this was a mother taking out the body of her only son for burial.

Luke says that when Jesus saw this brokenhearted, bereaved mother, *"he had compassion for her."* In spite of his being assailed continuously, every day, by pitiful people in need of help, he was not numb to the situation. The original language is more graphic; it literally says *"he was moved with gut-wrenching feeling for her."* That tells us something important about *compassion*. It always hits us in the gut. It's an internal yearning, a deep empathy for people which is so intense it affects us physically. Authentic compassion begins, first of all, with powerful feelings we just can't make go away.

Jesus called out, maybe from the roadside, to the poor woman and said, *"Oh, please don't cry!"* What could be more gut-wrenching than to hear the cries of a mother who has just experienced such a loss?

Jesus went over and stopped the procession. He put his hand on the bier and said simply, "Young man, I say to you, be raised." The man immediately sat up, alive, and began to speak. Luke says that Jesus "gave him back to his mother." The villagers were awe-struck. With their own eyes they had just seen the power of God at work, just as in the days of Elijah. And they ran to spread news of the miracle far and wide. We're not told anything else: not about anyone coming to faith, and not about the woman or the boy being grateful to Jesus. Nothing else, only this: *"He gave him back to his mother."*

Jesus' *compassion* for the grieving mother is the first thing the gospel-writer mentions, and it's the main point of the story. He was "deeply moved with gut-wrenching feeling" when he saw her tears, when he recognized her loneliness and sensed her anxiety for the future. A widow who had no son to be her protector was at risk in that ancient society. The woman probably had no idea who Jesus was, and the other people from Nain were as much in the dark as she was. They might have heard about a miracle-working prophet named Jesus of Nazareth, but they could have had no idea that this man was he. Certainly the weeping woman had no faith, no expectation that some stranger at the roadside could help her. She was absorbed in her own pain.—But Jesus felt compassion for her.

Compassion is a powerful emotion, but it's more than that. All the great religions describe *compassion* as one of the main attributes of God and as a quality found in holy people. But how do you and I acquire compassion? Can we *learn* compassion? I've never seen an advertisement for an educational video entitled *Six Weeks to a More Compassionate Me.* I've never read a how-to book on compassion.

Compassion is a gift. I believe that. Faith is a gift, too. But just as there are some things we can do to deepen our faith, I believe that there are some things we can do to deepen our natural capacity to experience and practice compassion. Here are three steps we can take.

The first step is TO DECIDE TO BECOME MORE SENSITIVE TO OTHER PEOPLE. I got this lesson when I was a senior in high school and was the editor of our high school paper. The journalism teacher who was the sponsor for the student paper said to me every day, over and over, "Bruce, you have to be sensitive to other people's feelings. Be sensitive to other people." Obviously, I was a typical adolescent, totally wrapped up in myself.

What we have to do is stop, and look around; take notice of others. Look them in the eye. We're often oblivious to what's really going on with our friends, much less with strangers. We keep wrapped up in ourselves, our ambitions, and our emotions. We don't always notice others' sadness; we don't perceive their pain. Or, if we do notice, we don't want to let it get to us because we think there's really nothing we can do to help. Besides that, we don't want to be intrusive. We want to respect their privacy. So we pat them on the back and go on about our business.—But compassion demands that we *allow ourselves be emotionally vulnerable,* that we share the other person's pain so much that we are inwardly moved, just as Jesus was.

That leads to the second step, which is A DECISION TO ACT ON OUR FEELINGS. Compassion is more than just feeling sorry for people. It requires that we get involved, that we do whatever we can do to help. Emotions come and go. But compassion, like faith, also involves an act of the will: the decision to *get personally engaged with the other person.* Peter Ustinov once said, "Charity is more common than compassion. Charity is tax-deductible. Compassion is time-consuming." Many bystanders were probably moved to tears as they watched the weeping mother following the body of her only son to his tomb. But Jesus didn't just weep, he didn't just have feelings; he did something. *He got personally involved.*

The third step in this process of growing our own capacity for compassion is TO BECOME FULLY AWARE OF OUR RESOURCES AND UNDERSTAND WHAT WE CAN PERSONALLY BRING TO BEAR WHEN WE DECIDE TO GET INVOLVED. After the South Asian tsunami in December 2004, there was a story in Newsweek about Rebecca O'Connor, a pediatric nurse in New York City. Seeing the reports of the terrible devastation, she and a handful of other medical professionals she knew in the city flew at their own expense to Sri Lanka to help. They staked out a location for themselves and began seeing as many as a hundred patients in a day.

After they'd been treating people for several days, they learned that there was a local hospital less than a mile away from them and another clinic, too. O'Connor asked a Sri Lankan friend, "Why are people coming to our little clinic here instead of going to the local hospital?"

The friend answered: "Because at the hospital, someone just asks them, 'Name? . . . Age? . . . Complaint?' and then gives them a sheet of paper and tells them to go take a seat somewhere. But you sit down with them, you ask them what's wrong, and then you treat them. *You listen to them.*"

O'Connor closed her interview by saying: "It seemed that the most valuable therapy we were providing had nothing to do with antibiotics or wound care. By listening to story after heartbreaking story, by admiring pictures of families once happy and healthy, and by playing soccer with kids who had lost everything, we were able to say, 'We care about you, and we share your grief,' without actually speaking a word."

Jesus dealt with needy people all the time. By rights, he should have had compassion fatigue. But he did what only *he* could do. He stopped the funeral procession, raised a young man from death to life, and gave him back to his mother. You and I might not be able to work miracles like that, but God has given us resources we can offer that have their own life-giving dimensions of compassion. Sometimes all a hurting person needs is for us to say, as I'm sure Jesus often did, "Don't be scared. I'm here, and I'm going to stay with you. I won't leave you alone" And, perhaps the simplest of all, after listening to a person who's down on his luck and ready to give up, we can open our checkbook and say: "Here, let me take care of that for you," and pay his debts.

I believe all disciples want to be like the Master. And, if we want to be like Jesus, that means we want to be compassionate.—But remember: *compassion is not just a feeling. It's a decision to get involved.*

36. IF YOU WANT TO WALK ON WATER, YOU'VE GOT TO GET OUT OF THE BOAT.

Matthew 14:22-33

After the famous 5,000 uninvited guests had all been fed by his disciples' little snack-pack of five loaves and two fish, Jesus told his friends to climb back in their boat and go on back home alone, ahead of him. It was sundown, but he wanted to go off in the hills by himself and pray. He'd walk back home when he was ready.

During the night, a big storm came down on the lake and the disciples' boat was caught in it. The wind was blowing, waves were high, and the boat was taking on water. It looked ready to sink.

The pictorial symbol of the Church as a *boat* goes way back. And, though the little picture of a boat by itself can't convey it, we should remember that this boat is always full of terrified Christians in a storm. When Matthew wrote his gospel the Church already had problems: enemies on the outside and friction on the inside. Traditional Jews had expelled Christian Jews from their synagogues. Jewish Christians weren't sure how to treat gentile Christians. Gentile Christians weren't sure how to get along with their still-pagan families. And Peter and Paul had fallen out with each another.—So when you hear about another crisis in the Church, keep in mind that this is nothing new. There's never been a time when the Church was totally free from one crisis or another.

Just before dawn on the morning after he'd sent the boys back home in the boat, Jesus came walking out to them, through the wind and rain, over the stormy lake. The men in the boat saw him out there on the water as he approached them, but in the dim light and falling rain they thought they were seeing a ghost. After all, flesh-and-blood creatures can't walk on water, so this had to be an apparition, maybe something evil. They were already scared the boat might sink, so when they saw a figure heading toward them walking on the water they were terrified. Then the "ghost" spoke, and the voice sounded familiar: "Have courage. It is I. Don't be afraid." It was Jesus. At least, he sounded like Jesus—but it was still hard to see clearly.

The main point for Christians as we hear this story again is that the Lord has promised to be with us forever. Forever. The Church—divided, weak and preoccupied with non-essentials as it now is—has been sent by Christ to do his work in the world. We're his chosen agents. In the time of our greatest need and most wrenching fear, when we're worn out either from "fighting the good fight" or fighting with each other, Jesus comes to us. So remember: this story isn't just about something that happened to the original Twelve disciples long ago, it's also the sign and promise of what Jesus will do for us when our boat is in danger. But, like the twelve scared men that stormy morning on Galilee, we don't necessarily always recognize Jesus when he shows up. Even when we hear his voice we can have doubts.

There's also a story-within-the-story here. The big story is that Jesus has committed his work to us. He has sent us out just as he sent the disciples out in their little boat. When we face storms and strife, Jesus promises to come to us. The story-within-the-story is about "Doubting Peter." (Everybody knows about "Doubting Thomas." This story is about "Doubting Peter.") Peter heard Jesus say, "Have courage. It is I. Don't be afraid." But he was skeptical. He wasn't totally convinced it was really Jesus, fifty yards away across the water, calling out to them. So he decided on a test. He hollered back and said, "Lord, if it's *really* you, command me to come to you on the water."

Jesus gave him a one-word answer, *"Come!"*

Now, why do you suppose Peter figured *this* was the acid test for whether the mysterious figure really was Jesus or not?—Why this?—I think it was because Peter knew his Master had the habit of insisting that his disciples do exactly what *he* was doing. He wanted them to imitate him. That's because Jesus expected his followers to *become like him.* (He still does.) That meant he assumed they'd take on missions that looked impossible—like feeding 5,000 people with five little loaves and two pieces of fish. Jesus had looked at the hungry crowd the day before and said to the disciples, "You give them something to eat." So it might have seemed logical to Peter that Jesus would say, "OK. You see me doing it. Now you walk on water." Peter knew something else, too: when Jesus told his disciples to do something, he always gave them the power to do it.

With this in mind, Peter climbed over the side of the boat and started to walk to Jesus. And, lo and behold, he was stepping on the water like it was dry land. I imagine he took one slow, tentative step at a time; he didn't break into a run. The water wasn't level, of course. Since the waves were high, Peter's stroll on the lake was up-and-down. But as long as he kept his eyes fixed on Jesus, he was fine: "Look at me, guys; I'm walking on the water!" After he was twenty or thirty yards from the boat—but still not all the way to Jesus—he must have looked down and thought about the two hundred feet of water directly underneath him. That's when he got scared. (Or, we should say, he got more scared.)

Something like that has happened to me before in airplanes. I'm scared of heights, but I usually manage well enough on a plane . . . unless I start looking out the window and thinking, "It's five miles down to the ground. Five miles."—That's when I want to press the button and have the cabin attendant bring me a parachute.

Anyhow, I think Peter took his eyes off Jesus—maybe he looked over his shoulder at the other guys who were in the relative security of the boat—and then he began to sink. I picture this as happening with unnatural slowness. If I stepped out of a boat into a lake, I'd go down like a rock. But Peter went down s-l-o-w-l-y. And as he was going down, he yelled, "Lord, save me!" Suddenly Jesus was right there and pulled him up to safety, saying "O, man of little faith, why did you doubt?"

Peter made an attempt and failed.—Or did he? He got out of the boat and walked on the water *part* way to Jesus. That's not total failure; that's partial success. He almost made it to Jesus, and *then* he got scared and lost his nerve. Then he began to doubt. Peter had both faith and doubt. Jesus didn't call him a "man of *no* faith." He called him a "man of *little* faith." At a crucial moment, the doubt won out. Here's something true I read somewhere: *"Every time you take a step in faith you run the risk of failing. But if you're afraid of failure, you'll never step out in faith."*

I think that maybe Peter had pretty substantial faith in Jesus, but not so much faith in his own ability to *do* what Jesus had told him to do. When he got out of the boat and walked a few steps, he started to doubt, not Jesus, but *himself.*

In principle, walking on water was like what all the disciples had done the previous day when they'd waded into the crowd and started breaking up the five little loaves and two hunks of fish that Jesus had prayed over, expecting to feed the whole mob with that little bit of food, just because Jesus had told them to do it. I stole the title of this sermon—and quite a few of its ideas—from a book by John Ortberg, *If You Want to Walk on Water, You've Got to Get Out of the Boat,* which is one of my favorites. John Ortberg says the story about Peter walking on the water isn't just about risk-taking; it's about *obedience.* Christians have to learn how to tell the difference between what God is telling us to do and what just might be a prideful impulse on our part. Courage by itself is not enough. Courage has to be accompanied by wisdom.

I believe the Lord wants our church to take some serious new steps in faith. I'm not sure what they are yet, but I feel certain that God will make his will clear before too long. *If you want to walk on water, you've got to get out of the boat.* Being a Christian doesn't just mean going to church services on Sunday, week after week, and that's it. It means a life of authentic faith, obedience—and risk. It means being willing to say, "Lord, tell us to come to you walking on the water." The kind of faith that gets us out of the boat is the only kind that will keep Christ Church in Aspen sailing into the future.

37. IS THAT "SOMEBODY" YOU?

Luke 9:51-62

Luke says that "as the days drew near for him to be taken up," Jesus "*set his face* to go to Jerusalem.*" He had a goal. And he was determined to reach that goal.

He *"set his face."* Isn't that a great expression? Like other grandparents (and parents, too, of course) Joan and I have seen our share of Little League baseball games. The look of determination on the faces of some of those scrappy little guys when they come up to bat is a perfect illustration (at the little kid level) of what it means to set your face.—Stance, expression, everything about the most serious of those pee-wee ball players says, "I'm gonna swing this bat and get a big hit!"

Aspen is now playing host to hundreds of young musicians for the next eight weeks. Those gifted young people have the same kind of grit. You just don't become an accomplished pianist, or violinist, or horn-player, or singer without setting your face.

A compliment people often give—whether to musicians or athletes or scholars—is to say that they're *focused.* They have their eyes fixed on a destination in life—no matter how distant it might be—and they intend to reach it. Focus, commitment, dedication, stick-to-it-ivity—whatever you want to call it—is a virtue we admire in people of any age.

When Luke tells us that Jesus "had *set his face* to go to Jerusalem," he means that Jesus was resolved to do God's will—no matter what it might cost him. He'd already made clear to his friends that he was on his way up to Jerusalem and certain death. Jesus had enemies; and he had no illusions about what was waiting for him in the capital city. He knew that there was about to be an encounter between the incarnate love of God and the powers of this world's present darkness. And he knew that he was going to have to lay down his life, if the love of God was going to triumph over evil.

When we read Luke's gospel carefully, we see that much of it is a narrative of Jesus' journey from Galilee to Jerusalem—and the cross. He's always on the road, passing through countryside, towns, and villages. And as he keeps moving onward, we detect that neither his disciples nor the people who he spoke to along the road were really getting what he was telling them.

They knew he was going to Jerusalem, but they refused to believe that his journey to the capital was anything but a kind of victory parade. They figured that Jesus was so brilliant, so gifted, so charismatic, so awesome in everything he did and everything he said—how could he not be acclaimed by the leaders of the nation when he arrived on their doorstep? Some of the villagers tagged along, falling in behind Jesus and his disciples as they hiked along the road to Jerusalem. They wanted to be there to see this new prophet put a whipping on the Romans.

The character of Jesus as we see him in the gospel is always consistent. He's never wishy-washy.

He's never indecisive.—Always focused, *his face is set.*

He believed God had summoned him to walk the way of the cross, and he was doing it. The shortest route to Jerusalem took him through Samaria. As you know, Samaritans and Jews were ethnic cousins, but they had about as much affection for each other as Palestinians have for Israelis these days. So Jesus sent some of his friends on ahead to see if they could find everybody a place to stay. They discovered that no Samaritan would even give Jews going to Jerusalem so much as a pallet to lie on out behind the house.

James and John were enraged. Indignant. Insulted. They said to one another, "Don't these filthy Samaritans know who this is that's looking for rooms? These people aren't showing us any respect. We should nuke 'em!"—So they went back and asked Jesus if they should call down fire from heaven to burn up those Samaritans.

But Jesus had *set his face*. He had a destination, a goal, a purpose. He wasn't about to be distracted by hostility from anybody, and the very suggestion that he take violent revenge on his enemies disgusted him. One version of this story says he scolded James and John and told them, "You men don't know what kind of Spirit you're made of. The Son of Man has not come to destroy people but to save them."

I said that Jesus had been picking up a crowd as he moved along. Most of them were just admirers, what we'd call "fans" in our day, like the Boston people who came out to Denver this past week to watch the Red Sox play the Rockies. But a few of the people who joined him were more than merely fans.

A handful were deeply serious about forming a bond with Jesus and becoming like him. What do you think motivated those serious people? I guess I'm cynical, but most people who want to get on a bandwagon—political, religious or otherwise—are looking for some kind of personal advantage. When we feel that a régime change is in the wind, we know it can be profitable for us if we're pals with the new king—or president, or bishop, or whatever.

Jesus invited everybody to have a relationship with him, but he was never interested in merely casual or opportunistic followers. He had no time for fair-weather friends—the kind of people who wanted to follow him around so they could go "oooh" and "aaah" over his miracles or clap after his sermons. And Jesus made no glib, shallow promises to the crowd in order to curry favor. He was the total opposite of the successful politicians and so-called spiritual leaders we see today. He refused to exploit his popularity for political or financial gain, and he never soft-peddled the cost of discipleship.

To a man who said that he would follow Jesus anywhere, Jesus said, "Oh, you will, will you? . . . Even if you have to sleep by the roadside? . . . Even if nobody in town will rent you a room because you're with me? Keep in mind, my friend, that the Son of Man—on this very journey—has not even had a place to lay his head."

The level of devotion Jesus asked for was 100%. To the man who said that he'd follow Jesus after he'd buried his father, Jesus said, "Come with me and leave the dead to bury their own dead." To one who just wanted to run back to his village first and kiss mom and dad good-bye, he said, "Nobody who puts his hand to the plow and looks back is fit for the kingdom of heaven."

This was the clear message: If you really want to be Jesus' disciple, not just a fan or an admirer, he expects you to *"set* your *face"* the same way he set his own. The truth is that Jesus has always attracted more admirers than disciples. More fans than followers. Then and now.

Admirers of Jesus are everywhere, and they always have nice things to say about him, such as "He was a wise man, a good man, the best man who ever lived." Or "He was noble, kind, compassionate, self-sacrificing, and full of love for everybody." (After all, what's not to admire about Jesus?)

But *admirers* are not *disciples*. Here's the difference:

- Admirers just want to observe. They want to watch, listen, and applaud.—Disciples want to get involved.

- Admirers want to appreciate Jesus.—Disciples want to imitate Jesus.

- Admirers can lose interest fast when they're no longer being entertained or stimulated . . . or when they're not hearing something new . . . or when there's no immediate personal pay-off.—Disciples want to go where Jesus goes, even if the path leading there is paved with broken glass.

- Admirers have no responsibility to Jesus. They're passive except for cheering when they're happy.—Disciples accept a responsibility to Jesus. They know their job is to reproduce the life of their Master.

We are a little, rather conventional Christian church in a very sophisticated town, in a world which has truly become a spiritual marketplace. This spiritual marketplace is an inescapable aspect of our consumer-oriented age, an expression of our demand for choice, our need to celebrate our personal preferences. Having freedom to choose is a good thing, not a bad thing.—But what do we choose? And why do we choose it?

Around us and among us one may find preachers and gurus and spiritual entrepreneurs of many kinds: Christian, pseudo-Christian, and non-Christian; teachers of eastern religions, advocates of western secularism, or even people trapped in the lunacy of cults. It's a carnival of souls out there.

We all have friends who are shopping and hopping from one religion or cult or church to another and back again, looking for somebody to provide the custom-crafted spiritual high they're after, and who will give them absolute certainty that they are now, *finally*, on The One True Path.—Last time we talked to those folks, they were Episcopalians, but now they're into Tantric Buddhism. I guess next year they'll be studying Scientology. After that, who knows? (Maybe Wicca?)

I want to tell you something this morning, and when you hear it you'll know in your heart that it's true: The greatest peace, the most "centered" place, is found only when you commit to one Master and stick with him. You will never find peace if you're always looking for someone or something new: A *new* teacher. A *new* hero. A *new* way of life.

For me, and for many of us here: Jesus is The One. He's not looking for another admirer. He has plenty of them, and always has. But Jesus is always looking for another *disciple*, somebody who's ready to commit, somebody who's able to be focused, somebody who can *set his face* (or "her face") and keep going with him the whole way, no matter how tough things might get along the road.

To steal a line from an old love song, and a love song is exactly what's appropriate here: *"Is that 'somebody'* YOU *?"*

38. WHAT WILL IT TAKE FOR JESUS TO GET THROUGH TO YOU?

John 6:24-35

"*What are you looking for?*" Those are the first words spoken by Jesus in the Gospel according to John. In your red-letter Bible (you *do* have one, don't you?), these are the first red words in John. Theologians think that question is a key to understanding everything else Jesus says or does in that gospel.

What are *you* looking for? I believe most people come to church because they're looking for something. Maybe some just have the church habit, so they arrive here automatically on Sunday mornings. But I think most of us—at some level—are looking for something when we come to church. A few might just be trying to find a congenial group of people to be friends with. But I suspect the majority of us are here because we're looking for something else, we *want* something else. Maybe we're not entirely sure what that "something else" is. If we don't find it the first time we come, we might come back a few more times . . . or we might not.

So: What are *you* looking for today?

- Maybe you're looking for INSPIRATION: you want a word from the Bible or a word from the preacher or a prayer or something that will help you get out of bed on Monday and go about your business with a spring in your step and peace in your heart.

- Maybe you're looking for GUIDANCE: how do I cope with what my wife and I heard from the doctor this week? She has Alzheimer's. . . . What can I do to help my son get his messed-up life straightened out without completely alienating him?

- Maybe you're looking for MEANING in your life: I'm bored and depressed; what am I here for? . . . Is there something I'm supposed to do other than make money and play golf? . . . I need a reason to keep going.

- Maybe you're looking for HEALING or HELP: I have cancer, and I'm scared. . . . Do miracles still happen? I'm on my last month of severance pay, but haven't found a new job yet. . . . What do I do now?

I read a story this week about a young woman in southern California who had everything she once thought she wanted in life. At age 25 she was earning a good six-figure salary. She owned a string of properties—including her own fine home with a silver Mercedes sport coupe parked out front. She had both youth and wealth. Most people would say that she had everything in life going her way. To be doing so well in this economy at age 25 is amazing. But she drove that Mercedes to a Laguna Beach hotel, checked in, and then checked out of life with an overdose of pills, leaving behind a note that said she was committing suicide because, and this is what she wrote, "I am so tired of clapping with one hand." I'm not sure what caused her to make a reference to the famous Zen *koan*, but this successful young woman was obviously looking for something she couldn't find. So she gave up and decided to die.

If you're looking for something—and you haven't found it yet, but you're here in church on Sunday morning—*what will it take for Jesus to get through to you?* Hang on to this question, and I'll come back to it in just a few minutes.

Last week, we read John's story about Jesus feeding five thousand people with a little boy's picnic lunch of five barley rolls and two pieces of dried fish. The child shared what he had; Jesus gave thanks for it; and then Jesus personally handed out the bread and fish to the whole crowd. You remember. The people who were there had as much to eat as they wanted, and then Jesus' disciples gathered up a dozen big baskets of leftovers. The hungry crowd figured that anybody who could do that ought to be running the country, so they decided to take Jesus down to Jerusalem and put him on a throne. He didn't like their idea, so he ran off and hid from them.

Today we read about what happened after that. Jesus crossed back over to Capernaum, his home town. Some of the people out of the crowd he fed on the other side of the lake arrived there, looking for him. (Now, don't forget. Jesus' very first words in John's gospel are the question, "What are you looking for?") When they find him, he says, "You're looking for me, not because you saw a sign from God, but because I filled your empty stomachs—and for free. Don't waste your energy striving for food like that. Work for the kind of bread that lasts, food that will nourish eternal life in you, bread the Son of Man wants to give you."

We like people who give us free food. That's why one of the first rules I learned as a youth minister back in 1974 was: "Always provide food." Teenagers are perpetually hungry, and they'll come to youth group for food, if for nothing else. Kids want pizza. That's easy. ("Hello. Is this Dominoes? Great. I want a dozen large pepperoni with extra cheese. And fast!")—What do adults want? . . . Whatever it is, we tend to like people who give us what we want. Especially for free.

The crowd originally followed Jesus over to the other side of the lake because they'd heard he was a healer, and many of them were sick. They were deaf, or blind, or lame, or disfigured, and they wanted him to make them well. Those who weren't sick were curious to see what would happen, so they could go "Oooh!" and "Aaah!" and "Look at that!"—By late afternoon they were hungry, and so he fed them. The next day they rowed across to his home town, looking for him. To be fair, they were mostly people who lived a subsistence lifestyle, literally living from one meal to the next. (Like people in Haiti.) Who could blame hungry people for looking for more free food? And who could blame sick people for traveling across country to seek out a man with a well-earned reputation for healing the sick? They had real life needs. And Jesus—in their minds—was obviously the man who could (and did) meet those real-life needs.

But, of course, their diseases that needed healing and their hunger that needed satisfying kept them from being able to think much about their other needs, deeper needs—soul needs—that Jesus had come into the world to meet. That's why he said, "You people are looking for another free lunch. But God sent me here to give you a totally different kind of 'bread'."

Poor people. Poor hungry people. They didn't get it. They were not in the mood for metaphors. They could not see what they were not looking for, even though it was hiding in plain sight. They started asking him to give them "a sign," talking about Moses and manna from heaven.—Hello? . . . What were they thinking? What just happened? Jesus had just fed five thousand people with five dinner rolls and two pieces of fish, and now they want a sign? They couldn't grasp what was really going on. They couldn't see what they weren't expecting. Jesus was not getting through to them.—Oh, my. Oh, my.

They didn't get it. But do WE? This brings me back to the question I asked a couple of minutes ago: *What will it take for Jesus to get through to you?* What will it take?

Do you think Jesus could get through to you if you witnessed a really-truly, honest-to-God miracle? If so, I have to tell you something from my own experience as a pastor who has seen really-truly, honest-to-God miracles: *Miracles won't satisfy your hunger for God.* Sometimes miracles get through to people, and sometimes they don't. A miracle will only get through to us if we're able to see *beyond* the miracle itself. A miracle—whether we're talking about a healing for a sick person, or a job for a jobless person, or a meal for a starving person—is *a road sign that God puts up, pointing further.* It's a flashing red neon arrow that says, "Look! Here's a gift. Now go this way to meet the Giver."

Jesus did not come into the world in order to do miracles. His miracles—like miracles today—were just road signs, arrows pointing the way to go. Road signs are necessary, but they only work if we're able to follow directions. Jesus came into the world to draw us to God: the fulfillment of all our hungers, all our hopes. The people who wanted a sign asked Jesus what they needed to DO in order to be doing the "works of God." He gave them a very simple answer: "Believe in the one whom God has sent." Come to *me*. Put your trust in *me*. I am the Bread of Life, and I am putting myself in your hands.

I have to confess, I'm a perceptually challenged person. I don't see what I don't *expect* to see, even when it's right in front of my eyes. I can't see what I'm not looking for. This happens over and over again. For example, Joan asks me to set the dinner table, and when she makes the request she puts a stack of plates out on the counter below the cabinet where they're kept. I say, "Okay, honey," and go into the kitchen, and the very first thing I do is take another stack of plates out of the cabinet. I'm standing directly in front of the plates she has already put out for me. They're hiding in plain sight. I have eyes, but I don't see. Why? Because I can't see what I don't *expect* to see. This has been going on for all of our married life, but every time she asks me to set the table I still expect to find the plates in the cabinet, not on the counter.

So, I ask you again: *What will it take for God to get through to you?*

39. WHO DO WE WANT ON OUR GUEST LIST?

Luke 14:1, 7-14

A few years ago, Joan and I were having dinner with some people who visit Christ Church regularly from out of state. When these folks come here, they always have questions about our church, and the conversation that evening touched on our First Sunday Breakfast. They had been present at the breakfast, and they'd observed that there were some apparently homeless people there who just came in off the street for the meal, and then departed without even coming to the church service.—"Was that right?" our friends asked.

I said, "Yes, that's right. There were several homeless people eating with us last Sunday morning."

The questioner then asked, "You mean just *anybody* can come to your breakfast?"

I smiled at the question and said, "Well, yes. This *is* the church, after all. 'Just anybody' can come." Then we all had a good chuckle, because the people who asked the question are devoted Christians. And they said, "Well, good for Christ Church."

In the Bible it says "God is no respecter of persons." That means kings, queens and homeless people, corporation presidents and kids who work in the mail room, movie stars and pre-school teachers, archbishops and church janitors, are all the same in God's eyes. There is no divine preference for the rich and powerful. Instead, if we really believe the Bible reveals the nature of God, it looks as if there might be a divine bias in *favor* of the disadvantaged, the poor, and the rejected of the earth. Remember the words that Mary the Mother of our Lord sang after the angel Gabriel told her that she would bear the Messiah:

"The Lord has scattered the proud in their conceit;
He has cast down the mighty from their thrones and has lifted up the lowly.
He has filled the hungry with good things, and the rich he has sent away empty.
He has remembered his promise of mercy."

The mission of our church is to be an *outpost* of the Kingdom of Heaven—to be part of the answer to what we ask every time we say the Lord's Prayer: "thy kingdom come, thy will be done on earth as it is in heaven." In the Church, our standards, our way of thinking about ourselves and other people, are set by the Biblical vision of the Kingdom of God.

Jesus intends that anyone who experiences the hospitality of his disciples—anyone who comes into a service on Sunday or who spends time in the company of Christians at events like our First Sunday Breakfasts—should taste the reality of the Kingdom of God. We could say that they should "experience heaven" when they're here with us. And that heavenly experience has nothing to do with great music, or an interesting sermon, or the beauty of the building. No. It has to do with the loving acceptance, compassion, generosity, and contagious joy displayed by the followers of Jesus.

Bishop Tom Wright, whom I have quoted to you before, says that Luke's gospel has more meal-time scenes than all the other gospels. He says, "If Luke's vision of the Christian life, from one point of view, is a journey, from another point of view it's also a *party*." In Luke, Jesus seems to be eating all the time, and when he's not eating, he's *talking* about eating. He gets invited out to dinner a lot, frequently to the home of a prominent person.

The Bible's most common symbolic picture of heaven, its most frequent metaphor for the Kingdom of God, is not a city with streets of gold, but a *wedding feast.* The reason for this symbolism is that poor people in Bible times rarely had enough to eat. Some days, they just had a handful of parched grain, four or five olives, and a piece of cheese, washed down with goat's milk. They might have had a few sheep and goats, but they raised those animals for their wool and milk. They rarely butchered them. Therefore, ordinary Galilean peasants almost never had meat to eat except at Passover or a wedding feast.—So their idea of paradise, of "heaven," came to be a big party that included lots of delicious food, abundant wine, music, dancing, laughter and fun. (I like to point that out to people who think Christians should be puritanical and boring.)

That's also one of the reasons why our Sunday worship centers on a meal. The Eucharist, the sacrament of the Lord's Table—though now it's only a symbolic meal—is an anticipation of heaven. The question the Lord is asking us today is: *"Who are you inviting to your banquet? Who do you want on your guest list?"* In other words, who are the people we'd like to have come and share our Sunday feast, week after week—both the abundant breakfasts like the one we're going to lay out next Sunday and the sacramental meal which is the symbolic bond of our fellowship week-in and week-out?

Who do we want on our guest list? Let's think. Why, I guess the first people I would put on our guest list would be ones who have the potential to make big pledges to help pay for this building . . . and all the monthly bills, too. This is stewardship season, and the Rector is thinking a lot about money.

Along with people able to write big checks, we'd also like to invite those who have time and talent to help with Godly Play, serve on the Altar Guild or Vestry, and volunteer for the tutoring program or Holiday Baskets or the homeless shelter or other outreach ministries. On our dream guest list we'd like to have people who are able to keep Christ Church a successful parish. Then we'd round out the list with busy young, high energy couples with cute kids, people who one day might take over the work of the church from us graybeards.—If we're totally honest, those are the kind of people we'd LIKE to invite to sit at our banquet table.

We aren't likely to go looking for illegal aliens, bag ladies, high school dropouts, or people who just got released from the county jail.

BUT: If we're going to take the gospel seriously (and God help us if we don't!) . . . If we're going to take our status as an outpost of the Kingdom of Heaven seriously . . . If we're going to recognize this altar, seriously, as the banquet table of the Lamb of God . . . Then maybe we should pray and ask Jesus who he has on *his* guest list.

What would happen, do you think, if we took Jesus' words in today's gospel literally and intentionally went looking for modern day equivalents of "the poor, the maimed, the lame, and the blind" that Jesus talked about to the rich Pharisee? Who might be 21st century counterparts to those New Testament-era "undesirables"?—Maybe ex-convicts, delinquent teens, ski bums, the hopelessly unemployed, and people who sleep rough under bridges or down by the river. Maybe people who clean the rooms and make up the beds down at the Little Nell.

If we sought out marginalized people like those to invite to our weekly banquet, do you think we'd ultimately find that our resources were tapped out? Do you think the generous givers we depend on for resources would abandon us and go looking for a church where everybody else at the Table looked just like them and nobody ever showed up who hadn't had a shower and put on clean clothes?

Or would maybe something else happen? . . . something of a revelation? . . . something of a miracle? . . . something that would show that Christ Episcopal Church in Aspen is, indeed, an outpost of the Kingdom of God?

Jesus is asking us to put some so-called marginal characters on our guest list, to include them in our lives, not for their benefit, but for *ours*. Here's the thing: If seats at the heavenly Marriage Supper of the Lamb of God are assigned by God's grace, and not by our own this-worldly standards, then you and I are going to find heaven to be a very surprising place when we get there.

But maybe, if we choose to see our guests as Jesus sees them, we can make heaven happen right here. After all, won't we pray once again, in just a few minutes, as we do over and over in church: *"thy Kingdom come, thy will be done, on earth as it is in heaven"*?

Remember, remember always, what Jesus said: "The Kingdom of God is in *your* midst."

40. THE SPIRIT HELPS US IN OUR WEAKNESS.

Romans 8:26-28

Most of us admire strong people. I'm not talking about physical strength—though we can be impressed by that. I'm talking about the strong character of people who stick to their principles and always do the right thing, no matter what (like an incorruptible New York City police detective who can't be tempted by money and really goes after the Mafia) . . . and the dedication of people who won't allow themselves to be beat down by adversity, but keep coming back—ready to fight on (like the man who builds a great company, loses it in a financial disaster, then starts all over and builds a new one from scratch) . . . and the strong leadership of people who can project such a courageous vision of the future that everyone else rallies behind them (like Winston Churchill in World War II).

I'm also talking about the strength of Christians like Mother Teresa who gave forty-plus years of her life in service to the poorest of the poor strictly out of love for Jesus, but in all those years received only a few fleeting moments of what we'd call "spiritual reward."

We admire strong characters. But if we're honest, we'll admit that *we're* not always strong. We're not often heroic. We admire strong people, and we'd like to be strong like them. But, in fact, most of us are weak more often than we're strong. We fall into temptation and compromise our principles, or our values, or even our faith.

When we have a scary diagnosis from the doctor, or if we lose our job, or if we lose a lot of money, we can plunge into depression. We look at what's happening in our life at times like that and despair. We say, "I can't take this anymore."—"I don't have it in me."—"I wish I could just run away." Or we beat ourselves up and say "If I had only done this instead of that!" Or "How could I have been so stupid?"

The apostle Paul, knew first-hand about rejection, failure, danger, and fear. He wrote: "Five times I have received from the Jews the forty lashes minus one. Three times I was beaten with rods. Once I received a stoning. Three times I was shipwrecked; for a night and a day I was adrift at sea; on journeys in danger from rivers, danger from bandits, danger from my own people, danger from Gentiles, danger in the city, danger in the wilderness, danger at sea, danger from false brothers and sisters; in toil and hardship, through many a sleepless night, hungry and thirsty, often without food, cold and naked. And, besides other things, I am under daily pressure because of my anxiety for all the churches. Who is weak, and I am not weak?" [2 Cor. 11:24-29]

He tells us today how he was able to cope with all that. He says, *"the Spirit helps us in our weakness."*

When we're feeling strong, purposeful and self-reliant, totally in control of everything and confident that we can overcome every obstacle, we're pretty much shut off to the Spirit and operating strictly on *ego*. But when we have our back to the wall and feel empty and helpless—*that's* when we're open to God in a way we could never be otherwise.

Paul says there was a time when he was tormented by what he called "a thorn in the flesh, an emissary from Satan." [2 Cor. 12:7-10] We don't know if this "thorn in the flesh" was a disease Paul had, or a difficult person who caused him trouble. He says he begged the Lord three times to deliver him from this situation, and God's answer was this: "My grace is sufficient for you. My power is made perfect in weakness."—*God's* power is manifested in *our* weakness.

"The Spirit helps us in our weakness; for we do not know how to pray as we ought, but that very Spirit intercedes for us with sighs too deep for words."

There have been times in my life when I really didn't know how to pray. Life was just too confusing. Or I couldn't pray because I was just spiritually empty. (Yes, that happens to priests, too.) There are times when words of prayer fail us all, when we can't express the depth of our desire for the peace the world can't give. Paul says those are the times when "We don't know how to pray as we ought, but the Spirit prays within us with sighs that are more profound than words."

It's when we're weakest that we can, in fact, find ourselves closest to God—in the best position to be lifted up by the Spirit. Do you know what's the most effective prayer in our darkest moments? It's the *prayer of letting go*, when we stop trying to impose our will on the circumstances of life and start trusting that God is God, and that he holds us in the palm of his hand.

Admission of our weakness opens us to God. It also opens us to other people. When we're always in control, tough, strong, and sure we can handle everything, we make it impossible for anybody else to help us—or even love us. But when we admit our weakness and need—and let the Spirit pray within us—God can bring people into our lives to help us. These people are the answer to the Spirit's wordless prayer rising from the deepest place of our soul.

We hear something else from Paul today; it's one of the most powerful verses in the whole Bible. If you've never memorized it, memorize it now. "We know that all things work together for good for those who love God, who are called according to his purpose." Or, you can learn this abbreviated version, which works just as well: "In all things God works for good for those who love him."

This doesn't mean that everything should be seen as being in some way "good." Obviously not.—It's in no way good that tornadoes ripped through nine New Hampshire towns on Friday and killed someone. It's not good that thousands of people are still suffering from the earthquake that hit China and the cyclone that hit Burma months ago. It's not good that people in Darfur are still afraid that government-backed raiders might swoop down and destroy their village.

"In all things God works for good for those who love him" is the assertion of a person who understands the ways of God. It's a proclamation of faith, the strongest proclamation anybody can ever make: "We know that in all things—all circumstances, even the terrible ones, even the frightening ones, even the evil ones—God works for good for those who love him, who have responded to his call." Paul says we know this to be true. We don't know it as a scientific certainty, but as an article of faith—forged in the fire of our own tribulation.

I like to say that "God takes the garbage of our lives and turns it into fertilizer," so that out of even awful events some good may come. But this requires our willingness to do two things. First: surrender ourselves to God in deliberate acts of submission and trust. And, yes, I said "acts." Plural. It takes more than one. The constant theme of our prayer needs to be: "Whatever may happen, dear God, I want not my will but *yours* to be done. I turn my life over to you and I trust you for the future, absolutely."

And, second: let the Spirit of God lead us to reflect on our lives in such a way that we finally can see our experiences the way God sees them. Without the Spirit's help, we see just the surface of events. God wants us to see the deep reality. People with such faith tell us about painful experiences, experiences that were impossible to understand at the moment—but through which they were later able to perceive that they had been given something else that was precious. With the Spirit's help they were able to ponder the darkest moments in life and see them from a perspective of faith, in the light of God.

This perspective of faith, with its confidence that for those who love him, God is at work for good in *all* things, is the secret of the Kingdom of Heaven.

For those who have discovered this precious pearl, this priceless treasure, every moment of closeness to God, every happy circumstance, and every joy—as well as every weakness, every failure, every sacrifice and every sorrow—is being used by God to transform them into the likeness of Christ. And that's our destiny.

41. GOD IS LOOKING FOR SPIRITUAL ENTREPRENEURS.

Matthew 25:14-15, 19-29

There's nobody more respected in American culture today than a successful entrepreneur. They're the heroes and heroines of capitalism, business world counterparts to the saints, the heroes of faith we talked about last Sunday.

The entrepreneur starts out with a good idea, then works hard and takes the risks to convert that good idea into a hugely profitable success.—Think about Andrew Carnegie, Henry Ford or Thomas Edison in an earlier generation and people like Bill Gates, Wayne Huizenga, or Oprah Winfrey in our day. These are people with brains and talent—but maybe not much money to start out with—who built incredible businesses. In a town like Aspen, you can run into entrepreneurs every day. Why, we've got a bunch right here in our own congregation, maybe nobody quite like Henry Ford or Bill Gates, but still cut from the same cloth—just a smaller pattern.

Jesus' parable of the talents is one of those stories everybody knows, even if they don't read the Bible very much. It's a part of scripture that's embedded in our culture, in our folklore, like the parable of the Good Samaritan. You don't even have to be a Christian to know Jesus' story about the three servants whose master gave them his money to manage.—In fact, this parable became internalized in our culture so long ago that it loaned our language the word "talent" itself.

I mentioned entrepreneurs earlier because in the parable of the talents Jesus seems to be offering compliments to people who show an *entrepreneurial attitude,* people willing to take risks in order to be successful. Look at the story. An obviously very rich man goes away on a long journey and gives three of his high-ranking slaves money to invest on his behalf.

According to Jesus' story, the man gave one slave five talents to invest, another two talents, and another one talent. A talent was a unit of weight—of anything really . . . iron, copper, bronze, silver or gold. The most common monetary reference was to a talent of silver, and that's probably what Jesus had in mind here. A single talent of silver was the equivalent of about 16 years' wages for the ordinary worker. That was a lot of money. Let's compare it to today's economy: in 2004 the median income in Colorado for a family with one wage earner was about $40,000 a year. Sixteen times that is $640,000. That's not chicken-feed. And that's the modern value of just *one* talent. That was the amount the rich man entrusted to the number three guy. *Five* talents would be worth $3,200,000—80 years' income for the average person. So the rich man gave his three slaves some serious money to work with while he was gone.

When the master returned from his journey—probably years later—he called in the three slaves and asked for them to report on what they had done with the money he gave them to invest. The first two—the five-talent man and the two-talent man—had doubled their money. Obviously they had to take some risks in order to make a 100% profit. Investing was no more of a sure thing in A.D. 29 than in A.D. 2005. The master praised and rewarded them. He told them how happy he was with them. As a reward, it looks as if he let them *keep* all the money . . . both the principal and the profit.

But the one-talent man hadn't made a single shekel for the boss. This was *not* good . . . not good at all.—What had he been *thinking?*—He knew what kind of man he worked for, a man who expected to "reap where he hadn't sowed." But that seems to have scared him, so he became unwilling to take chances of any kind. He just dug a hole and buried the money.—Of course, he took a chance that the boss might feel sorry for him and let him off the hook. Maybe he'd get to keep the money. But in that respect, he made a huge mistake. He was left in the end with nothing at all.

O.K. Jesus didn't tell this story to encourage investors to take risks. He wasn't addressing himself to estate managers and high-ranking slaves, offering a kind of first century b-school case study. He had another point, of course, and it was—naturally—a *spiritual* point. It's a point I'd summarize this way: *The Lord is looking for spiritual entrepreneurs.*

Luke records a saying of Jesus that I think is pertinent here. In Luke 12:48 Jesus says, "From everyone to whom much has been given, much will be expected; and from the one to whom much has been entrusted, even more will be demanded."

The Lord has entrusted us with the truth of the Gospel. He has endowed us with the gift of faith. These are treasures of incalculable worth. Along with these assets, God has given each of us a range of innate abilities and skills, and on top of those he has blessed us each with spiritual gifts. No two people are exactly alike. Obviously some people are more gifted than others, but there's nobody with *no* gifts at all. And those who might think of themselves as being like the "one-talent man" have to recognize that even the *one* talent man had actually been given a great deal of money to invest. One talent was worth sixteen years' wages.—The reality is that God has been very generous to *all* of us.

The Lord is looking for spiritual entrepreneurs. He has entrusted much *to* us and it's pretty clear that he's expecting a lot *from* us in return. This parable is not about the stewardship of money; it's about our stewardship of the Good News of Jesus Christ. It asks: What are you going to do with your faith? Are you just going to sit on it? . . . Bury it in a hole in the ground? The Lord is saying to us, to you and me, to Christ Church in Aspen: "I'm looking for risk-takers, for adventurers in faith. You've shown that you know how to do that in the business world. So now show me that you can do it in the realm of the spirit, too.—What are you afraid of?"

This parable also tells us that there's ultimately going to be a day of reckoning. The master returned from his long journey and ordered his three trusted slaves to render an account of what they'd achieved with the wealth he had put into their hands. We're making a colossal blunder—as big as the mistake of the one-talent man in the parable—if we imagine that the Lord is not expecting us to do something with the faith and spiritual gifts he has entrusted us. Remember: "From everyone to whom much has been given, much will be expected."

What kind of risk in faith are *you* willing to take today?—Maybe we're back with Peter stepping out of the boat in the teeth of a storm, trying to walk on water. The principle is not too different. There are as many ways to step out in faith as there are people in the church. But there are some things we all can do. Here's one of them: *pray for healing for the sick.* We have a healing service here every Wednesday at noon. The average attendance is about six, with more in the summer and fewer now. Last Wednesday there were only three. But we believe in stepping out in faith, and we've heard reports of miracles.—And, no, miracles don't happen every time. Just like investments, some prayers for healing result in a bigger return than others. But we keep investing in faith-filled prayer.

Here's another way to step out in faith: *go to your friends and invite them to come to church with you some Sunday.* (That's really risky, because you might get labeled as being "religious.") Not every investment will pay off. An insurance man I know said once that this was like making cold calls trying to sell accident insurance. You have to make ten of them in order to get one new customer. But that's o.k. You're doing this in faith—investing what God has given you. And the potential reward is great.

"From everyone to whom much has been given, much will be expected." The Lord is looking for spiritual entrepreneurs.—Are you ready to be one?

42. YOU CAN'T SERVE GOD *AND* ANYTHING ELSE.

Deuteronomy 11:18-21; Matthew 6:24-34

When I was in first or second grade in Sunday School, we did a craft activity imitating what Moses told the Israelites to do before they came into the Promised Land. First we took pencils and laboriously copied out on lined paper these words that the teacher had written on a blackboard: "You shall love the LORD your God with all your heart and with all your soul, and with all your might." Then we folded our paper up really small and put it into a matchbox we'd already decorated with construction paper and strung on a long piece of ribbon. Our teacher tied these little boxes onto our foreheads, telling us that this was to remind us to love God more than anything else. Then we went into the church with our parents.

We were a bunch of little Christian children imitating what our Jewish friends do in obedience to the Law when they wear *tefillin* (phylacteries)—black leather boxes on straps not only around their heads but around one arm. We just read about this in Deuteronomy: "You shall put these words of mine in your heart and soul, and you shall bind them as a sign on your hand, and fix them as an emblem on your forehead. Teach them to your children, talking about them when you are at home and when you are away, when you lie down and when you rise."

This is what Moses told God's people to put in their heart and soul, bind on their hands and foreheads, nail to the gateposts of their houses, and teach to their children: "Hear O Israel, the LORD our God, the LORD is One. And you shall love the LORD your God with all your heart, and with all your soul, and with all your might." Moses warned them that if they turned away from loving God more than anything else, there would be sad consequences. And we know Moses told the truth: keep your focus on God.

In the Sermon on the Mount, Jesus is speaking just to his disciples—not to the crowds, not to humanity in general. This is wisdom directed to a group of people who've already made what I would call *the* most important choice in life—the decision to follow Jesus. He says: "No one can serve two masters. For a slave will either hate the one and love the other, or be devoted to the one and despise the other. You cannot serve God and wealth."

This may sound to you like a quaint saying, maybe appropriate to people in the first century but not to us. After all, we live in the age of multitasking. Many of us have worked two or even three jobs at the same time, had two or three bosses, and we've done fine. We liked them all, and working for several employers provided interesting diversity. If that's what you're thinking, let me offer you a different way of hearing what Jesus is saying.

First off, what he's really telling us in effect is: "You're not as independent as you think you are, or as you wish you were. You're not 'the master of your fate and the captain of your soul.'" He's saying, "The truth is that you are going to 'serve' some*thing* or some*one*. You're going to be under the influence, the guidance, maybe even the orders of some*body* or some *force* or some *values* that WILL shape your life. You're free to choose this person or power or value system, so be very careful."

"You cannot serve God and wealth" was not a caution directed just to wealthy people—or even mainly to wealthy people. After all, Jesus was talking to his disciples, and as far as we can tell he didn't have many rich disciples. (There were a few, but very few.) Most of the people who heard the Sermon on the Mount were small businessmen, humble craftsmen, fishermen, farmers, and housewives. There were no plutocrats among them, but there were many who only got by from day to day, living hand to mouth.

Jesus is warning about the disease of *materialism,* an affliction that has more to do with our attitudes than our affluence. It's counsel for all of us who live in this world of material necessities—whether we have enough money to indulge our whims or have to pinch pennies, whether we drive a Ferrari or a Ford. It's about getting our priorities in order. This applies to the rock star and the grocery clerk in equal measure. Materialism isn't only the rock star's insatiable craving for more and more toys—another yacht, another jet plane, another villa on the Riviera. It's also the grocery clerk's pervasive fear of never having enough—enough to pay the rent, enough to pay the dentist, enough to put gas in the Ford. Materialism is a distortion of values and a reversal of priorities. It is myopic and "this world" centered, ignoring the place of God in the universe and our mission as servants of God.

You can't serve God AND anything else. You can't serve God and the accumulation of more toys—or even God and the bare necessities. You can't serve God and your own ego. You can't serve God and the pursuit of power . . . or entertainment . . . or even a better job. Be careful about what worries you, consumes your energy, and is the subject of your nightmares, because—whatever that is—it can quickly become your master. And *"No one can serve two masters."*

Write this on your heart, on your arm, on the gatepost of your house: "You shall love the LORD your God with all your heart and with all your soul, and with all your might." Love the LORD, serve only him, and "Do not worry about tomorrow." A friend of mine says that people who worry think they're doing something useful: "Don't bother me, I'm busy worrying!" Jesus doesn't say not to think and plan for the future. He doesn't say not to be prudent. What he DOES say is not to worry. When we worry, we obsess about things that are beyond our control. We lose sleep over potential problems and possible disasters. And we forget that Jesus has promised to be with us always, even to the end of the ages.

If you find yourself consumed by worries, listen to what Jesus says in the Sermon on the Mount.

- First: GET YOUR PRIORITIES RIGHT. *"Strive first for the kingdom of God and his righteousness, and all these things shall be yours as well."* One author I read this week said, Jesus didn't say to "strive *only* for the kingdom of God" but to work for God's kingdom first. When you put God first, other things that should rightfully concern you will fall into their proper places.

- The second is related to the first: INVEST YOUR EFFORT WHERE YOU CAN REALLY MAKE A DIFFERENCE. *"Can any of you by worrying add a single day to your span of life?"* Worrying drains your energy. That's why people who worry think they're actually accomplishing something—they're tired all the time. There's only so much you can accomplish in a day or a year or a lifetime. You have a finite amount of energy, and you need to direct your energy into projects that have the potential to bear fruit, projects chosen according to God's priorities.

- Third: LIVE ONE DAY AT A TIME. *"Today's trouble is enough for today."* In the real world, bad things *do* happen to God's people. Christians lose their jobs, contract diseases, and have problems in their marriages at about the same rate as everybody else. But Christians know that "in all things God works for good for those who love him." So we face today's troubles today, sleep peacefully tonight, and expect that the Lord will be there for us when we have to face whatever tomorrow may bring.

43. THOU ART THE JOURNEY AND THE JOURNEY'S END.

John 14:1-14

Recently we drove out to California to spend time with Joan's brother, who is very sick. I'd never made a road trip to California before, so I spent a lot of time on the computer, looking at MapQuest, and figuring out the roads and possible places to spend the night. I planned a careful itinerary. I wanted to go the fastest possible way—allowing for one night on the road since the shortest route is 1,200 miles.

We left here and went west on I-70, then diagonally southwest across Utah to Las Vegas. Leaving Vegas, we drove across the Mojave Desert, then up the central valley of California to Gilroy, "the Garlic Capital of the World." (Your nose can lead you there if you lose your map.) From the garlic-processing plants it's a straight shot over to San Jose at the southern end of San Francisco Bay.

The route included unforgettable scenery in Utah—spectacular canyons and fascinating rock formations. But it also included mile after mile of desolate, gray desert landscape in Nevada and California. When I look back on it, I see that route from here to San Jose as a good metaphor for life: some parts were exhilarating and others were miserable. We passed through some places so pretty that we decided we'd go back and enjoy them at our leisure in the future. Other places were so grim that I wanted to get through them as fast as possible and—if I have a choice—never come back.

There are people who like to drive. Maybe you're one of them. But not me. When we have to take a long car trip—which I always avoid if possible—I want to go the shortest, fastest way. When we have to drive rather than fly, I like to get on the Interstate, put the pedal to the metal, and get the trip over with.

Joan is different. If we never drove on a freeway, that would be fine with her. She likes the two-lane back roads that meander through small towns. Lots of stop lights. She likes to see every aspect of the countryside up-close and personal: farms and ranches, little mom and pop grocery stores, seedy antique stores, grain elevators, and roadside restaurants with funny names and gas pumps out front with signs reading, "Eat here, get gas". If it takes three days to make a one-day trip, that's o.k. with her. If we never go faster than 55 miles an hour that's o.k. too. In the Mojave desert she thought the Joshua trees were fascinating.

I can enjoy that sort of thing now and then if we're just exploring, just looking around and seeing the sites for the fun of it, as we hope to do some day in Zion National Park. But if I have a *destination*, I want to get there as fast as I can. Only when I reach my destination can I relax and begin to enjoy myself. When I have a destination, the journey there is a necessary preliminary to get through as quickly as possible—just something to endure, like a visit to the dentist.

But for Joan, the journey itself is something to enjoy. Maybe that's a girl thing. Or maybe it's a sign of her greater maturity. (Probably the latter.) There's something to value about every journey, even ones that take us through territory we'd prefer to have avoided and end up someplace that turns out to be quite different from what we had in mind when we started the trip. That's why stories about journeys are so common in all the great spiritual traditions. And when we're planning a journey somewhere, we need to choose a "way," a road, a route, a path to follow to our destination.

We've heard over and over, especially from people who tell us they're "spiritual but not religious," that all spiritual paths lead to the same place. They remind us that if we're seeking to have a relationship with the One True God, it shouldn't matter which path we take because they all lead eventually to the same place. I'm willing to admit that there's some merit in that. But if the journey is just as important as the destination, then finding the best path is essential.

It's easy to see why the passage from the Gospel that we read this morning is used at funerals. It's very comforting. Jesus says, "Do not let your hearts be troubled. Believe in God, believe also in me. In my Father's house there are many dwelling places. If it were not so, would I have told you that I go to prepare a place for you? And if I go and prepare a place for you, I will come again and will take you to myself, so that where I am, there you may be also."

The King James Version says, "In my Father's house are many mansions. " Those words made generations of Christians imagine that when we depart this mortal existence, Jesus will take us to be with him in heaven, where we'll each live forever in a place that looks like the plantation house in *Gone with the Wind.* That seems pretty fine. Folks where I grew up used to say, "Heaven is my home. I'm just passing through down here."

But the "passing through" part is a lot more significant than we think. If the journey is as important as the destination, then the path we take matters. The disciples asked Jesus for more information. Thomas said, "Lord, we don't know where you're going. How can we know the way?" Jesus said to him, 'I am the way, and the truth, and the life. No one comes to the Father except through me.'"

Jesus was telling Thomas and his friends, in effect: "I am the way, the road, the path. I am the Truth. I am Life. Nobody gets to know the Father except by me. And, if you haven't realized this before, I want you to understand it now: to see me is to see the Father. To know me is to know the Father. I am in the Father and the Father is in me. The Father and I are one."

Jesus spoke these comforting words to the disciples just before he went with them to the Garden of Gethsemane, to a time of agony and horror, to a time when he would ask his Father if there might not be some way of escaping his painful destiny. That may seem ironic, but it really isn't. To know Jesus as the Way, the Truth, and the Life is to discover in the life of Christ the deep meaning of our own existence; in his openness, the mirror of perfect integrity for us; and in his journey, our journey with him.
A Christian philosopher named Boethius, writing in that frightening time when the barbarians had taken over and Roman order was disintegrating in Europe, pondered the mystery of Christ and put that mystery into these

words: *"To see Thee is the end and the beginning. Thou carriest me and thou goest before. Thou art the journey and the journey's end."*

Alan Jones, long-time Dean of Grace Cathedral in San Francisco, wrote in his book, *Journey into Christ*: "The root meaning of the Greek word for truth is 'that which reveals itself.' Truth always uncovers itself; it never hides from view. Like Love, Truth cannot keep itself secret. When Jesus was sad, he wept. When thirsty, he asked for water. When troubled, he trembled. Yet in all of this he was still one with the Father; his life was a dimension of God's life. It still is. There are indeed other roads that wind their way toward God. But only Christ is both road and destination, journey and journey's end."

I know that we will have to drive that long road to California again sometime—pass through the beauty of Utah's canyons and cross the desolation of the Mojave. But when we travel that way once more, I will remind myself that every mile of every journey in life is a gift of truth and a revelation from God.

44. GIVE ME THAT OLD TIME RELIGION.

Mark 7:1-8, 14-15, 21-2

Please join me in praying again the collect for this Sunday. It's on the front page of your bulletin: "Lord of all power and might, the author and giver of all good things: Graft in our hearts the love of your Name; increase in us true religion; nourish us with all goodness; and bring forth in us the fruit of good works; through Jesus Christ our Lord, who lives and reigns with you and the Holy Spirit, one God forever and ever. Amen."

That's a beautiful prayer, mostly Thomas Cranmer's 16th century revision of an old Latin text. Among other things, we ask the Lord to "increase in us *true* religion." The Latin original just asked God to "increase in us religion." Archbishop Cranmer, with the combative spirit of a Reformation Era thinker, inserted the word "true."—But there's a world of difficulty in trying to determine precisely what constitutes "true religion," isn't there? At least for some people.

My grandma and grandpa McNab belonged to a little independent Christian Church where I would sometimes go with them to Sunday night services. It was the only place I ever witnessed a performance on a musical saw. (Have you ever heard one of those?) I remember a song that we'd sing at their church now and then. I'll bet some of you know it. Its chorus was *"Give me that old time religion. Give me that old time religion. / Give me that old time religion; and it's good enough for me."* I forget all the verses, but I remember *"It was good for the Hebrew children,"* and *"It was good for Paul and Silas,"* *"It will take us all to heaven,"* and every verse wound up with *". . . and it's good enough for me."*

The fact that my grandma and grandpa's church felt sure that "old time religion" demanded baptism by total immersion for adult believers (and no baptism for children) made their church different from the church my parents belonged to. In our church it seemed that baptism was mainly just for babies and required the use of very little water. The minister just dipped his hand into a silver bowl and then made the baby's forehead wet with it. I thought the song was fun to sing, but even when I was eight or nine I wasn't sure what the people at my grandparents' church might think I meant when I was singing *their* song.

The greatest divisions in society are often between people who agree on a common goal, but disagree about the best way to reach that goal. That is to say, they agree about the end but strongly disagree about the means to that end. That's one way of looking at the difference between Jesus and the Pharisees—who were disturbed because Jesus and his disciples weren't practicing what they believed was "that old time religion," handed down to them by Moses.

Good Pharisees sincerely wanted to honor and obey God. They aspired to live a holy life. They yearned for what 17th century Puritans would have called "godliness." Jesus completely agreed with their goal. But the Pharisees saw the means to that end as a meticulous observance of every religious rule and tradition—written and unwritten, significant and insignificant, that had come down to them from the past. For them, that was true religion. They were strict about traditional dietary laws, ritual cleanliness, Sabbath observance, tithing, marriage rules, and anything else that might be seen as a sign of obedience to God.

Pharisees wanted to separate themselves from anything not godly. They believed that if they touched anyone or anything impure, they'd be defiled, contaminated, and—therefore—unacceptable to God. Their old time religion treated ritual impurity the way we treat a contagious disease. Their goal was to keep themselves disease-free. For example, though they had no concept of leprosy as a disease, Pharisees would never dream of touching a leper—because, according to the Law, merely touching a leper would make the Pharisee unclean, unacceptable to God. Their guiding principle was "Be separate; be holy."

Jesus offered a different understanding of true religion. Jesus proposed that the only effective way of becoming holy was for people to imitate God's generous, open-handed love. He even said, "Love your enemies and pray for those who persecute you, so that you may be children of your Father in heaven: for he makes his sun rise on the evil and the good, and sends rain on the righteous and the unrighteous." That was what Jesus called a "righteousness that exceeds that of the scribes and Pharisees."

Jesus' treatment of lepers was the opposite from that of the Pharisees. Jesus reached out and touched lepers, and his touch healed them. The Pharisees taught that if a "holy" person touched an "unholy" person, the holy person would become *un*holy, be defiled. Jesus showed that when a "clean" person reaches out to an "unclean" person it's the *unclean* person who is transformed.

Jesus practiced the old time religion of the Hebrew prophets. He saw the Law as good, but taught that its right observance came only as the response of a renewed heart—as Isaiah had taught—and not from a zeal for separating holy people from sinners.

The story of Jesus' encounter with the Pharisees that we read this morning is dangerous because it can lead us to imagine that *we* are not like them, that we have moved beyond all that business of separation and purity and being defiled by contact with unclean people.—Hah! If we think the Episcopal Church has left Pharisaism behind and has become a superior kind of true religion, all we have to do is look at the current crisis (as well as earlier ones) in our branch of the Church and see that we haven't gone far. The debate about clean and unclean, holy and unholy, hasn't gone away, even if we don't use those exact terms of comparison. We're up in arms with one another—on both sides of the divisive issues—about whose approach to being the Church constitutes true religion.

There are still some of us who have a deep need to believe that we are the pure and others are the impure. We are the righteous, and others are the unrighteous. That's a way of seeing ourselves as *better* than other people, whether that means being more faithful to Old Testament laws about sex, or to teaching about authority, or to the prayer book and traditions of the Episcopal Church.

The heart of Jesus' problem with the Pharisees was their use of the moral law to identify a so-called holy community that could be proud of its superiority over the unholy. Eager to define ourselves as better in comparison with others, it's easy to forget that the Bible says "*All* have sinned and fallen short of the glory of God," and "*none* is righteous, no, not one."

Time and again Jesus spoke out against spiritual pride. He asked those who knew themselves to be without sin to cast the first stone. At the end of today's gospel reading, Jesus says that the things that defile us come from within us, not from contact with other people. Among the defiling things that come from human hearts he listed a number that most of us here can probably say we haven't experienced, like theft, murder, and adultery. But he extends the list to avarice, deceit, envy, slander, pride, and folly. I'm pretty certain that each of us here today is guilty of one or more of these faults, especially folly. (Who among us has never been foolish?) "All of these," Jesus says, "are evil things that come from within, and they defile a person." If Jesus is right, then we have to acknowledge that we're all "unclean." We *all* need forgiveness.

It was not the adulterers, fornicators and prostitutes, or anyone else guilty of sins of the flesh, who came in for scolding from Jesus. In fact, Jesus didn't reprimand any category of sinners at all. He just called everyone to repent and saved his scorn for those who imagined they had no need for repentance.

The gospel of Christ does not call us to create a "pure Church." Instead, it calls us to become a community of grace and forgiveness. This is the heart of true religion. I remember attending a Billy Graham Crusade at old Mile High Stadium down in Denver twenty-some years ago. After the altar call and people had come out on the field to give their lives to the Lord, Billy Graham told them that they needed to find a local church and live out their Christian lives in the fellowship of a worshiping community. But he told them not to go looking for a perfect church. He said, "There is no perfect church, so don't try to find one. Anyway, if there were such a thing as a 'perfect church,' it wouldn't be perfect after you joined it."

When Jesus said to his disciples, "The Kingdom of God is in your midst," he meant that the fellowship of his followers is the place where—right now—the redeeming grace of God may be found. This is where we can forget about who's right and who's wrong, who's pure and who's impure, whose religion is "true" and whose is not. Here in the Church is where everyone is welcome to come, repent, believe the gospel, and live a new life—a life characterized by unconditional love and mercy for one another.

We come to the Lord's Table today as sinners who know that Jesus loves us in spite of our sin, and that he died on the cross for our redemption. We come, remembering that at the Last Supper Jesus didn't even exclude Judas the Betrayer.

There's another song I remember from my grandparents' little church. It has a great and timely message, the heart of "that old time religion," *"Whosoever will, whosoever will," / Send the proclamation over vale and hill; / 'Tis a loving Father, calls the wanderer home: / "Whosoever will may come."*

Whosoever will may come.—Welcome, sinners!

45. WHAT GOES AROUND COMES AROUND.

Matthew 18:21-35

We all know the Lord's Prayer. Even people who don't usually go to church can say it. Maybe we know it too well and say it too easily—especially the part that says, "Forgive us our trespasses as we forgive those who trespass against us." Or as the version in Matthew's gospel—the one most familiar to our Presbyterian friends—puts it, "Forgive us our debts as we forgive our debtors." (More about debts and debtors in just a minute.)

There's not a person among us—old or young—who doesn't have to deal with forgiveness in some form. Wives have to forgive husbands, and husbands have to forgive wives. Parents have to forgive their kids. Kids have to forgive their parents. Brothers and sisters and neighbors all have to forgive one another. So the question Peter asked Jesus should be important to us: "If somebody sins against me, how often should I forgive him?"

Truth is that many of us are in the habit of imposing conditions before we'll grant forgiveness, or even offering rationales for why we "can't" forgive. We say (and I have heard these exact words from people) "I cannot, *in good conscience,* 'let this person off' without any consequences. That would be wrong."—I beg your pardon? Is this a way of saying that our *conscience* is what compels us to set limits to the practice of mercy? (Who shapes a "conscience" such as this? Mom and Dad? School teachers? Certainly not the Bible.)

Jesus says nothing about the limits of forgiveness or the scruples of legalistic consciences. Instead he tells Peter and the others a story, and—while it's a very complicated story—at least one point of it is clear. Just as the King's servant—who represented the governor of a province or some such figure—owed the King a huge debt he could not pay (a sum that would amount to hundreds of billions of dollars today), so *we* human beings owe God a debt *we* can't pay. That's what the Bible says.

Now here's a point to remember, and it's pretty simple. In the moral universe of the Bible a *sin*—an offense or transgression of any kind, either between people or between people and God—*always creates a moral debt.* Logically, then, a sinner owes a debt to the one who has been sinned against, a moral debt that's just as real as a monetary debt.

We apply that same logic in our own everyday lives. Think about it: if I hurt your feelings in some way or otherwise offend you, don't you say to yourself, *"He owes me an apology"*? When we talk about crime and punishment, about convicted criminals going to prison or paying a fine, don't we say they're "paying their debt to society"? We still live in the Biblical moral universe, whether we're Christians or not, a universe where transgressions against other people or against God put us in *moral debt.* If you offend against me, *you owe me.* I have a moral right to compensation of some kind from you, even if it's something as simple as an apology. I'm entitled. And if I offend against God, *I owe God.* God is entitled to compensation from me. (That's what gave rise to sin offerings in Judaism in the days of the Jerusalem Temple. And that way of thinking helps us understand the symbolic meaning of the cross of Christ.)

We human beings have grown into the habit of putting ourselves first and God and other people somewhere further down the line. We've exalted our judgment above God's judgment, our will above God's will. In fact, we have created all kinds of idolatries for ourselves. *But God in Christ has forgiven us.* That's what the death of Christ on the cross was all about. The Son of God dying on the cross for the sins of the world was, in effect, God *absorbing the loss* caused by the debt humanity could never pay. Paul said, "God was in Christ reconciling the world to himself."

Let's imagine I come to one of you good people and ask you for a personal loan, say $10,000, to pay an unforeseen expense. I tell you that if you'll lend me the money, I'll pay you back in one year with interest. Let's imagine you say, "Sure, Bruce," and write me a check for ten grand. A year later, when it's time to repay the loan, I come to you and say, "I'm really sorry, but I don't have the money right now. Can I have just six months more?" And then you, being a kind-hearted, Christian person, say to me, "Don't worry about it. Consider it a gift. You don't owe me anything." I'm tickled to death and go away dancing on air because this huge burden is now lifted off my shoulders. But what about you? You're out $10,000! You have to *absorb the loss.* You were entitled to repayment; you were even entitled to earn some interest on the loan. But, instead, you made it a gift and so you have to absorb the loss.

That's how I understand the cross. God, in Christ, *absorbed the loss* created by humanity's sin. Some people like to say that Jesus "paid our debt." I remember an old hymn they used to sing at my grandparents' church, *"Jesus paid it all, all to him I owe."* That's a good image, but I like to change it just a bit and say that God, in Christ, *absorbed the loss.* God was entitled to compensation from us. We owed him a moral debt. But he chose to forego his entitlement and absorb the loss. That's Christ on the cross.

This brings us back to the point of the parable we heard in the gospel this morning. We should treat one another as God has treated us—with mercy and grace, absorbing the loss, foregoing our rights and entitlements, and demonstrating readiness to forgive those who have sinned against us.

But there's another point to this parable. Put in simple, colloquial American it can be stated this way: What goes around comes around. If over a lifetime of faith and practice we prove unable to develop the habit of extending to others the mercy that God has given us in Christ, then on the great Day of Judgment we're liable to find our own forgiveness withdrawn and full restitution demanded.

If you don't think you're ever going to have to stand before the Lord and render an account of your life, then maybe you can ignore this sermon.—But are you willing to chance it?—The old saying has a lot of truth in it: What goes around comes around. That's not a Bible verse, but it could have been. It's just as true. In the Sermon on the Mount, after Jesus gives the disciples the model prayer that we call the Lord's Prayer, he says quite clearly, "If you forgive others their offenses, your heavenly

Father will also forgive you. But if you do not forgive others, neither will your Father forgive your offenses."

Listen to the voices around us in our culture. They say: "We want justice." "We believe in law and order." "Punishment should fit the crime." "Three strikes and you're out." This sounds right and good to us until *we* happen to become the accused offenders—until *we* get stopped by the police for DUI, or *we* get nailed for failing to follow through on a commitment, or *we* have a loan called by the bank and can't raise the money to pay it off. When that happens, we want mercy, not "consequences". We want understanding from the traffic cop or the judge or the banker. We want patience with our failures. And—please!—give us a second chance, or maybe even a third or a fourth. When *we're* the offenders, it's amazing how clear the extenuating circumstances are, how understandable our shortcomings, how obviously forgivable it all should be.

Forgiveness is not instinctive. It's not an innate human reflex. It doesn't come naturally to us. No. Vengeance, retribution, violent response to an attack—*these* are the natural human qualities. And so, because forgiveness *is* un-natural, we have to *work* at it. We have to practice it regularly, deliberately, intentionally, like any other spiritual discipline, 'til it soaks down into our souls and softens our hard, judgmental, vengeful hearts and re-shapes our consciences.

Gandhi said, "The weak can never forgive. Forgiveness is an attribute of the strong." It takes a strong person to forgive. It takes a strong person to absorb the loss caused by someone else's offense. Weak people demand their due, stand on their entitlements, and insist on getting their pound of flesh. You and I are called to stand in the strength of Christ.

From the cross, Jesus looked down at those who were crucifying him, not just at the Roman soldiers who were merely doing their jobs, but at all the people standing around there on the hill of Golgotha—the chief priests and Sadducees and other "good people" who really, truly thought they were doing God's will by punishing this terrible blasphemer, and he said, "Father, forgive them. They don't know what they're doing."

People who understand, deep down in their hearts, that they are offenders who have received God's forgiveness, hopeless debtors whose debts have been mercifully cancelled, these are the people who are strong enough to practice forgiveness and extend mercy to others.

What goes around comes around. It's a principle, almost a law of nature. We pass along to others what we ourselves have received. You and I have received mercy.—Let's pass it along.

46. WHAT DOES IT TAKE TO BE A SUCCESS?

Mark 9:30-37

I believe everybody has some kind of ambition; everybody wants to 'succeed' in life. We all have something we want to accomplish, or something we want to have, or someplace we want to end up. We all have a goal, but goals vary from one person to another.—One person wants to make a lot of money, another wants to be President, another wants to compose a great symphony. Other people's ambition is to get the approval of their parents or peer group. (By the way, if you're sixty-five years old and your parents are long gone, you can *still* be living for the approval of mom or dad. That's because they're always with us—in our heads—saying, "Way to go!" or, more likely, "Didn't I tell you *not* to do that!")

And then there are people whose idea of success is to stay safely in the background, never draw any criticism, and live long enough to retire to Aspen and live the good life. Now, if that was your own picture of success and you're already here, then it's time to set a better goal, otherwise the time you have left is going to very boring. All downhill.—And I mean *way* down.

What we want—our ambition, our idea of success—changes between childhood and old age. When I was ten years old I was big for my age, cross-eyed, and clumsy. My idea of success then was to not be the last guy selected when we chose up sides to play baseball. It was inconceivable that I might dream of hitting a home run. I just prayed to get a walk.

As I matured, my picture of success changed. When I was a graduate student my ambition was to become a popular university professor whose lectures drew such large crowds that they had to be held in the biggest auditorium on campus. (I've always been a ham.) And, of course, I would be interviewed on TV and write books.

A few years later, God dramatically changed my life and my idea of success. After that, I wanted to serve the Lord and his people and share my love of Jesus.—But even so, my hankering for recognition didn't go away, not for a long time. Maybe that just goes with being young, like the twelve who first followed Jesus.

There's something sad, even pathetic about the scene described in today's gospel. Jesus has reached the time in his ministry when his companions have recognized him as the heaven-sent savior of his People. But he has told them that the fulfillment of his mission includes being crucified and then raised from the dead, and that anybody who wants to be his disciple will have to shoulder a cross too. Jesus tells them this as they're on the way to Jerusalem—where these frightening things are soon supposed to happen. His twelve friends, full of idealism and dreams of personal glory, must have listened, but they didn't get it. Probably they didn't want to get it, because Jesus' picture of the future seemed too disturbing.—Betrayal to his enemies? Death on a cross? *No, no!*—So, when he finally quit talking this way and lapsed into silence, the disciples fell into a quite different conversation among themselves as they walked along, one that ultimately led to an argument.

When they finally got to Capernaum where they were going and were settled into the house, relaxing after the long walk with a glass of wine and taking it easy, Jesus asked: *"What were you fellows arguing about back there, as we were walking along?"* They didn't want to answer. They sat there, silent with embarrassment.

Their Teacher had been trying to explain to them that though he would be handed over to his enemies and crucified, God would raise him up. And he'd been telling them that if they wanted to continue as his disciples and do his work, they would have to face a similar fate.—But these twelve energetic, idealistic young people had ignored what Jesus was talking about and instead had taken up an old, long-standing debate about "Which one of us is 'The Greatest'?"

Maybe it was just because the Twelve were guys, but they were *competitive* with each other. They not only expected *future* greatness, they were comparing themselves with each another, arguing about which one was the "alpha disciple". For them, the big question was: *Who is going to be voted team MVP?*

This reminds me of how often I hear and repeat to others the words of Jesus, but still devote my energy to things that are the opposite of what he taught. (Does that happen to you?)—We may want to achieve good things in the Lord's name, but part of us also wants to see our name up in lights. (Or at least mentioned in the church bulletin.)

Most of us learn very slowly that we can accomplish the greatest things in life as long as we don't mind if someone else gets the credit. Jesus said: "Let your light shine before others so that they may see your good works and glorify your Father who is in heaven." Whatever we do in the Lord's name is to give him the glory, not us. The more we can get our egos out of the picture, the better.

Jesus took his friends to task and said, "Any of you who thinks you want to be the most important person in the crowd must take the least important role and become the servant of all." He took a little child and put the child in the center of their circle. Then he took him in his arms and said, "Whoever welcomes one such child in my name welcomes me, and whoever welcomes me welcomes not me but the one who sent me."

His point was not that the child was young or innocent or helpless, but that the role of a child was humble. A child's social status was zilch. People didn't sentimentalize childhood back then. In AD 29, as soon as a little kid had manual dexterity enough to do a simple job, he was put to work—washing dishes, wielding a little broom, coiling up a rope . . . anything—helping anybody else in the household who needed a hand.

It didn't register on his disciples at the moment, but Jesus was telling them that God had *sent his own Son into a world full of people who needed help*—not to be a celebrity among them, but to be that humblest child in the family whose duty was to be the servant of all.

We honor people like the late Mother Teresa who gave her life to serving the dying untouchables of Calcutta or Dr. Paul Farmer, the Harvard Med

School professor and practical-minded Christian who has dedicated himself to the task of bringing medical care to the poorest of the poor in Haiti and Africa. We're not so blind to holiness that we can't acknowledge it when it's right before our eyes. But how many Mother Teresas or Paul Farmers have *we* known? How many people are we *personally* acquainted with whose reputation is completely a by-product of their true Christlikeness and whose only desire is to achieve their godly goal, regardless of whether they get any recognition or not?—One? Two? . . . None?

Unfortunately, for most of us even our loftiest goals get mixed up with a desire for some kind of reward. We might start out eager to serve God and do something good just for others. But it's easy to end up distracted by a thirst for self-validation and lose sight of the goal, the cause, the calling.

I want to tell you a story I read this week. On the morning of July 4, 1952, the California Coast from Santa Barbara to south of Los Angeles was blanketed in heavy fog. Offshore, on Santa Catalina Island, a thirty-four-year-old woman waded into the water and began swimming to the mainland. Her name was Florence Chadwick, and she had already been the first woman to swim the English Channel both ways. Now her goal was to be the first woman ever to swim the twenty-two-miles between Catalina and the mainland.

The fog was so thick Florence could barely see the boats that were with her. But as the hours ticked by, she kept swimming. The water was bone-chilling, but she was never threatened by fatigue. She was strong. Her biggest problem was the *fog*. After more than fifteen-hours, her body numb from the cold, Florence asked to be taken out of the water.

As soon as she gave up and got in the boat, she learned that she was only a relatively short distance from the shore. Florence said, "I'm not excusing myself, but I know that if I could have *seen* the shore I might have made it!" Florence Chadwick was not defeated by the ocean or the cold, but by the fog. *It's hard to keep going when you no longer see your goal.*

Our world is easily driven by the politics of envy. People who start with high and unselfish goals, can get distracted by a hunger for the talents, possessions, privileges, power, or physical attributes of others. We see what others have and begin to crave those things for ourselves. We *do* want to be "real" Christians, we really do, and follow in the footsteps of Jesus, *but we lose sight of our Christ-centered goal amid the frequent heavy fog of ego-centered cravings.*

Success for you and me lies in walking the way of the cross, the way of humility, the way of simplicity, the way of lowliness, the way of sacrifice—not by default, but by *decision.* "Greatness"—if greatness is even the right word to use—for Christians or for a church can only come when we look around us at the world and ask the Lord this goal-focused question: *How do you want me to serve?*

Rest assured that if we're sincere with that question, God has an answer for us.—I hope we're ready to hear it.

47. TO SUCH AS THESE THE KINGDOM OF HEAVEN BELONGS.

Roundup Sunday Service and Barbecue
Matthew 19:13-26

It's wonderful that we have so many children here this morning, because the gospel we just heard is really about children. Oh, I know that it probably sounded as if it was mostly about not being focused on our material possessions. That is A point, but not THE point. The main point is about children. It's about childlikeness. It's right there at the beginning, and it's one of my favorite sayings of Jesus. It's found in Matthew, Mark and Luke: "Let the little children come to me, and do not stop them; for it is to such as these that the kingdom of heaven belongs."

At this point in his ministry, Jesus was passing through the villages, teaching. He seems to have been speaking to a market-place crowd this time—mostly if not entirely male, as was the custom. Itinerant rabbis or teachers did not usually speak to mixed company; they spoke to the men. But some mothers seem to have come up with their children, wanting Jesus to lay his hands on them, pick them up and hold them, hug them. *There was blessing in his touch.* The mothers knew that. No doubt some of these moms had toddlers in tow, little guys who were walking on their own, kids maybe two or three or four years old.

Who was annoyed by this? Not the daddies. Their wives were coming up to Jesus with their own sons and daughters. The daddies probably thought: "The Teacher is going to bless my child. How cool is that?" No, it was the disciples who turned grumpy. We've already seen how bossy they could be. Remember the hungry crowd of 5,000? "Send them away!" Remember the poor Canaanite woman who trailed after Jesus seeking his help for her daughter? "Send her away!" Now it's mothers bringing their little children up to Jesus. "You women, get these children out of here. They're disturbing the teaching. Jesus is talking to the men about important things. Go away."

But Jesus contradicted them. Flatly contradicted them. He said: Let these little children come to me. Don't stop them. Don't push them away. The kingdom of heaven belongs to such as these. Or as another gospel writer put it: Unless you become as a little child yourself, you will never enter the kingdom of God.

Which, of course, raises the very important question: What did Jesus have in mind when he said that unless we become like little children we cannot enter his kingdom?

What are the qualities we once possessed as little children that we should try to re-discover if we want to be fit for God's kingdom? And, mind you, this is a kingdom which is *already here,* a kingdom that's in our midst! This is not about pie-in-the-sky-by-and-by, not about going to heaven when you die. I'm talking about entering a life that is open to us, through the love of God and the sacrifice of Christ, *right now.*

Is there anybody here who knows absolutely nothing about children? Good. 100% of us here know *something* about children. After all most of us have had children. Many of us have grandchildren. And all of us were once children ourselves. (Is there anybody here who was never a little child?)

The first thing that I think of about little children is that they are *spontaneous.* They live in the moment. They aren't worrying about what didn't get done this morning. They aren't worrying about what has to be done this afternoon.

We had two of our little grandchildren, Lucy and Sam, with us last weekend at church, and we'll have another one with us next Sunday. (I wish they all could have been here today for Roundup Sunday. They'd have had such fun.) The two who were with us last Sunday are a perfect illustration of the kind of childlikeness that Jesus prized. Sam, the younger of the two, is not quite a year and a half old, and he has discovered the joy of mud puddles. It rained last weekend, as you remember. When afterwards we went walking down North Street to Triangle Park with Sammy, he had to stop and stomp in every puddle. Then he had to bend down and pat the puddle. If there was mud, all the better. He knew just where he could wipe it off. He had a great time. And his mom and dad handled all this in a relaxed way. Wet shoes and socks were no big deal.

To enter the kingdom of God right now, you and I have to rediscover our capacity for spontaneity and joy.

Another thing that characterizes children is that *they have no doubt about their importance*. For example: I can be sitting in my favorite chair in the rectory family room watching the Rockies' game on TV or reading the Sunday paper—which is a sacred activity for me—but if whatever grandchild might be in the house at the time comes up and asks, "Can I sit in your lap, Poppy?" do I say, "No, you'll block the TV? I might miss a pitch." Or, "No, I'm reading the paper." Of course not! I love it that they want to sit on my lap. I love *them*. These little children are more important than anything else, and they can sit on my lap anytime they want to.

To enter the kingdom of God, we have to accept that we're important to our heavenly Father. We're his children. He loves us unconditionally. We can crawl up and "sit in the Father's lap" any time we want to (even if we're over sixty). I do it myself, and I recommend it to you. Just use your imagination.

Another thing about little children's believing that they're important to God is that they don't have any trouble believing that God might do something special with them, or for them, or through them. God might even speak right to them. (Often kids can hear God much better than we do.)

Tony Campolo tells a great story about a friend of his who dashed upstairs to his five year-old little girl's room one night during a terrible thunderstorm, when the lightning was flashing and the thunder was crashing. The man was sure his daughter would be terrified by the storm and he'd find her in tears. When he got up to her room, he found her spread-eagled against the tall window in her bedroom, looking out at the lightning storm. He said, "Honey, what's wrong? Are you o.k.?" Without looking back at him, she said—with her little face still pressed against the window: "I think God is trying to take my picture."

Little children know they're important to God. *Do you know that, too?*

Another thing about little children that we need to imitate if we are to enter the kingdom of God is that *they have absolute confidence in the future.* When I was in seminary a long time ago I worked in the slums of New York City. If you asked poor, inner-city eight year-olds forty years ago or you asked similar kids today what they were going to be when they grew up they'd tell you: I'm gonna be a doctor. I'm gonna be a ballerina. . . . Or an astronaut. . . . Or a pro basketball player. . . . Or an explorer. . . . Or a pop singer. . . . *Anything!*

Little children believe in their own unlimited possibilities. They can do anything, be anything. They believe in the future. It's full of hope. The kingdom of God belongs to those who become like little children, little children who know that with God all things are possible. All things. All things. All things.

That brings me to the last quality I think Jesus was thinking about when he said that we had to become like little children if were to enter the kingdom of God, and that is *recognition that we are always dependent.*

Little children are dependent. *We* know they're dependent on us. And *they* know it too—even if they often wish it were not so. They know that little children can't do very much all alone. I am not talking about teenagers, of course. I am not even talking about a certain four year-old granddaughter of ours who, when her daddy drove her to the first day of pre-school this last week, insisted that he stay in the car and let her walk into the school all alone. "Daddy, I can do it by myself!" A four or five year-old might want to be "big" and independent. That's natural. But little kids usually know pretty well what they can do right now and what they can't do.

The rich man in the gospel story who asked Jesus what more good deeds he needed to do in order to inherit eternal life had the sense that he was totally independent. "Inheriting" eternal life—the way he had inherited the family fortune—was just a matter of following the rules, knowing what good deeds to do, what rules to keep, what lessons to learn.

Jesus played along with him, listed some of the Ten Commandments, and added also that he should love his neighbor as himself. (That should have been the kicker, right there.) And the man said, "Yeah, sure. I know about all that. I have done all of that since I was a little kid." Mark's version of this story differs from Matthew and Luke. Mark says that when the rich man (sometimes called "the rich young man") said these things, "Jesus looked at him and *loved* him." Not me. I would have said, "You're pretty cocky for a young fella, aren'tcha?" Or "Oh, yeah? Who do you think you're foolin'?" But Jesus just "looked at him and loved him."

And then Jesus said, "Well, if you want to be perfect, take all your possessions and sell them and give the money to the poor, and you'll have treasure in heaven. And then come, follow me." "Come, follow me" was the same invitation he had given to Peter and Andrew, James and John and the others of his most intimate circle. It was Jesus' invitation to share his earthly life, full-time.

But the Bible says that when the man heard this "he went away grieving, for he had great possessions." Or, we might say: "His great possessions had him." (Have you ever known anybody whose possessions possessed *them*? I have.) His possessions made it impossible for the man to give them up in order to share Jesus' life, full-time. He was not as independent as he thought he was. He could not achieve all that he imagined he could achieve. The one thing needed for his perfection was beyond him. And it's beyond us too. Achieving entrance into the kingdom of God was not possible for the rich man in the story that day, perhaps because he was the very opposite of childlike.

Unless you and I become like little children, we cannot enter the kingdom of God. And that's because we can't inherit it, or buy it, or earn our way into it. But if we become as little children are, we can climb up into our heavenly Father's lap and look into his eyes and ask him if we can come and be part of his kingdom—right now, today, this minute—and receive that from him as a gift.

The kingdom is beyond our attainment, but—paradoxically—it is within our grasp . . . *if* we are willing to receive it from the Father's hand. For all things, all things, all things are possible with God.

48. BREAD FOR THE LIFE
OF THE WORLD.

John 6:37-51

I love bread. I mean the hearty, heavy, whole grain, crunchy stuff, the sort where a loaf weighs about a pound and a half. I love it for breakfast, with butter and marmalade. I rate our local restaurants by the quality of the bread they put out for guests when they're first seated. The ones that bring out a nice basket of luscious *warm* rolls and sliced focaccia or wheat bread folded in a white linen napkin are the winners. *(Mmm. mmm.)* By the time my main course arrives I've usually eaten so much bread and butter that I don't have much of an appetite.

Back around '99—having reached the age that my waistline was advancing and my hairline was retreating, I decided to do something about the waistline and go on the Atkins Diet. I'm sure some of you tried that. (It was the low carbohydrate thing, remember?) It worked, but one of the things I had to give up was bread. On the diet I could only eat some awful stuff that was mostly cellulose and tasted like pine bark. I lost about 15 pounds, but eventually had to give up the diet. All the pork chops and cream cheese I could have were no substitute for bread.—I *need* bread.

We heard a familiar passage this morning from John's gospel. To understand John, we need to be aware that in nearly every situation, he's offering answers to the questions, "Who is Jesus? . . . Who is this man? . . . What is he all about?"—In John, Jesus answers these questions with repeated "I" statements. He says, for example, "I am the light of the world." "I am the good shepherd." "I am the way, the truth and the life."

Today Jesus tells the crowd (some of the 5,000 people he has just fed with five loaves and two little fish), "I am the bread that came down from heaven." He says again, "I am the bread of life." And he adds, "Whoever eats this bread will live forever; and the bread that I will give for the life of the world is my flesh."

Here we see that Jesus connects himself both with God and with the people who are listening to him. He says, in effect, "I'm here for you. I've come from God to be 'bread' for you. . . . to give myself for you."—In a sense, this identification with bread is very humble, isn't it?—He says that his work in the world is to be "bread"—the most ordinary, basic, simple food. Nothing special. He doesn't say, "I am caviar," or "I am filet mignon" (or whatever first century Galilean gourmet delicacies would have been). And he doesn't say, "I am the spice of life." He says, "I am bread." . . . Just bread.

But bread was THE necessity. It was the staple of everyone's diet. In Jesus' native tongue, the invitation to come and share a meal—even a very elegant banquet in a palace—was "Come and *eat bread* with us." So Jesus was saying *"I am the basic necessity of life."* And that's what Christians proclaim to the world. We say "Jesus is the basic necessity for Life. If you want to live, really live with gusto (which, in a sense, is what it means to have 'eternal life'), you need Jesus."—Clearly, not everyone would agree with that proposition.

Jesus acknowledged that not everybody was going to accept him; not everybody would come to him. Lots of people around him said, "Who needs this Jesus? . . . this carpenter turned preacher?" That's why Jesus says, in today's gospel, "No one can come to me unless drawn by the Father who sent me."

I want you to notice something important about bread: it's a means to an end. Food is eaten in order to give life.

Anorexia is a terrible disease. I imagine most of us know people who have suffered from it. I hear that it's rooted somehow in the person's self-image; anorexics have a fractured, false picture of the self. Years ago I had a woman in my parish who suffered from this condition. Where do you think I ran into her most often, other than in church?—At the supermarket! I remember encountering her once when I was doing the grocery shopping, pushing around a cart piled high with all kinds of goodies. (I love to eat, and I love shopping for food. What I forget to buy at the store is not food, but stuff like Kleenex and light bulbs.) This woman was at the fresh fruit and vegetable section, and her cart had just a few things in it—paper products and cleaning supplies, of course, no food.

After we'd exchanged greetings, she said to me, "Look at this Olathe sweet corn, isn't it gorgeous? And those cantaloupes . . . they are *so* perfect!" I said to her, "They look delicious. Why don't you get some? Can't you just taste them right now?"—She, like all anorexics, thought constantly about food. But she would not eat . . . or *could* not allow herself to eat, at least not enough to stay healthy.

Jesus said, "The bread that I will give for the life of the world is my flesh."

You've heard the old saying, "You are what you eat." We can't take that literally, of course, but in a profound sense it's absolutely true. We who feed upon Christ *become* the Body of Christ. We become, graphically, the "flesh" of Christ. And so, like Christ, *we* Christians are meant to become "bread" given by God for the life of the world.—How do we turn that idea into more than just another piece of religious rhetoric? I want to suggest four ways.

The first way: STAY HUMBLE. Stay basic . . . like bread. See your life in the world as meant for something beyond your own personal gratification. If you are to be "one who gives life to the world," that idea can charge your mind and soul with vision and purpose. God has a work for *you* to do, but it's probably not going to earn you a lot of public recognition. So stay humble.

The second way: LET YOUR CONVERSATIONS BE LIFE-GIVING. Does what you say to other people build them up? Does talking to you give other people joy and hope and courage and the ability to go on with their lives, especially if they've had hard times? Moses said that people "live by every word that proceeds from the mouth of God." What word does God want you to speak on his behalf to your neighbor? . . . your spouse? . . . your child? . . . or the stranger you meet at coffee hour when this service is over? What are these people hungry to hear? Perhaps they're starving to hear "I'm glad to get to talk to you." Or "I admire you." Or, maybe, "What can I do to help you?" Or just, "Have I told you lately that I love you? Well, I do."

The third way: ENGAGE IN LIFE-GIVING KINDS OF BEHAVIOR. If we're to be bread for the life of the world, we have to think seriously about the world and what it needs. And I'm talking about the *kosmos*, the physical world, as well as the people in it. (*Kosmos* is the Greek word that's used for "the world" here in John's gospel.) So, one part of what I'm talking about is compassion for the environment—making decisions and engaging in behaviors that nurture the earth. (I believe that mission is alive and well here in our town.)—And the other part of what I'm talking about is compassion for the more than 2.5 billion people who go to sleep hungry every night. I know it's hard to think about hungry people when we're surrounded here by world-class restaurants, but we have to *act* to give life to the physically hungry people of the world, and not just talk about how sad it is.

This leads me to the fourth and last way I want to mention that we can become bread for the life of the world, and that is: YOU CAN IMPLEMENT YOUR FAITH. Jesus said, "No one can come to me unless drawn by the Father who sent me." You might be the agent God has chosen to draw someone to Jesus. And the most effective means of drawing others to the Bread of Life is your life and what your life stands for.

Don't forget the famous instruction of St. Francis of Assisi to his friars. He sent them out, saying: "Go into the world and preach the Good News. If necessary, use words." Your *life* can be bread to feed a hungry heart.

Today we've come to where we might feed on Word and Sacrament. But there's nothing magic here. Sharing the Eucharist doesn't automatically lead to moral transformation. It's possible to hear the Gospel, yet not *listen* to it. It's possible to swallow the Sacrament, yet not be *nourished* by it.

Many of us suffer from a kind of spiritual anorexia. Like the woman I mentioned who spent so much time in the supermarket, some people come to church because they admire the gospel of Christ. After church, they say to the preacher, "What a wonderful message."—But they don't take anything in. They come and look, but never *taste* . . . never savor the goodness of the Lord . . . never feed on the Bread of Life in such a way that they *become* what they have eaten.

Today I invite you: Come and eat! "Taste and see that the Lord is good. Happy are those who put their trust in him."

49. WE NEED TO MOVE FROM DECISION TO ACTION.

Matthew 21:23-32

There's nobody more dangerous to the church than an immature, but very fired-up, enthusiastic Christian—especially when that immature Christian has a clergy collar and a license to preach. I'm talking about myself thirty-three years ago. When I was in my second year of work in a parish, I delivered a fire-breathing sermon about the demands of the gospel. I told the congregation of St. Paul's Church down in Lakewood that the Lord expected them to match their *professions* of faith with *lives* of faith. In the wind-up to my sermon, I said, "If you really don't intend to start obeying the gospel in an obvious way, why don't you just get up and walk out of this church right now? Why don't you have enough integrity to find something else to do on Sunday morning? The Church is meant to be the company of the committed, and if you're not *committed* this is not the place for you."

I looked over at my boss, Fr. Bob Royster, the rector who had hired me just out of graduate school a year before to come out to Colorado and be his assistant, giving me my first chance to work full-time in a church and introducing me to this beautiful state where we still live. He was hiding his face in his hands. But before he had a chance to get on my case, I was blasted at the church door by a young father, a man named Ben Simpson who was a little older than me and who had two boys a couple of years older than my own children. The encounter made an indelible impression on me. Ben was *really* mad. He told me that he was trying his best to be a good Christian and bring up his children to know and do the right thing, and it was (expletive-deleted) arrogant of me to tell people who weren't yet "perfect" that *they* didn't belong in church. He knew that he had a long way to go, but he said it looked like *I* had a whole lot further to go than I imagined.

In those days my boss and I would take turns being the preacher on Sunday morning—he would preach one week and I would preach the next. Every Sunday when I was the preacher, we'd have a sermon review session at the rectory on Sunday afternoon. This time, getting in my face, he said "I never *ever* want to hear you say anything like that again." Jabbing his finger in my chest, he told me, "When you say something like that you just hurt people. And your job is not to hurt people, but to *help* them." He was right. I was wrong. And I repented.

But the issue I was trying to talk about in that ill-considered sermon is still real. It's the challenge of putting our faith into practice—living it, not just discussing it. The challenge of "working out our own salvation" as Paul called it. It's often easier to *decide* what's right than to *do* what's right.

Next week there will be a baptism at 8:00, and we'll all join with the parents and godparents in renewing our faith by saying the Baptismal Covenant together. Anybody who has worshiped in the Episcopal Church for at least a year has recited this several times. Maybe the fact that it's so familiar makes it easy to say it without thinking too much. The Baptismal Covenant includes different things, but it ends with five questions about life as Christian people in the world. The third of the five questions is this: "Will you proclaim by word *and* example the Good News of God in Christ?" (That means, in other words, "Will you put your faith into practice, and not just announce it?") The answer to this question, and to all of the others, is: *"I will with God's help."*

If we apply Jesus' story about the two sons to ourselves, most of us would have to say that we're not like the first son, who flatly said "No," when his father told him to go pick grapes. We're more like the second son, who said "Yes, daddy," but actually never got around to doing anything. We *want* to follow through on our verbal commitments. We mean to. But we get distracted.—And why? I say it's because we're not *fully converted.*

I grew up in a home where my mother was a good church-woman and my dad was a cynic. He thought churches were full of hypocrites. But I know churches, and I don't think for a minute that the churches are full of hypocrites. We want to stand up for the truth, for things that are good and right and true. Our intentions are excellent when we say the Baptismal Covenant for the first time or for the 500th time. But we're distracted by other things, other interests, and other concerns in life. Ordinary daily life is complicated in the 21st century, and it's getting more so, not less. And so we get distracted. We mean well, but meaning well is not enough. Just answering formal questions correctly doesn't mean we've been *converted to the task* entailed by our answer. Take for example the question, "Will you proclaim by word AND example the Good News of God in Christ?"

In 1937 the Danish author Karen Blixen (writing under the pen-name Isak Dinesen) wrote a book called *Out of Africa*. It was made into a great movie, which I've seen many times, though I never read the book. I'm told, however, that in the book a young Kikuyu boy appears at Blixen's door to ask for a job in her house. She hires him, and he proves to be a good worker, but she's surprised when after only three months he asks for a letter of reference to Sheik Ali bin Salim, a Muslim elder living in a nearby town. Blixen offers him a bigger salary if he'll stay, but he says, "I am not interested in money. I have decided to become either a Christian or a Muslim, and I came to work for you so that I might see in person the ways of the Christians. Now I shall go and observe Sheik Ali to see how Muslims behave. Then I shall decide."

Blixen said, "Good heavens. You might have *told* me that when you came here."

It would be helpful to know whether someone is watching us because they want to "see in person the ways of the Christians." Might someone decide either to become a Christian or not on the basis of what they observe in *your* behavior? . . . not just what they know of your belief system, but how they see you put your beliefs into action? A few weeks ago I read a book that said younger people in America who are seeking a relationship with God are looking for a *way of life*, not just a belief system. When they check out a church, they're hoping to find a community of people who model a *way of living* they can understand and adopt for themselves.

In Jesus' story of the two sons, the one who refused to go work in the vineyard later changed his mind. When he had changed his mind—or *repented* as the Bible says—then he went to work. That's what I mean by being *converted to the task*. The same kind of conversion was possible for the other son, the one who gave a good answer but failed to follow through. If he had changed his mind, too, he might have been converted to the task. But that couldn't happen because his mind was on other things.

A similar repentance and conversion is possible for us, who believe in Jesus Christ and mean well, but have trouble transforming our convictions into behavior. Consider the answer we give to the questions we're asked in the Baptismal Covenant: To each question, "Will you . . . ?" "Will you . . . ?" "Will you . . . ?" We answer not just "I will," but *"I will, with God's help."*

We're engaged in a growth process: we're on a road from decision to action. At the end of today's reading from Philippians, Paul calls that process "working out our own salvation." And he promises that "God is at work in us, to will and to work for his good pleasure." The same loving Father whose amazing grace brought us to faith in the first place can also empower us to take action. And "we can do all things through him who strengthens us." (Phil. 4:15)

We have not yet become the fully-formed, Christ-like men and women that one day, with God's help, we hope to be. But we're on our way. We're working at it, just like Ben Simpson told me he was, back in 1975 when he nailed me for my arrogant sermon. That episode in my early life had a sequel just two years ago. In 2006 at our Colorado Diocesan convention, a young man in his thirties came up to me in the aisle during a break, stuck out his hand, and said, "Hello, Fr. Bruce, I'm Ben Simpson." I said, "Bennie! It's so good to see you after all these years." It was Ben Simpson, *Jr.*, son of the Lakewood parishioner I spoke about earlier. When I had seen him last, he was a first grader, and everybody called him "Bennie" to distinguish him from his dad. We had a good visit, and I learned he was now a young father himself and also a solid Christian, a member of the vestry in his church and clearly a man who was trying to live his faith.

We're all on a journey in this life, and we're at many different places on that journey. Some of us have had one conversion; some have had two or three. But the most important conversion of all is from decision to *action*. We're all here in the church to worship this morning because we have made a decision. But the place for *action* is not in here, it's out there—in the world beyond the church doors. Let's go out there and get to it.

50. CHOOSE WHOM YOU WILL SERVE.

Joshua 24:1-2a, 14-25; John 6:56-6

For almost every social phenomenon in our modern world there's a counterpart in the pages of the Bible. Today we heard from the Old Testament book of *Joshua*, Moses' successor. Sometime between 1500 and 1200 B.C. (no one really knows exactly when) Joshua led a great company of Hebrew people across the Jordan River into the land called Canaan—the land God had promised Abraham that he would give his descendants. These Hebrews were a rag-tag bunch, the children of former slaves, plus nomadic tribes who had thrown in their lot with them during their forty years of wandering in the Sinai desert after leaving Egypt.

The Hebrews proved themselves to be both cowardly and brave at different times during their desert sojourn. But through that whole time, God was always with them, always active and evident—in spite of the fact that they were often fickle. They always acknowledged the supremacy of God, because he had brought them out of Egypt—but they wanted to cover all religious bases, so early on they made themselves a golden calf to worship, and they hid little images of local fertility goddesses under their beds to ensure that they'd have lots of children.

In fact, the Hebrews were inclined to make offerings to any divinities they thought needed to be placated while they were passing through their territory. Of course, they continued to worship the God of Abraham, Isaac, and Jacob—at least in a formal way—but they weren't completely

242

convinced that this *one* God was enough. They felt like they needed other options. (We're a lot like them.)

When the Hebrews finally came to the boundary of the Promised Land, Moses died. Joshua, his lieutenant, then became their leader. Before the Hebrews started to settle the new land, Joshua called a great assembly where he put this proposition to them: "It's time to settle on *one* God," he said. "You've got to get rid of your idols and serve the living God. Or, if you won't do that, then pick out for yourselves a god that you *will* serve. *But as for me and my household, we will serve the LORD.*" We seek no other options.

"Oh," the Israelites answered, "We will serve the LORD too! After all, he brought us up out of slavery in Egypt. We will worship him. He is *our* God."

Notice what Joshua told them then: "You *can't do it*," he said. "The LORD is a holy God. He's a jealous God. He won't tolerate any rivals. If you abandon him and serve other gods, believe me, he is going to turn and punish you.—Mark my words, you'll be sorry."

"Oh, but yes." they countered, "We WILL serve the LORD." (Imagine the sons of Israel standing around Joshua, pumping their fists in the air like a bunch of frat boys at a football game, chanting "We will serve the LORD!" "We will serve the LORD!" "We will serve the LORD!")

"Very well then," Joshua told them, "You are witnesses against yourselves that you have chosen the LORD, to serve him. So now, get rid of your idols and incline your hearts to the Lord." Then Joshua made a solemn covenant with the people of Israel.

Here's the parallel with our age: Idolatry can run rampant, even among the people God has redeemed to be his own. People who consider themselves Christians fall into the comfortable habit of worshiping other gods alongside the Lord, exercising our freedom "to enjoy other options."

Let's not deceive ourselves about this, just because we don't call the objects of our worship "gods." Remember: *anything that defines* ULTIMATE VALUE *for you, anything that becomes the supreme guide for your life*—THAT'S *your "god."*

We worship a whole range of idols, including a variety of local or tribal deities, each one defining ultimate value for us in one compartment or another of our life.

Just for fun, let's give names to the local deities worshiped here in Aspen. One of the most admired of our tribal gods is *Human Intellect.* This is a form of self-worship—and self-worship is always *very* popular. Then how about *Entertainment?* Of course, she's adored everywhere, not just here. Everybody wants to have fun. Party, party. Then there's Entertainment's virile male consort: his name is *Recreation.* The local version of this divinity is the mountain god, whose chosen sacrifice is a broken leg, offered in winter. *Appearance* is another fashionable local goddess, and not just for certain body-conscious women, but many men as well. Appearance needs copious offerings of sweat in the gym, and she demands that her followers live exclusively on the sacrament of steamed vegetables and macrobiotic tea. Special priests called cosmetic surgeons assist the most serious devotees of Appearance with the offering of special, painful sacrifices.—Of course, along with these and other local deities I haven't named, we also bow down before the American pantheon of Power, Success, Social Status, Celebrity, and Political Correctness.

O.K., I'm teasing. But I believe that now, as much as ever in history, God's people need to renew their loyalty to him. And we in particular, here in Christ Church, need to renew *our* loyalty. In his sermon yesterday at the Service of Dedication and Blessing of this new building, Bishop O'Neill said that we have just come through our time of "exile," our period of "desert wandering," and as we have taken possession of our new and beautiful church building, we're something like the Israelites coming back to the Promised Land.

That's a good image to work with. If, as a community of believers, we are—symbolically—in the same position as Israel entering the Promised Land, then God is telling us the same thing Joshua told the people of Israel: "Choose this day whom you will serve." In other words: let's decide now what's really important. Let's make up our minds concerning where ultimate value is to be found for us. Let's make—or re-make—a spiritual commitment and live by it.—Let's choose one path and stick to it and turn our backs on the other options.

Jesus fed the multitude with five loaves and two fishes, but when he tried to make them understand that the food that had filled their bellies was not nearly as important as the Bread of Life that he was offering them, they didn't get it. They didn't like it. When he told them that if they wanted to have eternal life they would need to eat his flesh and drink his blood—which really meant that for them to have true Life, they needed to be filled with *his* life and become *like* him—they were shocked, and the majority of them left him.

The majority were unwilling to believe that the true Life of God had become incarnate in this carpenter from Nazareth, and that the only clear path to Life lay through becoming one with him. They were willing to go along with Jesus only so far, as one option among many. When he asked for ultimate commitment, they turned away.

It's a shock for people today to hear Jesus say that "the flesh," the stuff our world values the most, really has nothing to offer.—Is he telling us that all we've worked so hard to acquire, which gives us so much pleasure, counts for nothing in his eyes? To the former disciples who were leaving him to go seek other options, Jesus called out these words: "The Spirit alone gives Life; the flesh is useless. The words I have spoken to you are Spirit, and they are Life."

These ex-disciples had decided that his words, who he claimed to be, and where he said he came from were just too much for them to swallow: "Good-bye, Jesus. Thanks for the picnic, but we need to find someone with a totally different approach."

Jesus said, "No one can serve two masters." If we're truly committed to Christ and we take our Baptismal Covenant seriously . . .

- We can't render equal honor to the wisdom of God and the so-called wisdom of this age. One will take precedence over the other.

- We can't be submitted to the Word of God and at the same time be totally guided by the last interesting speaker we heard at a conference down the road. One will take precedence over the other.

- We can't say the Creed and receive Holy Communion on Sunday in church and then worship all the tribal and local divinities I jokingly described earlier, Monday through Saturday. To do so is apostasy.

Today, now that we have symbolically entered our "promised land," God is inviting us to make a fresh commitment of loyalty to him. After the other disciples had gone away and left Jesus alone in the Capernaum synagogue with the Twelve, Jesus turned to them and said, "Well, do you want to leave me now, too?" Peter said, "Lord, to whom could we go? You have the words of eternal life. And we have believed and come to know that you are the Holy One of God."

If we have believed and come to know that Jesus is the Way, the Truth, and the Life for us, then we have to make a choice about the direction our lives are going to take and what our lives are going to mean hereafter. If we believe that the Light Christ has kindled in us is the one, true Light of God, we cannot permit that light to be dimmed by any form of idolatry, no matter how seductive our regional deities might be.

Knowing what you believe is important. But there's a difference between belief and commitment. *Commitment is belief in action.* Jesus calls us to belief in action, to make the choice that will shape all other choices we ever make—a commitment that will interpret life's experiences for us and move us to action. To service.

Joshua said, "Choose this day whom you will serve. But as for me and my household, we will serve the Lord."—How about you?

51. JESUS IS OUR PEACE.

Ephesians 2:11-22

Tradition says that Paul wrote his letter to the Ephesians from a prison in Rome to a church far away in Asia Minor (modern Turkey), a church he had helped to start. He was reaching out to people he knew and loved—and who had a strong emotional bond with him, too. One of the main reasons Paul had for writing his friends in Ephesus was that their church was coming apart at the seams. They'd lost their unity. They were quarrelling with each another. They had developed factions and chosen sides. Partisanship was getting out of hand.

Their divisions and loss of love for each another grieved the Apostle who had brought so many of them to faith in Christ. In this part of his letter, Paul was offering assurances to the Gentile Christians, whom he had gone out on a limb to welcome into the young church as equals with Jewish believers in Jesus as the Messiah.

It's hard for us to imagine how difficult it was for Jewish Christians to welcome Gentiles into their fellowship. In that era, Jews were taught to regard Gentiles as completely outside God's covenant. They were alien, unclean. Jews alone were God's people. "Gentile sinners" was the common way they spoke of non-Jews.

This way of thinking wasn't just crude prejudice; it was rooted in the Hebrew Scriptures and the traditions of the Elders. Four hundred and fifty years earlier, when they returned from their exile in Babylon, Ezra the Scribe compelled Jews who had married Gentiles during the exile to divorce their spouses and send them away. Gentile wives would "contaminate" the holiness of the People of God. That kind of thinking was not easy to break.

We can take cold comfort from remembering that the church has had factions and disagreements since the days of the New Testament. But we know that Jesus prayed for his disciples to be united, asking "that they all may be one, as you, Father, are in me and I am in you."

Factions are a plague. But we have to admit that factions are also a logical product of human nature. We like to have things our own way, and so we sift ourselves out into groups (and further into *sub*-groups) that share a common culture, or the same way of thinking about a specific issue, or the same political goals, or the same religious convictions. "Birds of a feather flock together," as they say. So we might even assume that factions are normal.—But, then, war is normal too, isn't it? . . . Like cancer. Or lust. Or greed. The fact that something is normal makes it understandable, but doesn't make it *desirable*.

There's nothing wrong with people having different ideas about things. People *are* different. Diversity is not a choice; it's built into our nature. But *factionalism* is a giant step beyond diversity. Factionalism is more than peaceful association with like-minded people or friends with similar interests. Factional rivalry goes beyond advocating one school of theological opinion or one particular interpretation of the Bible. Factions—in politics or in the church—strive for control and domination. Factions want to impose their views and values on everyone else. Factions want to *win*. Winning, though, presupposes "enemies" and the need to defeat them. For Christians, as essayist Tom Ehrich wrote in a recent column, "a focus on winning can lead to arrogance and cruelty, and it sees people as expendable in the great work of fighting the enemy."

Jesus prayed that his followers would have the same kind of unity with one another that he had with his heavenly Father. Paul told the Ephesians that Jesus "is our peace." He even said that "He has abolished the law with its commandments and ordinances, that he might create in himself one new humanity in place of the two, thus making peace, and might reconcile both groups to God in one body through the cross." Those are powerful words. Paul saw the death of Christ as the birth of a New Humanity. All the old divisions and hostilities and barriers to fellowship were abolished. In another letter, Paul says, "Male and female, slave and free, Jew and Greek—all are one in Christ Jesus."—Oh, if only we could live that way.

Natural, human inclinations have led Christians to split into sects based on our differing interpretations of the Bible (interpretations which we proclaim as revealed truth, repudiating all other plausible interpretations). Or we separate from one another based on competing visions for how the church should be ordered (condemning other views than our own as revisionist). That's precisely what Christians have done for hundreds of years—and are doing still. But the Bible tells us that God wants the church of Jesus Christ to be *different* from the rest of human society. These days, any difference is hard to spot.—That must grieve the Spirit of God.

Unity is only possible in the church to the extent that we recognize that *Jesus* "is our peace." As Paul said about Jews and Gentiles, we all "have access in one Spirit to the Father." And at the Last Day, he alone will be our judge. Christ did not send his disciples out to be judges, but to herald the presence of the Kingdom of God and by their lives give testimony to God's power to transform sinful human beings. But the current hatefulness and bitter language towards one another within the church testifies that we have not been transformed in any obvious sense.

It strikes me that all the differences among churches and church people matter a lot more to *us* than they do to our heavenly Father. We're *going* to have these differences. It's unavoidable. Our differences won't go away, but they don't have to make us enemies, not if we believe that the redeeming death of Jesus has made us into a single New Humanity.

I have little expectation that the Episcopal Church or the Anglican Communion is going to look the same in the year 2016, ten years from now. Some kind of realignment is coming; many would say that the realignment has already begun. The center seems to have collapsed, and all of the energy in our church is out at the opposite edges—the hard right and hard left, or (as they call themselves) "the traditionalists" and "the progressives." I've always believed that it's more important to build bridges than walls, so the most recent developments in our church depress me.

But I'll tell you this: Though I'm sad and disappointed at the current state of the Episcopal Church and the Anglican Communion, I'm not alienated from anybody in this church—either on the left or the right of the current issues. Personally, I'm a relatively conservative, evangelical Anglican. But I don't have to win. I can love people with whom I have sharp disagreements about many things, and I can be part of a single family with them in Christ, a New Humanity. If they can't accept me as a brother or love me back, that's more their problem than mine. If we profess faith in one Lord Jesus Christ, as we say in the Creed, that's enough for me.—If it's not enough for them, I'm sorry.—I pray that many of you here today agree with me, but if you don't, that's o.k., too. I still love you.

I believe we can have real unity and yet agree to disagree about serious issues. We can have real unity and also advocate differing interpretations of the Bible or Christian doctrine (or anything else). We can have real unity and also be free to believe that we're right and others are, possibly, *not* right.

Consider this: the Pharisees and Sadducees in Jesus' day were at least as different from one another, or more so, than Bishop Bob Duncan and Bishop Gene Robinson are today. The Sadducees only accepted the first five books of the Bible as inspired by God, and they didn't believe in prophets, or angels, or the resurrection. And they collaborated with the Romans. The Pharisees believed in the Law and the Prophets and the Writings and treated the teaching of their Elders as inspired. They believed in the resurrection of the dead and they hated the Romans.

But Pharisees and Sadducees worshiped in the same Temple together and shared a single, burning loyalty to the God of Abraham, Isaac, and Jacob. They argued about almost everything, but neither ever pointed the finger at the other and said, "*You're* not a Jew. I can't worship at the same altar with *you*!" They knew they were one People, one Family, the children of Abraham. That was enough.

Only love for one another will have the power to keep Anglicans together when everything else fails. If we accept that God loves us and that Christ died for us so that we could be one in him, how can we *choose* not to love one another? And real *love* isn't just a word—it's a way of life. It's embodied in how we actually behave toward others, especially people with whom we have many differences.

Love makes me look at the people I disagree with and say, "No matter what happens, you're my sisters. You're my brothers. We're one family."

Jesus is our peace.

52. WRITE THE VISION.
MAKE IT PLAIN.

Habakkuk 2:1-4

One essential for any kind of achievement is a *vision*. That is: to make progress, we need a mental picture of where we're going and how we're going to get there. To succeed, we need a vision of what success will look like. The entrepreneur building a new business, the educator establishing an experimental school, the physician treating a patient, the parent raising a child—all these build on a visionary sense of what the outcome of their efforts will be (God willing), if they do things right. Or, to choose a different example: Michelangelo—starting out to carve an angel from a shapeless block of stone—said that from the beginning he could *see* an angel in the marble; his work was simply to release it from the stone.

We read a passage from the Book of the Prophet Habakkuk this morning. Habakkuk—like Amos earlier and Ezekiel later—was a visionary prophet. That is to say, God gave him a vision—a mental picture—of what was going to happen to Israel. God showed Habakkuk how he would purge his people of their sin and gave him a vision of the healing that God would provide for them, once they'd been purified. And the Lord commanded the prophet to write the essence of the vision and make it plain, to write it on tablets in letters so big and bold that even a runner passing by could read it: *the righteous shall live by faith.*

In every instance, the vision of a prophet like Habakkuk was a way of making the promise and purpose of God concrete for his people—so they could hang on to it, believe it, and know when it had been fulfilled.

I believe that it's important for a pastor to ask God for a vision for his church. Such a vision, such an inspired picture sent from God, can give pastor and people a sense of direction. A vision enables a church to know when we're succeeding and when we're failing. It's both a promise from God and a call to obedience. It's a standard against which we can test ourselves, asking "If we do thus-and-so, are we being faithful to the vision God has given us?"

I do not claim to be a prophet like the ones whose books are in the Old Testament, but I do believe that from time to time God has given me a definite message to share. And I believe that now, as we are moving towards the end of my first year as your rector, the Lord has given me an unambiguous sense of what he is looking for from our church. This is a vision, and its central element is a picture of Christ Church in Aspen as a *community where people meet Jesus Christ*.

I believe that what God wants is for us to be most of all a fellowship of people where both we and those who come to us from around the country can encounter Christ in a deeply personal, entirely authentic, life-transforming way.

The vision of our church as a community of where people meet Jesus Christ is a composite picture, sort of like a photo-montage. First, IT'S A PICTURE OF WORSHIP THAT UNITES US WITH JESUS . . . that communicates his undiluted love . . . that lifts us into his presence in the power of the Spirit . . . that refreshes us as those were refreshed who came to him on the Galilean hillsides and lakeshore . . . that heals the hurting hearts and bodies of those who come into his presence . . . and—most of all—that inspires us to imitate him.

IT'S A PICTURE OF TEACHING THAT IS GROUNDED IN THE BIBLICAL GOSPEL, the record of the words and works of Jesus, the Son of God . . . that connects discipleship with daily living . . . that equips every participant in a Bible study or class to be an informed and faithful witness for Jesus . . . and that supplies us with the only kind of moral formation that will allow us to find our way safely through the minefield of temptations and delusions which we know as contemporary American society.

IT'S A PICTURE OF SERVICE TO OTHERS AS THE NORMAL CHRISTIAN LIFE . . . a life shaped by the pattern that Jesus taught when he asked his followers: *"Who do you* think is greater, the person who sits at the table, or the person who serves?" Then he said, "Surely, the one who sits at the table is greater. But I am among you as one who serves," The normal Christian life is a life that's other-oriented not self-centered . . . a life that's lived in optimism about what those who believe in Jesus can accomplish, rather than pessimism because the task before us is daunting.

IT'S A PICTURE OF A CHURCH WHERE CHRIST IS REALLY TREATED AS HEAD, AS LORD . . . where no decisions are made without prayer . . . where each person great or small, young or old, local or part-timer, is treated as if he or she were the Lord himself—with respect, dignity, and care . . . where Jesus is the reconciler of our differences and the focus of our unity . . . and where there is a collective zeal to invite others to join us, not for our sake—because we want them to provide financial support or help with programs—but for theirs, because what we're experiencing is so valuable we want to share it.

The vision God has given for Christ Church is that it be just that: *Christ's* Church.—Centered on him.—Trusting in him.—Empowered by him. In worship, in teaching, in service, and in community life. That's the heart of the vision, and as God commanded Habakkuk, I want to make the vision simple, clear, and plain. I wish I had a big marker board up here by the pulpit so I could write this for you in bold letters: "CHRIST CHURCH: CENTERED ON HIM, TRUSTING IN HIM, EMPOWERED BY HIM."—But we need to remember that a vision from God like this one is not a picture of things as they are. No. It's a picture of *things as they can become* if the people of God respond in faith.

We have a daunting task. There's plenty of evidence that Aspen is not a religious town. According to survey data, roughly 75% of the people who live in Pitkin County profess no faith of any sort and are, in fact, "faith resistant." That is to say, three quarters of the people who live around us have no religion and no interest in religion. Churches are not on their radar screens. For them, "Jesus" is just the name of a man who lived a long time ago. The Bible is a boring book they have no interest in reading.—So there's the challenge God has for our church: to be a community of encounter with Christ in the midst of an environment where most people are not looking for him.

Next Sunday is Pledge Sunday. When we talk about pledges in the church, we're usually referring to written promises to support the church with our money, time and effort. And we're certainly asking for those kinds of pledges. We need them. But I want you to look towards next Sunday with a much bigger understanding of what it means to make a pledge than simply to promise to donate money and time. I want you to think about your pledge as being like what happens when a man and woman marry and make a commitment, a pledge of faith to one another, for better for worse, for richer for poorer, in sickness and in health, until they are parted by death. I want you to think about your *pledge* as being like what we mean when we put our right hands over our hearts and pledge allegiance to the flag of our country.

Pledge Sunday is the time for us to pledge ourselves to follow the vision God has given us: a time to renew our commitment to be a community where people meet the Lord Jesus Christ—right in the midst of a deeply secular, faith-resistant society. The money that we promise to give to support the church's work in the coming year or the tasks that we promise to do as part of the church's ministry are not really the substance of our pledge, they are simply the tangible signs, the proof we might say, of our real pledge: a pledge of our faith in Jesus, the Son of God, who has called us to follow him and be his disciples. Our true pledge is to go where he leads us. And he has given us a vision to show the way.

The word of God to the prophet long ago is a word that rings in my ears as if spoken this very morning: "Write the vision; make it plain . . . For there is still a vision for the appointed time; it speaks of the end, and does not lie. If it seems to tarry, wait for it; it will surely come, it will not delay. Look at the proud. Their spirit is not right in them, but the righteous shall live by their faith."

53. BONE OF MY BONES
AND FLESH OF MY FLESH.

Mark 10:2-9

Anybody who likes comedy knows that writers can always get some great humor out of stories about marriage. Shakespeare did it. And stand-up comics have done it with one-liners like Rodney Dangerfield's classic "Take my wife . . . Please!" Or little jokes such as: "What's the difference between a husband and a house cat?—One is a finicky eater who's impossible to please.—The other is a furry pet that purrs."

We can get some laughs out of marriage situations but marriage is also the major context for a lot of great drama too—from Homer to Sophocles to Shakespeare to Tennessee Williams.

And the reason for this is easy to see: *marriage is the primary human relationship.*

The Bible tells us this at its very beginning. The creation stories in Genesis are wonderfully profound. It's unfortunate that people often want to disregard them or make jokes out of them because they're unscientific. These are "mythic" stories, and I mean that in the very best sense. They're revelations of God's truth, but not descriptions of phenomena that could be substantiated by archaeology. Beginning with the statement that, "It isn't good that the man should be alone," we hear how the partnership between man and woman is fundamental. The two have the same nature.

Here's something interesting: the very first sentence the newly created Adam speaks in the Book of Genesis is the happy recognition of Eve as "bone of my bones and flesh of my flesh." And the story draws the following conclusion as a principle of creation: "Therefore, a man leaves his father and mother and clings to his wife, and they become one flesh."

Notice this: the Bible shows us that there's no subordination between male and female. There's only partnership, unity, and sharing. "Bone of my bones . . . Flesh of my flesh." In the Biblical narrative, subordination of woman to man—which was typical of ancient, patriarchal societies—comes into practice later on, as a result of human sin. This kind of subordination is not portrayed as part of God's original plan. There's a lot of bad teaching out there in some conservative churches, asserting that the Bible teaches the subordination of women to men, but that isn't what we read in the creation story. I read a comment somewhere that said the Genesis story doesn't intend that the female be subordinate to the male because she was made from his rib any more than it intends that the male be subordinate to the soil because he was formed from the earth.

The Genesis story is the basic revelation of God's truth that Jesus built on when he was confronted by the Pharisees who wanted to trip him up on legal technicalities. You know this part: As Jesus became popular and word of his teachings and miracles spread, members of the 'Religious Establishment' decided it was their job to put this carpenter in his place.

The Pharisees were the experts. They knew the law. They were the custodians of the sacred traditions of the People of God. They knew God's will was revealed once and for all in the writings of Moses. So they decided to trick Jesus into saying something against the Law. If they could demonstrate that he was blaspheming against the Law, then they could discredit him before the crowds who were hanging on his every word.

So the Pharisees asked him: "Teacher is it lawful for a man to divorce his wife?" They knew it was lawful. Deuteronomy said so. The only debating point was what constituted proper grounds for divorce.

Jesus answered: "What did Moses command you?"

The Pharisees replied: "Moses allowed a husband to divorce his wife as long as the husband drew up the necessary paper work."

And Jesus answered back: "Why did Moses allow this? He allowed it because of your hard hearts. But God's perfect will is revealed in creation where the man and the woman are one flesh . . . not two, but one. Therefore, what God has joined together, let no one else separate."

The Law permitted divorce. It still does. But Jesus refused to be tricked into betraying the intent of God. He told them that the Law permitted divorce because human beings have hard hearts. We're sinners. We fall short of God's dreams for us, God's ideal for us and for our lives together. It was true then, and it is true now.

Until not long ago, statistics showed that half of all marriages in America end in divorce. That ratio has improved, but only because many more people than ever before have started living together without getting married. The divorce rate is still high. And why? Because we fall short of God's dreams for us, short of God's intent for what marriage should be. For example, people sometimes marry hastily and for the wrong reasons. Husbands and wives change and grow apart. Couples become cruel to one another and forget they are "one bone and one flesh." They begin to destroy their marriages, not conscious that destruction of a marriage is a kind of self-destruction. Some marriages have to end in order to keep the self-destruction from eliminating the possibility of a future life for either partner.

We're human. We're sinners. We fail. But that doesn't change God's plan. God's plan and purpose is for a man and a woman to be life-long partners, one flesh. Marriage is *meant* to be an indissoluble bond.

The Pharisees wanted to trick Jesus. They wanted to make him say Moses was wrong in permitting divorce. But Jesus didn't say Moses was wrong. He just said that Moses allowed divorce because of men's hard hearts—but divorce was not God's original intent or plan.

People have asked me whether I "believe in divorce." They ask me this because I have been divorced and remarried. They say, "Since you're a priest and you've been divorced and remarried, you must 'believe in divorce.' Right?"

I say, "No. I do not 'believe in divorce.' I believe in Jesus." I think people who have been through a divorce would agree. It's not an easy solution to interpersonal problems. It's radical surgery—the last resort. The bishop of Singapore once asked me whether, since I was a divorced priest, I would recommend divorce as a solution for the troubles of married people who came to me for counseling. I told him that nobody who had ever been through a divorce would be quick to recommend it to anyone else. But there are circumstances when it's the only solution—like radical surgery for cancer.

I believe God intended marriage to be life-long. I believe divorce *always* involves failure, involves sin, and involves terrible human brokenness. But I believe in a God who sent his son into the world to deal with human sin and brokenness—including divorce. I do not "believe in divorce," but I do believe in the forgiveness of sins and in the new life that Christ gives those who turn to him in faith after the grief and pain and death that is divorce. Divorce is not the unforgivable sin.

I speak from personal experience. This isn't something I read in a book. A new life doesn't come from what we do, but from what Christ does in us—*if we let him.*

You remember the story of Jesus' encounter with the woman at the well in Samaria, found in Chapter 4 of John's gospel? Jesus was thirsty from a long walk when he met a woman at a well, and since she was drawing water from the well he asked her for a drink. She said, "How is it that you, a Jew, ask me, a Samaritan, for a drink?"

Jesus replied, "If you knew who it was that was asking you for a drink of water, you would ask *him* for a drink, and he would give you living water. . . . And that water would become a spring within you, welling up to eternal life."

The woman said, "Oh, give me this water always." Jesus told her to go get her husband, and she answered, "I have no husband."

Then Jesus said to her, "You told the truth there. You've had five husbands, and the man you're living with now isn't your husband." He noticed her marital disorder, but he didn't scold her about it. Instead, he offered her new life, new hope. So she believed in Jesus and brought the whole village with her. That's the hope Jesus offers everyone who—in the midst of their human failure and weakness—has turned to him.

The Lord's expectations of us are high, but he picks us up each time we fall, sets us up right on our feet, and says *"Try again . . . with me at your side."* I don't believe in divorce; I believe in Jesus.

God of creation, when you made us human beings in your image and created male and female to become one flesh in marriage, we know that you didn't expect us to hurt and wound one another. Give those who are married the gifts of tolerance, patience and generosity in their life together. And teach us how to regard those whose marriages are troubled, and those who are suffering through divorce, not with judgment but with compassion and love. Make us more like Jesus, for we pray in his name. Amen.

54. WORSHIP, A SACRIFICE
OF PRAISE.

The Song of the Three Young Men, 29-34

I want to begin by asking you a simple question: "What did you come here expecting to *do* this morning?" Notice, I'm not asking *why* you came. Maybe you're here because a friend brought you, or because you came out of duty, or because you're a member of the church and you always come on Sundays. I'm asking, "What did you come here expecting to *do*?" Think about how you might answer.

When we began our service, the first thing we did was to sing the great old hymn that goes *"Holy, holy, holy! Lord God Almighty! Early in the morning our song shall rise to thee. Holy, holy, holy! Merciful and mighty, God in three Persons, blessed Trinity."* That's one hymn everybody can sing—not just us, but all the Protestants and the Catholics too. Everybody knows it. Surveys say it's the most popular hymn in America—#1 on the "Hymn-singers' Top Forty."

After the Old Testament lesson, we stood and recited an ancient canticle—but in modern English. It comes from a little book in the Apocrypha that says it was sung by the three young Hebrews after Nebuchadnezzar threw them into the fiery furnace. "Glory to you, Lord God of our fathers; you are worthy of praise; glory to you. Glory to you for the radiance of your holy name; we will praise you and highly exalt you forever. . . . Glory to you, . . . glory to you, . . . glory to you."

I haven't always been an Episcopalian. Until I went to college I was a Presbyterian, and as was true back in the 50's for all good little Presbyterians, when I turned twelve our pastor expected me to memorize the Westminster Shorter Catechism. I'll never forget the first question in that little booklet. It was: "What is the chief end of man?" And the answer was: *"The chief end of man is to glorify God and enjoy him forever."*

"Glory to you, Lord God of our fathers . . . we will praise you and highly exalt you forever."

When I was twelve, I wondered: How do we "enjoy God forever"? I still wonder about that.—If we're not "enjoying" God now, how do we get started? I think the main reason we're here this morning is to enjoy God. And that enjoyment begins with *worship*.

When you see a cartoon picture of people with haloes, floating on clouds, wearing long white robes, and playing harps, you know it's supposed to represent heaven. Cartoons are meant to be funny, but—like other kinds of humor—they convey some truth. The reading from Isaiah we heard earlier and the long passage from the Book of Revelation are word-pictures that try to open a window into heaven, where the main activity is not exactly harp-playing, but rather *worship* . . . which—according to the Book of Psalms—includes not only harp-playing, but organ-playing, and trumpet-playing, bell-ringing, cymbal clanging, hand-clapping, singing, dancing, and shouting. (Sounds like fun, doesn't it? It's probably what those 17th century Presbyterians had in mind when they said we were meant to enjoy God forever.)—It reminds me of kindergarten, when the music teacher gave all of us kids rattles and drums and noise makers to play within the rhythm band. Of course, that was before we got old enough to be very self-conscious. We just made a joyful noise and had a good time.

Maybe we need to remember that Jesus said we had to become like little children if we wanted to enter the Kingdom of Heaven.

When Biblical writers tried to convey a vision of heaven, their vision always centered on worship and praise being offered to God by angels, archangels, cherubim, seraphim, and the white-robed assembly of the redeemed, gathered around the throne of God. So: If we're Christians who believe that heaven is—in some sense—our destiny, then we have to believe that our destiny also must be, as the old Calvinist catechism puts it, "to glorify God and enjoy him forever."

And that *glorifying* and *enjoying* starts here, with the people of God gathered for worship.

Pardon me for getting academic now, but at this point I think we need a definition. So let's think about the meaning of worship. "Worship" is short for *worth-ship*. (Stay with me here.) Worship is an activity that acknowledges the worth, value, dignity, or status of something or someone. In the religious sense, every act of real worship reinforces our sense of the ultimate value—the top rank or transcendent worth—of God.

In fact, whatever is the focus of my conscious valuing activities—that means what I spend most of my time, imagination, money, and energy on—*that* is my god. Therefore, when the focus of my valuing activities is something *other* than the All-Holy One-in-Three to whom we have been singing and praying here this morning, I am practicing what we can only call *idolatry*. I'm worshiping something that does NOT have ultimate, transcendent worth. I am offering sacrifice to a false god . . . or maybe a whole pantheon of false gods.

Here's another definition: *A sacrifice is a costly gift, joyfully given.* Worship must include the *offering of sacrifice*—the glad giving of a precious gift—because that's the only act which can certify the ultimate value that belongs to what I worship (that is, to my God). So, if I say that I believe in the One True God, Father, Son and Holy Spirit, but I offer God nothing of genuine value to me—like my time, or my intellect, or my money—my claim is invalidated, and I'm shown to be a fraud. My behavior gives the lie to what I say. Instead, it demonstrates that my *real* value-focus is elsewhere. When my most precious offerings are given to something else—like improving my appearance, or getting rich, or acquiring influence over other people, or seeking entertainment and pleasure—then that "something else" is my false god, my idol.

Worship is something we *do*. It calls for effort and concentration. In America our attitude toward many things has been formed by the experience of being passive spectators—sitting in front of the TV. Authentic worship, though, has to be participatory, not passive. It demands that we be focused, engaged, and active. However, more often than not we come to church looking for somebody to inspire, instruct, or entertain us.

But, you know, worship isn't about *us*. It's about God. It's an offering whereby we confess and reaffirm the worth of God and importance of God for us. Americans revere "the market," and the market says we reveal the value of something to us by how much we're willing to pay for it. Common sense and analogy with the rest of our lives tells us that if we don't put anything *into* something, we're unlikely to get anything *out of* it. We invest ourselves deeply only in things that really matter to us.—If education matters to you, when you were in school you studied. If a sport matters to you, you practice so you can play well. If your investments matter to you, you take care to manage your money.—And if God matters to you, you're serious about worship.

We work at what counts to us, and worship calls us to work. It's a sacrificial offering of our mind and imagination and energy to God.—Here's a paradox, though: God is the focus and recipient of our worship, but worship really only benefits *us*. After all, if God is truly God, he doesn't need our praises. God has no deficiencies. God isn't like an insecure human being who will wither unless we give him lots of positive strokes.—But our souls will wither if we *don't* worship.

Worship is like giving a special gift to the person we love the most. Don't we always want to give great gifts and do wonderful things for our beloved? Cost or personal effort is no obstacle. Love inspires us to sacrifice.

Do you remember the gospel story of the woman who broke the alabaster bottle of precious perfume and poured it over Jesus' feet? The *only* person who objected to such extravagance, the only person who said, "What a waste!" was Judas Iscariot.

Those who love the Lord are ready to "waste" their time, money, creativity, energy and intellect on him. Our songs of praise, our prayers, our acts of devotion—even something as simple as coming into the church a little early and getting down on our knees is costly perfume poured out on the Lord . . . just because we love him.

There's a void in the human heart that every person alive is trying to fill with something. There's an empty shrine in the center of our souls. That's the place that was made for God, because God made *us* for himself. God intended from the dawn of creation to make his home in our hearts, so we might "enjoy him forever."

Worship opens the door and lets him in.

55. AMAZING GRACE.

Matthew 20:1-16

I read a story recently about a woman in an airport who was waiting for a "red-eye" flight. It was around midnight. The woman was tired after a long day at the office, but she was hungry, too, and had a craving for something sweet. So she bought herself a little box of gourmet cookies in one of the shops on the concourse. She sat down in the departure lounge and opened her hand bag, looking for a book she'd brought along to read. A man sat down one chair away from her, and the next thing she knew he'd put the box of cookies on the seat between them, opened it, and was eating one!

This upset the woman but she didn't want to create a scene. Besides, she thought, "He's only eating *one*." But then he took another one. Rather than make a big issue of it, the woman simply took a cookie for herself. Then the man took another one, and she took another one.

This kept up for the next half-hour. He ate one and then she ate one, until there was only a single cookie left in the box. The man picked up the final tasty little cookie and, smiling at her, said to the woman, "Would you like to split it with me?"

She was so mad that she snatched it out of his hand, took her handbag and stormed away. Later, when she got on the plane, she was still fuming. Before she sat down, she opened her handbag to get out her book. But what she pulled out instead was the box of cookies she'd bought, and it was still unopened. *Oops!* The man she'd been so mad at had been generously sharing his (identical) box of cookies with her.—Very embarrassing.

In today's parable Jesus invites us to question our values as well as our assumptions about other people.

Some of the most beautiful poetry in the Hebrew Bible is found in the 55th chapter of Isaiah. Here are three familiar verses:

> "Ho, everyone who thirsts,
>   come to the waters;
> and you that have no money,
>   come, buy, and eat!
> Come, buy wine and milk
>   without money and without price." [55:1]

> "My thoughts are not your thoughts,
>   nor are your ways my ways,
>   says the Lord.
> For as the heavens are higher
>   than the earth,
> so are my ways higher
>   than your ways,
> and my thoughts
>   than your thoughts." [55:8-9]

God's ways are higher than our ways. The Bible is chock full of stories that communicate the truth that God is *not* like us. God is generous, merciful, patient, and kind, while we are—to put it gently—different in many ways. *God's ways are higher than our ways.* Jesus' parable of the workers in the vineyard is one of many he told to demonstrate that God sees life differently from the way we do. There are similar illustrations in all the gospels.

Luke's gospel tells about the shepherd who left ninety-nine sheep on the hillside while he went searching for one that was lost. That bothers me! What if something had happened to the ninety-nine while the shepherd was off looking for the one? You and I tend to be bottom line types. I'd guard the ninety-nine and write off the one, wouldn't you?

From John comes the story about a woman who poured a pint of Chanel Number Five—or something similar—on Jesus' feet. On his feet! That perfume was worth a year's wages!—Wouldn't an ounce of perfume on Jesus' feet have been plenty? (After all it was on his *feet*, for God's sake!) The rest could then have been sold and the money donated to charity or put in the local synagogue building fund. That would have been *my* advice—same as the advice of sensible Judas.

In Mark there's the poor widow who put her last two tiny copper coins into the Temple offering box for love-gifts—free-will offerings, not tithes, not dues. Jesus praised the woman who, despite her poverty, offered all she had. But he belittled the rich men who were ostentatiously pouring in whole bags of money because they still had plenty more where that came from.—Unlike Jesus, *I* know that a church can't make it on just "the widow's mite." It's a nice gesture, sure, but churches need generous givers of big gifts if we're going to keep our ministries afloat, right?

Finally there's the parable we hear today from Matthew, about the vineyard owner who hired workers to pick grapes. He went to the local marketplace and hired some laborers at sunrise. He went back at midmorning and hired some more, and still others at noon and mid-afternoon. He even went back and hired some more not long before quitting time. At quitting time, he paid everyone a full day's wage—even if they'd only worked an hour. We hear this story and say: "That's just not fair! What about 'an honest day's pay for an honest day's work'"? (Isn't that right there in the Bible along with "God helps those who help themselves"?)

Jesus says our God is One who values the solitary stray as much as he does the whole flock, and who prizes a poor widow's love-gift of her last pennies above rich men's millions, a God who rewards latecomers as generously as the early birds. What employer in his right mind would pay the same amount for one hour's work as for twelve? Jesus' story makes no human, economic sense, and that was exactly his point. It's all about *grace*, you see, and grace can't be calculated like wages. Grace can't be calculated at all. It is, quite simply, *amazing!* The parable of the generous vineyard owner tells us about a God whose heart's desire is to bless his people, not to measure out his love according to some contract, in careful spoonfuls.

Keep this in mind. In Jesus' day, most men in Galilee were landless laborers. They would gather in the market square every day before dawn, waiting to be hired. Landowners would come and hire some workers for whatever tasks needed doing that day. The most able bodied men and those known as good workers were always hired first. Landowners would agree to pay them the standard minimum wage for a day's work: one denarius.

In Jesus' story, the compassionate vineyard owner goes back to the market square several more times—mid-morning, noon, mid-afternoon, and even late in the day. Each time he returns, the men waiting to be hired are ones who have been waiting there since dawn. They've not been hired because they're not able-bodied. They are the weak, the old or the very young, the lame or those of bad reputation. But they're all *poor* men, and if they do not work their families will not eat. Each time the vineyard owner returns he hires those whom others have passed over, workers deemed less likely to be productive. When he hires them, he offers no contract. He simply says that he "will pay them whatever is *right*." They trust his promise and follow him into the vineyard. Notice: they *trust his word*, and follow him! (Hello? This is *Jesus* talking!)—At day's end, he pays every worker a normal day's wage—starting with the last-hired and ending with those who'd been there since dawn.

The landowner, who clearly represents God, gives what he deems "right" to the workers who have trusted him—a full day's pay for only a few hours' work. However, what is "right" in God's eyes seems arbitrary and unjust to workers who have labored since sun-up and see themselves as having a fair claim to more.

Jesus has a way of using outrageous events in his stories, and proposing ideas that challenged the conventional wisdom of his audience. *God's ways are different from our ways. God's ways are higher than our ways.* This story of the workers in the vineyard has a point in common with the parable of the prodigal son, who was welcomed home by his father and treated to a lavish party, leaving his always faithful older brother complaining that their father was unfair.

Now, isn't this the kind of thing that gives us trouble? We're willing that the vineyard owner should be generous to the men who worked fewer hours, but we think those who worked *longer* deserved a bonus. Maybe that's because we identify with the ones who had labored all day.—But is this accurate? If we're realistic about ourselves and our own relationship with God, we might consider that most of us are really more akin to those hired later, even at the end of the day. Are we not people who have received God's gift of grace in our time of need, not people who have "fulfilled our contract" with Him? Let's ask ourselves, have we "given God his due"? Have we truly loved Him with all our heart and soul and mind and strength and our neighbors as ourselves? Have we? Can we say, "O.K., God, you *owe* me?" I think not.

The message of the parable is this: It's by God's grace—and not our merit—that we enjoy his blessings, that we are welcomed into his Kingdom. *The great task for us is not to be good enough to earn God's favor, but to be humble enough to accept God's favor as a gift.* And if you need it spelled out, the moral of this story is this: We who have received God's grace are meant to share it.

56. THE PHARISEE AND THE
TAX COLLECTOR.

Luke 18:9-14

Jesus begins his story about the Pharisee and the Tax Collector by saying, "Two men went up to the Temple to pray." That was not the same kind of thing as us going to church on a Sunday. And they were also not going to the Temple because it was the expected thing to do and lots of other people were doing it, the way Christians fill the churches at Christmas and Easter. These two men went to the Temple deliberately and privately on a very ordinary day. Both of them went alone, seeking to draw near to God as best they could.

We know God is everywhere and we can pray anywhere. (That is, we *can* if we *will*.) But in Jesus' story the Pharisee and the Tax Collector came to the House of the Lord to present themselves before God, both spiritually and physically. Jesus says they "came to pray," not to make an offering. They didn't arrive with sacrificial animals or money to put in the collection box. To pray means to enter into a deliberate communion with God, a deliberate opening of the soul to God. Both men came for the same reason.—So far, so good.

The Pharisee came to give thanks to God. But when we look at it, the Pharisee's thanksgiving prayer seems focused more on himself and his achievements than on God whom he's supposed to be thanking. Notice how often he uses the first person singular: "I thank thee that I am not like other men. I fast twice a week. I tithe on all my income." The law required Jews to fast once a year and to tithe on agricultural produce only. The Pharisee is calling God's attention to the fact that he's doing much more than God requires.—He reminds me of a child riding his bike with no hands, calling out to mom or dad to notice. "Lord, look at what *I'm* doing! . . . See? . . . See? I'm a really *good* person, right? . . . *Right?*" There doesn't seem to be much that God needs to do in the life of this Pharisee other than agree with him.

Most of us have had to write a résumé at one time or another when we've applied for a job. I've written my share, the last one in 2003 when I applied to become rector of this parish. When I look at that old résumé it seems to resemble the Pharisee's prayer a little bit. Lots of "I" statements. It tells the reader that I'm a superior, competent, experienced priest whom this parish should be excited to call as rector. I emphasize my many accomplishments, my numerous skills, and I suggest that the wonderful things I have done elsewhere I will probably do here, too.

All of the stuff in that résumé was true enough, *but*—as with all résumés—there was no mention of the things I can't do, or don't do very well, or all the mistakes I've made. (And there have been plenty.) There was a list of references, people who were sure to say good things about me if asked, but there was no list of people whose observations might have been unflattering.

In Jesus' story, the pious Pharisee notices that there's a Tax Collector there in the Court of Israel with him. (I'm not sure how he could identify anyone as a Tax Collector, since they didn't wear uniforms. But this is, after all, just a *story*, not a news report.) The Pharisee is up front, as close as a lay person could get to the Holy of Holies. The Tax Collector is "standing far off"—maybe in a back corner by himself. The Tax Collector figures correctly that any worshipers who recognized him wouldn't want to stand close to him. So rather than push his way up front and watch other people flee as if he had the plague, he seeks a secluded spot.

The Pharisee includes a reference to the Tax Collector in his thanksgiving to God. He says, "I thank thee, dear God, that I am not like that Tax Collector."—What arrogance for the Pharisee to assume that he knows enough about the Tax Collector to recognize that he doesn't want to be like him. Maybe the Tax Collector is a wonderful husband and a good father. Maybe he's generous to the poor. Maybe the Tax Collector tithes on all his income, too. Maybe he fasts three times a week. (He probably doesn't, but the Pharisee has no idea, really.) The Pharisee doesn't know anything about the man except that he's a Tax Collector, and is therefore—*ipso facto*—a sinner.

The Pharisee seems to have come up to pray at the Temple in order to maintain his positive self-image, to reassure himself (and God) that he is, indeed, a righteous man.—But what about the Tax Collector? Why is *he* there in the Temple on this ordinary day?

The Tax Collector gets off by himself and won't even presume to lift his eyes toward the Holy of Holies. He strikes his breast with his fist and prays a simple prayer, "God, have mercy on me, a sinner."—No résumé. No thanksgiving, even. He's just asking for mercy, asking God to supply what he lacks, because he's very much in touch with his own deficiencies, which he appears to think are too numerous to name. The Pharisee came to stroke his ego; the Tax Collector came to get help. The obvious question for us is: what do we want from God when we pray, approval or mercy?

The Pharisee wasn't lying to God. He really did fast twice a week. He really did tithe on all his income. He set himself apart from others by his total faithfulness to the Law of God. By the standards of his religion, he was a righteous man. There were not many Pharisees, and other Jews treated them with great respect and deference. No doubt, he wanted to set a good example for others. Wanting to set a good example for others is a worthy ambition, as long as we don't go around saying to people, *"Don't you think I'm setting a good example?"*

All we know about the Tax Collector is that when he was standing in this holy place, in the presence of the Holy God, he felt only his deficiencies. In the House of the Lord, he felt like a sinner. He probably looked up at the righteous Pharisee and thought, "Oh, how wonderful it would be to be as close to God as *he* is!"

The hook in this story may be our own temptation to identify with the Tax Collector rather than the Pharisee, although we probably resemble the Pharisee in more ways than we'd like to think. Haven't most of us occasionally looked at someone else and thought, "There but for the grace of God, go I"? That may seem o.k. at first. After all, we're giving (some) credit to God. But comparing ourselves with others is always dangerous. Always.—Are we presuming that *we* know how to accept God's grace, but *that* poor soul doesn't? . . . Or can't? . . . Or won't?—How do we know? God may well be working in that person's life in ways our eyes are unable to see.

The nature of grace is paradoxical. It can only be received by those who have learned empathy for others. Only the merciful can receive mercy. Here's how this parable nails most of us: As soon as we fall prey to the common temptation to divide humanity into distinct groups—such as "the blessed people" and the "un-blessed people", those who are "open to God" and those who are "not open to God"—we've joined up with the Pharisee, who can't see that there's anything he personally needs from God other than a reassuring pat on the back.

This parable is about how we *pray* . . . how we most honestly present ourselves to God. Sincere prayer has to begin with a realistic appraisal of who I am before God. And if I'm going to be realistic, then I will always recall that I'm a sinner in need of a Savior. I can't lift myself to heaven by my own bootstraps.

Even if I have "let my light shine" in such a way that everyone around me can see my good works, it's important for me to understand (and make clear to others) that my good works are actually God's work *in* me, not my personal accomplishments. The glory belongs to our Father in heaven. Even if I do have much to be thankful for, I can't ever forget that God sees beyond my résumé. He knows that I'm likely to yield to temptations and am always in need of his mercy and forgiveness. Like the Tax Collector in Jesus' story, all of us come to God empty, in need of being fed. Filthy, in need of being washed. Ignorant, in need of being taught. Sinners, in need of being forgiven.

The Pharisee came to give thanks. Thanksgiving is good, but prayers of thanks go best if they're something like this:

"Dear God, I thank you that I'm just like everyone else. I've been shaped in your image, with a mind to know and a heart to love. Thank you that like everyone else, I've been embraced by the crucified arms of your Son who died to take away the sins of the whole world. So, now I too can claim Jesus as my brother. Thank

you God, that you judge me as you do everyone else, not by my appearance, or my bank account, or my race, or my politics, or the number of my good deeds, but by the love that's your free gift to all your children. You choose to treat me so much better than I deserve. Thank you, Father. Thank you.

God, I thank you that, despite our many differences, I am in fact remarkably like everyone around me in this world. Thank you for making me the same as everybody else, because that means I'm closer to your Son, who became what we are: completely and wonderfully human. Thank you for letting me see today that there is a little bit of the Pharisee in me. I'm sorry for that. I hope that there might be some of the Tax Collector in me, too, to make up for it.

If I am to thank you for making me different, let it be that because of your mercy I'm different from what I would have been if I had been left to my own devices, without your Son in my life. I'm always in need of your mercy. And, please God, help me to be as merciful to others as you have been to me. I pray these things In Jesus' name."

Can we say "Amen" to that?

57. TAKE TIME TO BE HOLY.

All Saints' Day
Wisdom of Solomon 3:1-9

I borrowed this Methodist hymnal from the Aspen Community Church last year when we were having our services in their building, and I haven't returned it yet. I think I'm going to have to go over and give Pastor Jane twenty bucks so I can keep it, because I like it. This week I was flipping through it and noticed that there's a whole section entitled "Personal Holiness." I thought: "How appropriate. Sunday will be All Saints' Day, and *'saints'* means 'the holy ones.' And to be "holy" means to be *given to God.* I bet there's a sermon idea here somewhere."—And, sure enough, there was.

Now, as a rule, folks don't hear a lot about personal holiness from Episcopal pulpits. The expression "personal holiness" makes Southern boys like me remember ladies with beehive hairdos, wearing long-sleeved dresses and no makeup. These would have been women from the holiness churches—mothers of some of our school friends. They were definitely not the style-setters for our crowd.

There's no special section in our own Episcopal hymnal where we can go to look up songs meant to inspire us to be holy. So I looked in the "Personal Holiness" section of the Methodist hymnal, and the very first song was one called, *"Take time to be holy."* The second verse goes like this: *"Take time to be holy, the world rushes on; / spend much time in secret with Jesus alone. / By looking to Jesus, like him thou shalt be; / thy friends in thy conduct his likeness shall see."*

"Take time to be holy; the world rushes on." We don't like to take much time for anything. We don't like to *wait*. We want what we want when we want it; and we mostly want it right now. Don't you think? "Taking time" is alien to our culture. We're all about "rushing on."

We associate waiting with *waste*—wasting time. "Time is money," the saying goes. Most of us have enough real money (though many would like to have more), but nobody has more than 24 hours in each day. We can accumulate money, but we can't accumulate time in the same way. So we save time by traveling on Interstate highways rather than country roads on our vacation trips because "we just can't wait to get there." People save time by sending text messages instead of making phone calls, by having an instant lawn put in, and by talking on cell phones while they drive to the pick-up window at Taco Bell—so they can munch their tacos in the car while driving to the mall for a little one-stop shopping during lunch hour.

Advances in technology have made it possible for us to have swift gratification of almost every wish. Some people think it all started with tea bags. (Do many tea-drinkers still boil water in a kettle on the stove, then pour it into a teapot and wait for the tea to steep? Only in Britain.)

I remember the laborious process of typing term papers in college on my faithful old Smith-Corona portable—doing my final draft, then discovering errors or mis-arrangements of paragraphs which forced me to re-type the pages. Now I get frustrated when the spell-checker in my computer can't catch all my mistakes (because that mis-used word *is* still a correctly *spelled* word), and so I have to go back and insert my own corrections.

Speaking of computers, I used to drum my fingers with impatience while I waited for my old inkjet printer to perform its task. It could only produce six pages a minute or just four if I used color graphics. (Ink *"jet"* indeed!) It was too slow; it made me wait. I don't like to wait, so I bought a new, faster printer.

Holiness can't be hurried. . . . That is, *if* you want to be holy. That's why the song I found is entitled *"Take Time to be Holy."*

But the question is: do you *want* to be holy?—Maybe you never really thought about it. Or maybe you have thought about it, but decided a long time ago that "holiness" was not something you personally wanted to aim for—particularly not if being holy might require you to quit your job and go to work in a leper colony or give up booze and your monthly poker night. Or both.

But I'm here today to ask you to think about it again, because every Christian is called to a life of personal holiness. No exceptions. Including you and me.—And don't worry, *holiness* will require you neither to leave home nor become a teetotaller. *But you will have to learn to pray.* And I'm not just talking about saying prayers. I mean learning the kind of praying that builds a relationship of loving daily intimacy with God.

Relationships like that are not formed overnight or on a weekend retreat. All loving relationships—both in the merely human sphere and in the *divine*-human sphere—can be developed only if we're willing to waste time with one another. Learning to pray will require you to spend quality time just sitting there with God.—Holiness can't be hurried.

Holy people are the ones among us whose lives are marked by a passion for God. They are given to God. They perceive instinctively, as Gerard Manley Hopkins wrote, that "the world is charged with the grandeur of God." They see God in mud puddles and sunrises, traffic jams and babies' smiles . . . Everywhere! For holy people, every bush is burning. To borrow from Shakespeare, they read books in running brooks, hear sermons in stone and see God's hand in everything. Their ears are attuned to the whispers of heaven. And the main thing they want to experience in life is unity with God. They want to be like Jesus.

Holy people sometimes have a marvelous knack for unabashedly, but kindly, telling us the painful truths we need to hear—even if we didn't know we *needed* to hear them 'til we heard them. They have the kind of courage only found in single-minded people, people who are serving just one Master and feel answerable only to him.—Would you like to be that kind of Christian? Would you like to be a *saint?* . . . A holy man? . . . A holy woman? *I* would.

Every culture, every age, and every religion has had its holy men and holy women, its saints. And we're no exception. We celebrate and give thanks for them today, on All Saints' Day. I'm not talking about the "Sanctimonious Suzie" or "Holier-than-Thou Harry" types, the characters that populate novels written to skewer religious hypocrisy. Of course, we've all known people like them. And I'm not talking about professional holy men or women, who cultivate a national following and have their own TV shows (or in some cases even their own networks). That's just show biz. I'm talking about men and women who will never be on TV or write a best-seller, but whose holiness shines out from their ordinary lives and exerts a powerful attraction on us. Hypocrisy is repulsive; but holiness is magnetic.

I was reminded the other day of something that Fr. Terry Fullam used to say. Back in the seventies and eighties Terry wanted to set the Episcopal Church on fire for Jesus, to move Episcopalians out of our traditional state of intellectual skepticism and emotional detachment into a passionate engagement with God. Terry used to say, "You know, there's nothing more nominal than a 'nominal' Episcopalian!"

I don't want us to be a community of nominal Episcopalians here in Aspen. Let's not be just a polite religious society. *Let's be holy people. Let's be saints!*—That's our calling. That's what we're meant to be. Sure, we're imperfect. But God isn't finished with us yet.

To want to be holy is not a spiritually arrogant goal. Holy people don't set themselves up on a pedestal. Saints aren't isolated from life. They don't think of themselves as unusual. The fact is, they don't spend much time thinking about *themselves* at all. Instead, they reach out to you and me—sometimes without even knowing it—and draw us into a relationship with them and, therefore, with God. They are *given to God* and they share that sense of givenness, that sense of joyful belonging, with us. It is incredibly attractive.

Jesus asks us to aim high, to aim for holiness, and *holiness takes time.* Hurried people, caught up in the rushing around that our world takes for granted, can't muster much more than lukewarm, nominal allegiance. But Jesus wants our time. As the song I found in the Methodist hymnal says, "*Take time to be holy, the world rushes on; / spend much time in secret with Jesus alone.*"

God wants us to put spending time with him first on our to-do list every day. Sure, God will forgive us if we go for it with all our heart and yet fall short of the mark. But he doesn't want us to give up trying. Saints keep trying, no matter how much time it takes.

Let's do it. Take time to be holy, starting today.

58. COME TO ME, AND I WILL GIVE YOU REST.

Matthew: 11:25-30

Our usual 8:00 service here is the Holy Eucharist, Rite One. Part of that service—just as in earlier Books of Common Prayer all the way back to the very first one in 1549—is a section that used to be called "the Comfortable Words." It comes right after the Confession and Absolution, and it's a collection of verses from various places in the New Testament. It starts off with a verse from the gospel for today—but in King James Version language. "Come to me, all ye that travail and are heavy laden, and I will refresh you." . . . Or, as our modern Bible translation puts it, "Come to me, all you that are weary and are carrying heavy burdens, and I will give you rest."

I wonder how many of us here this morning have a sense of being weighed down by circumstances in our lives. Jesus spoke these words originally to townspeople and peasants in Galilee who had a variety of different burdens to bear. First, they had the daily burden of survival in a subsistence economy. Famine was always just around the corner, and nobody except the very rich could be sure that they'd always have enough to eat. Many of them worked on large estates, owned by foreigners; their economic future was always insecure. They lived under the heel of Roman conquerors who imposed heavy taxes and whose soldiers could require forced labor from them without prior notice.

In addition, they went to the synagogue on the Sabbath and heard the Pharisees and Scribes urging them to be more zealous and meticulous in keeping all the requirements of the Jewish Law—observances that were commonly described, even by the Pharisees themselves, as a "yoke," the "yoke of the Law." This portrayed the practice of religion itself as a kind of burdensome servitude.

The people Jesus taught and touched were people who—for the most part—obviously did not have an easy life. They had all kinds of burdens to bear. . . . But what about us? Our lives are nothing like the lives of Galilean peasants in the year A.D. 29. Do *we* feel "weighed down"?

I know a woman (who, by the way, does *not* live in Aspen or visit here) who has no job and no significant volunteer work that she does. Her only burden—if you can call it that—is traveling around the country to visit her family, planning the next vacation, and organizing social events to fill her calendar. People who don't know her, or know other people like her, might laugh and say that they'd like to be as *un*-burdened as this woman. But, in fact, her idle life itself is a burden because it's so empty. I think she's looking for something to give meaning to her existence.

We all know people who have burdens they would never label as burdens. For example: What about persons who carry the burden of needing to stay in perfect control of themselves—and also need to control everyone else they know? What about the people who always have to be right and never make a mistake? (Being perfect is quite a burden.) And there are individuals who always need to win, always be successful, and never be seen to fail or show any weakness. There are people who have a compulsive need to prove their worth over and over again by ever-greater achievements in making money or climbing the corporate ladder or in some other realm where they're competing with others.—Of course, these people's burdens are all neurotic. But they're still *burdens*. . . . And aren't all of us just a little bit neurotic?

When I think about it, I really can't think of any people I know who are NOT burdened in some way. The people who aren't obviously neurotic are mostly either facing financial problems, business problems, marital problems, addiction problems, have troubled children to deal with, or have a health crisis to face. And then there are the people—maybe some of you here this morning—who bear the heavy burden of leadership. When you're the boss, you're in charge. You live in an environment where everybody is looking to you for answers, or at least for guidance.

Heck, even we pastors have our burdens.—There's nothing that makes me feel more weighed down than to be invited to speak somewhere and be told (as if this would make the job easier), "We just want you to come and give us a little inspiration."—Do these people think I can be inspirational on demand?

Jesus said, "Come to me, all you that are weary and are carrying heavy burdens, and I will give you rest. Take my yoke upon you, and learn from me; for I am gentle and humble in heart, and you will find rest for your souls. For my yoke is easy, and my burden is light."

When I feel like I'm being asked to produce inspiration on demand, I have to remind myself that I'm not on my own in this ministry. I'm a servant of Christ. I'm under *his* yoke. He's steering, not me. Anything I have to say that's inspirational at all, or that's even worth hearing, can only come from him. My job is to keep the ears of my heart open so I can hear him and repeat what He says.

It's the same way with all the burdens we carry. Even the neurotic ones—maybe even *especially* the neurotic ones. Jesus says, *"Come to me . . ."* One of the important things that Christ does in our lives is to show us the difference between the kinds of things we have to carry if we're normal human beings, and the neurotic things that neither we nor anybody else should try to carry.

People who can't figure out what to do with their lives need to come to Jesus. People who are struggling with trying to be perfect, or who feel the need to control their lives and the lives of others, or who need constantly to be proving their value as human beings again and again need to come to Jesus. People who feel like they're really losers unless they can win every contest need to come to Jesus and listen to what he has to say: "You don't need to prove yourself to me by your achievements, and there's no other Judge whose opinion is more important. I don't expect you to be perfect, just to admit that you need help. And if you feel like your life is empty and meaningless, come, follow me and I'll help you fill your idle hours with the joy of serving others."

Notice, Jesus doesn't say "Come to me and I'll make your burdens disappear." He doesn't say "I'll carry your load for you," though that's a common piece of conventional pulpit rhetoric. But what he does say is "By placing *my* yoke on your shoulders, I'll give you the means of carrying everything else that you *need* to carry."

When we have legitimate burdens: like the responsibility for raising and educating children, taking care of a sick spouse or parent, meeting our financial obligations, teaching students, or running a business, the Lord doesn't make those responsibilities disappear. But he comes alongside us and says, "Take my yoke upon you."

In Hebrew the ordinary word for "yoke" means an ox-yoke—and these yokes were always double. Nobody plowed with a single ox. The common expression, "a yoke of oxen," always meant *two* animals. When Jesus says, *"Take my yoke upon you,"* he's asking us to be teamed with him. He says, "Learn from me, for I am gentle and humble in heart, and you will find rest for your souls." He's the Lord of All, but he cares about ordinary people like you and me. He wants to give us rest.

Come, learn from Jesus. The plow-man teamed a young, untrained animal with a trained animal. Yoked with Christ, we learn from him. He carries our load with us every step of life's way, and in every step he's teaching us.

Sure, this "yoke" thing is a metaphor. Christ is not going to appear in your office on Tuesday to sit down and help you figure out how to finance the new plant. He's not going to take the kids to day camp or drive your mother-in-law down to Grand Junction for her appointment with the eye doctor on Friday. You're going to have to do those things yourself.

But if you come to him, his Spirit will give you the support you need in order to live your life and carry your load with peace and serenity—even in the most trying of situations. With Jesus at your side, the load will never be too much. And when that burden is a cross you are carrying for others' sake, you will taste the mercy of the Lord.

59. BY THEIR FRUITS
YOU SHALL KNOW THEM.

Luke 13:1-9

Most of Jesus' neighbors believed the Near Eastern folk wisdom that *bad things happen to bad people*. If somebody died because of an earthquake or was stricken with leprosy, there was bound to be a person nearby to remark, "See! He's a sinner. He's being punished by God."

Imagining other people's misfortunes as consequences of their moral failures wasn't just an ancient Near Eastern trait, as we all know. The habit lingers in 21st century America. (Just remember the blather from people like Pat Robertson when the Haiti earthquake happened.) And haven't you heard people say things like: "Most of those people in the shelters wouldn't be homeless if they had any gumption. They're just lazy and want other people to provide for them. They probably spend every penny they get on booze." That kind of thinking, aside from being both self-righteous and judgmental, illustrates a phenomenon we call "blaming the victim."—You hear it all the time.

But if something bad happens to us—if we get a scary diagnosis from the doctor or we wreck the car—don't we think, "Why me? I don't deserve this." And we probably don't. Of course, if you continue to smoke after being told it could cause lung cancer, or if you're texting on your iPhone while driving the car, you might anticipate some adverse consequences.

We don't inhabit a simple cause-and-effect moral universe. The truth is that bad things happen to good people about as often as they do to wicked people. The innocent sometimes suffer. The guilty sometimes escape punishment. Honest, hard-working folks get laid off and can't find new jobs, while sleazy characters hustling questionable products seem to be finding new ways to make a buck, regardless of the recession.—And we sigh, "It's not fair."

Our lives, our welfare, our health, our economic system—all of these depend on people and circumstances beyond our control. Philosophers say we live in a contingent universe, and for there to be authentic freedom in the universe there needs to be as much liberty for evil as for good. (Now *there's* some food for thought.—But those thoughts will have to wait for a different sermon.)

Jesus disagreed with "bad things only happen to bad people" thinking. He said that the Galileans whom Pontius Pilate slaughtered in the Temple and the Jerusalemites who were walking by the tower at Siloam when it fell on them weren't any worse than other people. We're all sinners of one kind or another. Those people didn't meet their unhappy ends because they were more wicked than anyone else. God wasn't punishing them; they were just accident victims. "But," Jesus said to the crowd of bystanders, "If you don't repent, you'll perish too."—What did he mean by that?

I think he was saying that while misfortune and natural disaster are in the natural, random order of things in a contingent universe—and not instances of divine judgment—we still mustn't think that there will never be *any* consequences for our disobedience to God's will. Jesus said that God looks for *fruit* from our lives the way the gardener in his parable looked for fruit from the fig tree in the vineyard.

Remember, Jesus said, "By their fruits you shall know them."

The first thing to notice is that the production of fruit is natural for a tree. It's expected. A mature fruit tree—whatever the kind—is naturally going to bear its fruit in due season. The more mature the tree, the more plentiful the fruit. (Those of us with gray hair need to take notice. Maturity and moral productivity are supposed to go together.)

God expects that we human beings are going to produce something good, something desirable in our lives. That means it isn't enough for us simply to abstain from evil. God is looking for positive good from you and me. He's looking for *virtues*. That's the word: virtues. And it's as logical for God to expect this as it is for a Mesa County orchard owner to look at a mature peach tree and expect that—in the proper season of the year—his tree is going to have good peaches on it.

Now the wonderful thing about the parable of the fig tree in the vineyard is that *it shows us the character of God.* It's not God's nature to rush to judgment. It IS God's nature to give us another chance. It's his nature to consider what might help us be the fruitful people he intended us to be.

When we look at this parable, some readers think they see God in the person of the vineyard owner and Jesus as the gardener who asks God to delay his judgment for a while. But look again. Look at the owner: he is demanding and impatient; he wants fruit right now; and he's ready to cut down the fruitless tree. That doesn't sound like the character of God shown in the New Testament.

No, in this story I think the character of God is portrayed entirely by the Gardener. The Gardener cares for the barren fig tree and nurtures it. He begs for leniency, compassion, and—above all—patience from the owner. He's willing to give the fig tree another chance to show its potential. *God is like that.*

Who is like the vineyard owner? We are. We'll give people a little extra time, but we're ready to write them off if they fail to measure up to our expectations fast enough. We're ready with our axes sharpened to chop down the ones we judge to be inadequate, or non-productive, or even just *not what we want.*—Fortunately, God is not like *us.*

God is patient and gives us what we need in order to start bearing fruit. He helps us. And that's where the fertilizer the gardener put around the tree comes in. The way I interpret Jesus' story, the *fertilizer* that God wants to use in our lives is produced by our repentance. The Biblical word for "repent" used here means "a change of mind," a new way of thinking. We need to change our minds and turn away from sterile, self-centered and judgmental thinking that makes us look for happiness in all the wrong places—such as fleeting physical pleasures and transitory material stuff, or in putting other people down in order to build ourselves up. My home-grown metaphor for the process is to say that "repentance takes the garbage of our lives and turns it into fertilizer," fertilizer that can help us bear the fruit God wants.

God wants to bring out the best in us. So he helps us as we work through the process of repentance, the process of living into a new way of thinking that produces fruit, the harvest of virtue in our lives. A modern paraphrase of Romans 12: 2 puts it like this: "Don't become so well-adjusted to the world that you automatically conform to it. Instead, fix your mind on God. When you do, you'll begin to be changed from the inside out. Recognize what God wants from you, and decide to do *that*. Unlike the world—which tries to drag you down to its level—God will bring out the best in you."

I don't want to end without offering a few examples of the fruit that the Lord is looking for from you and me, once our thinking has been transformed. The main fruit God wants, I think, is constant HUNGER FOR AN EVER-DEEPER CONNECTION WITH HIM. Isaiah said, "Seek the Lord while he wills to be found. Call upon him while he draws near. Let the wicked forsake their ways and the evil ones their thoughts; and let them turn to the Lord, and he will have compassion." How many of us—even us church folks—have made a serious commitment to be God-centered people?

A second fruit is MERCY. Jesus said, "Be merciful, as your Father in heaven is merciful." Mercy is the flip-side of unselfishness; unselfish people are usually merciful people. To show mercy to another person simply means to meet that person's needs. So, if *I'm* hungry, and *you're* merciful, you'll feed me. If *I'm* lonely, and *you're* merciful, you'll spend time with me and be my friend. If *I'm* wracked with guilt, and *you're* merciful, you'll forgive me and set me free.

A third fruit is FAITHFULNESS. Fidelity, or faithfulness, is an essential Christian virtue. The Bible shows that our God is a promise-keeping God. It's *God's* nature to be faithful. *We're* the fickle ones. Think how different our world would be, how different our country would be, how different our church would be, and how different our families would be if all of us just *'kept faith'* with one another . . . if we simply lived up to our commitments, our

promises, our duty. . . . Our baptismal vows. . . . Our marriage vows. . . .
Our ordination vows.

God is willing to be patient with you. So you need to decide to be patient
with yourself and other people. It takes time for fruit to develop. Virtues
don't manifest themselves overnight. Don't get in a hurry. Repent. Change
your thinking. Center your mind and heart on God and make union with
God your highest aim.—Fruitfulness will follow. I promise.

60. LET'S DEVELOP THE HABIT OF THANKFULNESS.

Sunday before Thanksgiving Day
Philippians 4:4-7

Two good ol' boys climbed a fence and began hiking across a pasture one day when—suddenly—they realized that there was a bull in that pasture, and he didn't like trespassers. They started running for the next fence, but the bull was closing on them fast. It seemed obvious they wouldn't make it. One of the two terrified guys hollered to his companion—who was a regular churchgoer—and he said, "Start prayin' Bob! He's gonna get us."

Bob answered, "I can't pray. I'm not used to saying my prayers out loud." (He was obviously an Episcopalian.)

"You've got to," his friend panted, "This bull is gainin' on us."

"O.K., fine," Bob panted, "I can remember one: *For what we're about to receive, O Lord, make us truly thankful!*"

That was supposed to be funny; I guess you must have heard it before. But even a stale joke has a grain of truth: thankfulness is an attitude to *all* of life. It's a commitment to discovering how to get in touch with the wellsprings of authentic gratitude—even in the midst of unpleasantness, even in circumstances of grief and loss. In our Eucharistic prayers for both Rite One and Rite Two, we ask that God will accept our "*sacrifice of praise and thanksgiving.*" We don't ordinarily think of thanksgiving or praise as a sacrifice, do we?

A *sacrifice* is "a costly gift, joyfully given." Are there times when giving thanks to God feels *costly* and the *joy* of it isn't really there? I think the answer to that question is yes—particularly when we're facing painful, uncertain, or frightening circumstances. Those are times when the punch-line of the silly joke I told carries a new kind of meaning: "For what we're about to receive, O Lord, make us truly thankful."

The truth of Christian experience is that we daily receive from God all we need in order to have a spiritually full life, even when we're nearing that life's end. Sometimes God gives us experiences that teach us the virtue of patience, or that will help us learn how to bear pain or adversity, or that will test our faith, so that it can grow strong. Not every gift of God for which we should give thanks is something which—in the moment of our first experiencing it—strikes us as something naturally pleasant or desirable. Usually it's in retrospect, in moments of spiritual reflection, that we look back and recognize certain disagreeable incidents in our lives as mysterious gifts—as, in fact, blessings. We have a common expression to describe those incidents. We call them "blessings in disguise."

If we haven't cultivated the capacity to perceive the variety of blessings that God gives us—in both the joys and the woes of human life—we miss a lot. We get bitter. And we feel cheated. As the Holy Spirit works in our lives and we mature in faith, we hope to arrive at the point where we're able to look for and find a blessing hidden in experiences that we might otherwise regard as only disasters. There might be disappointment or frustration or grief, but God can show us the gift, the blessing, that's there along with it.

Martin Luther said that "to thank God with all your heart is an art that the Holy Spirit teaches." (I occasionally need the Spirit to give me a personal tutorial.)

In his Letter to the Philippians, Paul says, "In everything by prayer and supplication with thanksgiving let your requests be made known to God." I've noticed that when we offer an opportunity for the congregation to offer their own prayers aloud during the intercessions at the Eucharist, there are always requests, always supplications (to use Paul's word), but few thanksgivings—sometimes none—even though the Bible tells us to let our requests be made known to God "by prayers and supplications with thanksgiving." Does this mean we're more focused on what we need (or want) than on what God in his providence has already given us? Probably.

Here's a way to start developing the habit of thankfulness. (I've done this myself from time to time, and it really works.) Decide to make *thanksgiving* your only kind of prayer for a set period of time, like a week. Since we're about to celebrate Thanksgiving, that might be a good day to start this discipline, if you want to give it a try. Starting this Thursday and for a week thereafter, don't *ask* God for anything. And unless you've committed a mortal sin and need to ask forgiveness, don't make any requests. Just say, "Thank you, God," and be *specific* about what you're grateful for.

Following this rule sharpens our powers of observation and hones our spiritual sensitivity. It makes us *take notice* of the diversity of gifts that God provides, but which we overlook because we're accustomed to taking them for granted. It's amazing how many things we take for granted, how much we consider ourselves *entitled* to. For example, in the material realm, we Americans are accustomed to first class domestic amenities: spacious housing, central heating, pure drinking water from the kitchen tap, electricity on demand 24/7, and relatively cheap fuel—even at $3 a gallon—for our cars, trucks, and snowmobiles.

When we get spiritually sensitized to all the "good gifts around us"—including the secret blessings that can come through frustrations and disappointments—we can begin to give thanks to God with greater fluency. And, by the way, in case you're afraid God might think your prayers this week are pretty monotonous, don't worry. It's perfectly O.K. to repeat ourselves, to thank God every day for the very same things. Remember: like telling your wife or husband "I love you," *"Thank you"* is a sentiment that bears frequent repetition—both in prayer to the Lord, and in conversation with your mate.

Developing the habit of thanksgiving is important, but it won't eliminate life's problems. Consider our Pilgrim fathers and mothers. By the grace of God they survived the awful winter of 1620 and celebrated the first

Thanksgiving. But they had to endure another hard winter in 1621.—And probably in 1622. Simple survival didn't get easier for those tough New England colonists for a long time. Diseases were rampant. Supplies from home were slow in arriving. But in the midst of their privations, they thanked God, and their thankfulness was a sign of their trust. Cultivating the habit of thanksgiving alters our perspective on life.

The attitude of thankfulness can lead to more than just an improvement in the quality of our prayers. I believe that authentic thankfulness leads us to become what I call "agents of grace," Christians for whom generous acts of compassion, service, and giving come naturally.

If we're truly grateful to God for what he has given us, we're going to be on the lookout for opportunities to be givers ourselves. We're going to look for ways to benefit those who need what we can freely supply. That generosity of spirit, arising from thankfulness, is the attitude of grace. It's what Jesus was talking about when he said to "be merciful, as your Father in heaven is merciful."

I believe that we're usually the most thankful for unexpected, undeserved gifts—the kind that come without warning and which we know we haven't earned. Twenty-two years ago, a man in my parish—someone I hardly knew other than to say "hello" at the church door—came to see me and told me he wanted to give me a new car! He was a wealthy man, and he said, "Go anywhere you want and pick out anything you want. Price doesn't matter. Just shop around 'til you find exactly what suits you. Then call me, and I'll pay for it.—But don't tell anyone. This is to be our little secret. And I'm giving this to you personally, not to the church; I don't want a tax deduction."

I was overwhelmed. I had done nothing for this man. I hardly knew him. But the truth was that I *had* been trying to figure out how to afford a bigger car because I had four growing children.—This gentleman was an agent of grace. And I was grateful.

If we're the most grateful for gifts that are unexpected and undeserved, maybe we can stimulate gratitude and thankfulness in one another by demonstrating unexpected, unmerited generosity to each other. And the beneficiaries of our grace will—we pray—become agents of grace themselves. If we do that, we'll fulfill Jesus' commandment to love one another as he has loved us, for the most precious gift we've received, a gift we could not have earned and did nothing to merit, is our Lord's gift of himself on the cross for us.

So what do we conclude? Simply this: we're the beneficiaries of God's generosity. And we're called by Christ to give generously to those who don't expect it and probably don't deserve it. If we do that, we'll discover that gratitude and grace are multiplied. And we'll prove ourselves to be children of God and disciples of the One who freely gave himself for us.

61. THE KING OF TRUTH.

Christ the King Sunday
John 18:33-37

E ugene Peterson's contemporary translation of the New Testament, called *The Message,* offers this version of some of the dialog between Jesus and Pontius Pilate that you just heard:

> Pilate said to Jesus, "So, are you a king or not?"

> Jesus answered, "You tell me. Because I am King, I was born and entered the world so that I could witness to the truth. Everyone who cares for truth, who has any feeling for the truth, recognizes my voice."

> Then Pilate said, "What is truth?"

What is *truth?* We have just endured another political campaign season. I say this every two years, but I believe it more every time: political campaigns are getting nastier and nastier. Four out of six TV ads this year—for all candidates—consisted exclusively of negative, hostile, almost slanderous remarks about the opposition. They offered almost nothing positive about the person whose candidacy was being promoted, just depressing, often malicious claims about the foolishness, shortcomings and moral failures of the other guy. And of course, we all asked ourselves: Is this believable? How much of this stuff is true? I read about a candidate for the U.S. House of Representatives somewhere in the northeast who decided to run only ads that told about what he hoped to achieve as a congressman, saying absolutely nothing negative about the opposition. He lost.

When I have listened to a speech by any President (either Mr. Bush or any of his predecessors of either party) I have wondered, "What's the *truth*? Is this an accurate portrayal of the domestic or world situation, or is he just giving us a collection of partial-truths and outright lies told for political reasons?

On any given subject—whether it's politics or advertising or debate about global warming—there are competing voices all claiming to present the facts, the hard data, the real skinny. Most people with good sense and a little bit of sales resistance are properly skeptical about such so-called *truth*—because truth in these situations really stands for whatever the advocate can persuade us to believe for a while—until we buy or vote or donate to the cause. This kind of truth is measured only by whether it succeeds in manipulating us.

It's hard to blame Pontius Pilate for being cynical when the Temple authorities brought Jesus to him and accused him of claiming to be a king. Pilate was a Roman governor, and he was accustomed both to hearing lies and telling them himself—lies that purported to be the truth. His was the pragmatism of the ruler, the governor, or the boss, either in the 1st century or the 21st century: "Truth is whatever I need to say in order to stay in power and get things done."

When Pilate asked Jesus if he were the King of the Jews, he wasn't inquiring about *facts*. He was asking about claims. Not truth, really, but something else. Jesus answered, in Peterson's version, "My kingdom doesn't consist of what you see around you. If it did, my followers would fight so that I wouldn't be handed over to the Jews. But I'm not that kind of king, not the world's kind of king. I was born and entered the world so that I could witness to the truth." And then came the kicker, both for AD 31 and for our age: "Everyone who cares for truth, who has any feeling for the truth, recognizes my voice."

Jesus proclaimed himself as King of Truth, the one whose word, whose very person is Truth, with a capital "T." But our world is more confused about the meaning of truth than even Pontius Pilate was.

When we were little kids, truth for us was whatever mom and dad said. When we got to be teenagers, truth was whatever our peer group said. As we grew older and went to college, we were taught that truth is to be known through rigorous application of the scientific method—using research tools to discover an observable, provable correspondence between material reality and hypotheses about that reality, the kind of *truth* that can be verified in a laboratory and tested consistently by ever-newer research techniques. Once we arrived at that point, science and scholarship seemed to offer deliverance from all the other so-called "truths" we had grappled with growing up.

But, as it turns out, scholarly and scientific truth doesn't help very much when we're trying to make moral decisions, when we're trying to decide right from wrong. It might offer interesting (perhaps accurate) information about who killed JFK, or the structure of the atom, or the human genome, but it doesn't help us live fulfilled and meaningful lives. It doesn't engender *hope*. It doesn't lead us to *love*. It doesn't help us *face death*.

Postmodernism is the contemporary movement in philosophy. Postmodern philosophers start from the question, "What can you truly *know*?" They say Reality is read differently by each knowing self that encounters it. Thus, so they say, there is no single meaning of the world, no single transcendent center to reality as a whole. Truth, the Postmodernists say, depends on your point of view. *It depends on the community you belong to.*

I'm not here to make a case for Postmodernism, but maybe they have a good point. Truth—the kind of truth that really makes a difference in our lives, the kind of truth that shapes us as moral creatures—is defined within a community. In fact, agreement about this Truth is what creates the community. The community we belong to celebrates the Truth that Jesus Christ embodies: the enfleshed reality of God's love and purpose for his creation. Jesus told his disciples, "I am the Way, the Truth, and the Life." He told Pilate, "Because I am King, I was born and entered the world so that I could witness to the truth. Everyone who cares for truth, who has any feeling for the truth, recognizes my voice."

So Jesus is our "King," not King of the Jews, but King of Truth. We're the community that believes in him, the community that—in a profound sense—*knows* him in a way that those who are not of our number can never know him. We're convinced that the birth of Jesus, the acts of Jesus, the words of Jesus, and the death and resurrection of Jesus reveal God. His person shows us Truth, and to encounter him, in the power of his Spirit, is to come face-to-face with a Reality that transforms us and makes living a fulfilled and morally meaningful life possible, makes *hope* possible, makes courage in the face of death possible. We, the Community of the King of Truth, are a community with these convictions, and the truthfulness of any set of convictions is discerned in the sort of lives they produce. As Jesus himself said, "By their fruits you will know them."

There's a wonderful logic in our focusing on Truth as the theme of the Kingship of Christ on this last Sunday before Advent, because King Jesus summons us to hear his voice, believe his words, know and love him, and—thus—to know the Truth that sets us free:

> . . . the truth that this world and its proud power are already passing away—setting us free from fear of what any political or economic or terrorist power in the world can do to us.

> . . . the truth that a meaningful life is found in loving God and one another—setting us free from both moral despair and the tyrannical need to look for meaning in the acquisition of more and more toys and baubles.

> . . . the truth that we were created to share eternity with God who gave us life and has promised in Christ to save us from death—setting us free to live a different kind of life right here, right now.

In the earliest days of the Christian community, there was conflict between the kingdom represented by the followers of Jesus and the kingdom represented by the Roman Empire. Rome tried to eliminate its rival by brute force. The Roman soldier proclaimed, "Caesar is Lord." and put his boot on the neck of his Christian victim. The Christian, from a heart of faith, cried, "No, Jesus is Lord." then bowed his neck to the Roman sword, and died.

Two thousand years later, whose kingdom is still visibly advancing and whose kingdom is known only from history books? Which kings exited the world stage long ago, and which one is alive forever more? Caesar has been gone a very long time, but Jesus, the King of Truth, rules the hearts of men and women on every continent. Thousands of new immigrants arrive in his realm each day. The sun never sets on his dominion.

And still we pray, while ages roll, "Thy Kingdom come."

62. ARE YOU THE ONE?
OR SHOULD WE KEEP LOOKING?

Matthew 11:2-6.

" **A** re you the one who is to come, or are we to wait for another?" John the Baptist, locked up in Herod's prison, sent messengers to Jesus to ask him this. *"Are you the one? Or should we keep looking?"*—Strange questions, coming from John the Baptist.

After all, John was Jesus' cousin and had baptized him. He'd seen the dove descend upon him. On that occasion John had announced to everyone that Jesus was "the Lamb of God who takes away the sins of the world." Concerning himself, John said that he was not the Messiah, just the advance man for him, the warm up before the main act. But now he wasn't so sure. He was plagued with doubts.

John had always been what folks down South used to call "a screamin' preacher." He blistered people's ears. Everywhere he went, his message was the same: God was about to send his Messiah to punish evildoers and vindicate the righteous. So, sinners needed to get baptized and put their lives right with the Lord or else when the Messiah came they'd feel the flames.—We heard a few lines from one of John's classic sermons last Sunday: "You brood of vipers. Who warned you to flee from the wrath to come? Bear fruit that befits repentance."

In spite of his hell-fire and damnation preaching, John drew big crowds. And he made converts. Lots of people were baptized in preparation for the advent of the Lord's anointed. John had seen Jesus as the long-expected deliverer of Israel, the One who would purge his people with Spirit and fire and usher in the age of God's direct rule.

So John, sitting in his prison cell, must have thought (and must have said out loud to his disciples when they visited him), "If Jesus *is* the Messiah, what am I doing locked up in Herod's dungeon? How come he hasn't called down fire from heaven to burn up Herod and his soldiers and set me free? How come there hasn't been an earthquake or a whirlwind or something awesome to show what he can do?—Could it be that I was wrong? He's not doing things the way I expected he would. Maybe Jesus isn't really the Messiah, after all. Maybe we should keep looking."

Is he the one? Or should we keep looking? This is something people ask about Jesus today, isn't it? There are many in America (and elsewhere) who are looking for something, looking for some*one* who can help them make sense out of life . . . who can offer a vision for tomorrow that isn't just "life is hard and then you die," or "the one who has the most toys wins." Whether they use this word or not, I'd say most spiritual seekers are looking for *salvation*—an experience of wholeness, fulfillment, and peace that doesn't vanish when a chemically-induced euphoria wears off, or the money is all spent, or the contests have all been won, or the sensual thrill *du jour* stops being a turn-on.

Since Christianity is the dominant religion in America, most seekers in our country started out as at least nominal Christians. But at some point—maybe when they went to college—they dropped out. Did they do that because Jesus hadn't fulfilled their private expectations—or was there another reason?

No doubt, some turned away because what they remembered from Sunday School didn't fit with what they were learning at the university, and nobody seemed interested in trying to answer their adult questions. Some dropped out because what their church offered them or required from them didn't seem to work; it didn't fill the emptiness they felt inside. Or—perhaps for some—the simple, black-and-white, binary moral universe described by the local preacher didn't deal with the gray areas and ambiguities they came across in real life situations. For others, the mountaintop experience at an evangelistic service wasn't followed by what they'd expected. There had been an emotional high, but no enlightenment. Some had prayed for a miracle and when no miracle happened, they turned away. Others couldn't cope with the mystery of suffering—how terrible things could happen to innocent people.

For whatever other causes (and there are many), what some people experienced in church didn't bring them what they felt like they needed. I think a major reason is that many times churches are unable to *connect* their people personally and effectively with Jesus. They can't make the sort of "introduction" that works. Therefore, for some folks brought up as nominal Christians, Jesus always remained a stranger.—So some of them abandoned Christianity and latched on to something else—maybe a form of Buddhism, or Transcendental Meditation, or Scientology, or the occult, or you name it.

These people at some point asked the question, *is Jesus the one? Or should I keep looking?* And they decided to keep looking.

It's interesting that when the disciples of John the Baptist came to Jesus with their master's question, "Are you the one?" Jesus didn't reply, "Of course I'm the one. And here are reasons one, two, and three." He didn't offer his Davidic pedigree. He didn't mention that he was born of a Virgin and angels heralded his birth. He didn't remind John of the Voice that had spoken from heaven at the moment of his baptism. Instead, he replied, "Go and tell John what you hear and see: the blind receive their sight, the lame walk, the lepers are cleansed, the deaf hear, the dead are raised, and the poor have good news brought to them. And blessed is anyone who takes no offense at me."

In effect, he told John's messengers to go back to their imprisoned leader and tell him what they had experienced—what they had seen with their own eyes and heard with their own ears. The blind, the lame, the leper, the deaf and the dead were symbolic of sinners and excommunicated outcasts—and they were at the heart of Jesus' ministry. Isaiah had long ago said that the redemption and healing of such as these would be the sign of God's saving work. With Jesus, the pariahs and the outsiders were finding their condition was no longer a barrier to experiencing God's love. As had been promised, weak hands and feeble knees were being strengthened, and fearful hearts were finding courage in Jesus' presence.

"Go and tell John what you hear and see. And blessed is anyone who takes no offense at me."

John had expected and assumed that God's Messiah would come to humanity in a display of terrifying power, smiting the wicked with the iron rod of his righteous anger. Instead, Christ came in quietness, humility, and healing love. He didn't push people around. He just said "Follow me." When people followed, their lives were changed. They didn't get rich. They weren't spared suffering. They didn't stop making mistakes.—But they found a center for their souls. They found "the peace that passes all understanding," and when they did, they were able to give themselves away in selfless love for others.

We have a challenge today. How can we answer a seeker—maybe someone who has left the church or who is about to leave—who asks us, *is Jesus the one? Or should I keep looking?* Before we answer, perhaps we have to ask first, have you really *met* Jesus yet? What are you expecting?

For those of us who have come through our own experience to believe that Jesus is indeed "the One," I think the only honest answer we can give to the seeker's question has to be a version of the answer Jesus sent to John the Baptist. We have to say, tell me what you hear and see. We have to ask, what do you hear in the conversation and see in the behavior of men and women who truly follow Christ? Look at them. Listen to them. Do you notice the fearful who've grown bold and the greedy "takers" who have changed into "givers"? Do you see the proud who have become humble, the cruel who now are kind, and those once drowning in despair who've been filled with hope? Look at all the restless, driven souls who've discovered peace, the lost who've been found, the dead in heart who are now vibrantly alive.

Those who honestly look at the lives of Jesus' disciples can't avoid this perception: *Jesus changes people.* And the people Jesus changes change the world around them.

You can't be neutral about Jesus when you meet him and it finally dawns on you what he's really all about. Then, you find that either you must embrace him as Lord and Savior, or you must do your best to discredit him. Nobody in human history has ever compelled such a response from people. And why is that? I believe that it's for just one reason: Jesus is God incarnate, God in our flesh, God *with* us—yesterday, today, tomorrow, and forever.

63. FOUR WAYS WE SHOULD BE LIKE MARY.

Luke 1:26-38

In the busy Israeli Arab city of Nazareth today there's a vast, modern Roman Catholic church—the Basilica of the Annunciation. You can see it from miles away because its dome dominates the skyline of the town. The basilica was built in 1969 over the site that ancient tradition says was the home of Mary, the mother of Jesus.

Some distance away is another, older church—the Greek Orthodox Church of St. Gabriel, which was first built in the 2nd century, destroyed many times and most recently re-built in 1767. It is quite small and not very impressive. It's built over a well, fed by a spring whose waters bubble up into a natural trough in the rock. According to ancient local legend, it was here—when Mary came to draw water—that the Angel Gabriel appeared to her and told her that she was going to be the mother of the Messiah.

For those who visit it, this little church, with its grotto enclosing the ancient water supply of Nazareth, can capture the imagination better than the big, modern church up the hill. We can envision the spring there among the rocks, feeding its water into the well as it did 2,000 years ago, on the edge of the little village, and a well-worn trail leads down to it.

We can imagine Mary coming down the trail to the well not long after sunrise, probably barefoot. Other women would be there on the same mission. She would dip her jar into the pool by its cord and then draw it up. If time permitted, maybe she stopped for a while and sat on one of the boulders nearby, just to enjoy a moment of quiet in the sunshine of early morning after the other women had gone on their way. I like to think that it was then that she was visited by the angel who told her what we heard in today's gospel, that she was chosen to be the mother of the Son of God—to be the one that Greeks call "the God-bearer."

It really doesn't matter how we re-create the scene in our minds, or dramatize the story that Luke gives us. What does matter for Christians is that the Bible offers Mary as a model for our own relationship with God. You see, there's a sense in which we can think of Mary as the first disciple, the first person to believe that Jesus was the Son of God and Savior of the world.

These verses weren't in today's gospel, but just a little further on in the same chapter it says that when Mary went to visit her cousin Elizabeth (soon to be the mother of John the Baptist), Elizabeth said about her, "Blessed is she who believed that there would be a fulfillment of what was spoken to her by the Lord." Mary was a believer.

In the gospel account of the Annunciation, I see four characteristics of Mary that we might take as goals for our own discipleship.

First: SHE WAS LISTENING FOR GOD'S WORD. Wherever she was, in fact, when the angel came to her—whether sitting for a moment beside the well in the cool of the early morning, or out in the busy village market buying vegetables, or folding clean clothes by lamplight before going to bed, I believe Mary was listening to God with heart and mind. Angels are messengers of God, and the messages of angels don't usually come with a flourish of trumpets. Their announcements are not necessarily proclaimed loudly. Some of God's most important communications to humanity have come in whispers or even in dreams—and these words might have been missed by one who wasn't listening. But Mary was listening. Of course, the message that came to her was unexpected. It was surprising, even shocking. But she didn't seem to doubt for a moment that it was from God.

I believe that one reason why Mary *"found favor with God"* (as the gospel says) is because she spent her prayer time not telling God what she wanted, but asking him to tell her what he wanted from her. She was a listener.

The *second* thing about Mary which we might take as a goal for our own discipleship is this: MARY WAS HONEST WITH GOD ABOUT HERSELF. She was afraid. She was perplexed. And she didn't pretend to be otherwise. She didn't hesitate to say to the angel, "How can this be?" Mary was formally engaged to Joseph. But, in careful obedience to the Law, she was still a virgin, living at home with her parents until the formal wedding celebration. So she asked the angel: How can this be?

We don't doubt that God knows our secrets, even if we fail to tell him. He is (as we say) the One "to whom all hearts are open, all desires known, and from whom no secrets are hid." But spiritual integrity for a Christian demands that we consciously open our hearts to God—owning before God all the realities of our thoughts and emotions, the good and the bad alike, including our fears, our frustrations, our questions, and our doubts. The Lord works with power in our lives when we offer him absolute honesty, when we have no illusions about ourselves.

The *third* aspect of Mary's relationship to God that we can see as a model for ourselves is: SHE BELIEVED GOD'S WORD. As her cousin Elizabeth said, "Blessed is she who believed that there would be a fulfillment of what was spoken to her by the Lord." A woman who believes that she is going to have a baby even though she has had no contact with a man is a believer.

As far as Mary was concerned, God was quite able to fulfill his promise. She did not doubt that. His word was enough for her. Believing God is what we do when we trust Christ for salvation, for our eternal security, rather than assuming we have to find some other path by using our own creative intelligence.

The fourth and most significant thing about Mary which we can take as a pattern is: MARY WAS SUBMITTED TO GOD. She was yielded to God's will for her life, *even though she didn't understand it.* Her answer to the angel's announcement was very simple, direct and humble: "Here am I, the servant of the Lord; let it be with me according to your word." The word "servant" in our English version is a concession to modern taste. The actual word is "slave." She said, "I am the slave of the Lord." A slave has no private will that counts for anything; only the will of the master matters.

And here's something that I think is important: *God did not force his will on Mary.* To use a current expression, we would say God respected Mary's "right to choose." I think that once she had heard what the angel had to say, Mary could have folded her arms and said, "No. This is not for me. You must find another woman. I can't do it." And if she had said that, God would have found someone else.—But, of course, before he sent Gabriel to her, the Lord knew Mary's heart. She had already found favor with God.

Mary said, "Let it be with me according to your word." Those words of his mother, spoken when he was conceived, find an echo in Jesus' own prayer in the Garden of Gethsemane on the night before he went to the cross: "Not my will, but yours be done."

If we *listen* for God's word to us; if we *believe* that word; if we are *honest with God* and with ourselves; then we need to follow through by *yielding* to God—let's call it *making ourselves available to God,* as young Mary did—if we are to experience the fruit of God's presence in our lives.

When Mary said her "yes" to God, "let it be with me according to your word," she had no idea what the future would be, either for herself or for her Son. All she knew was that God had chosen her to be his partner in bringing God's own life into the world in a unique, yet paradoxically very ordinary way. God's grace, God's favor had been granted her . . . for a purpose. And Mary said "yes" to God without asking what such cooperation might ultimately cost her. She simply said, "I am your servant, Lord, your slave. Let your will be done."

Greek Orthodox Christians call Mary the Theotokos, the "God-bearer." God summons us to be like her, to be "God-bearers" ourselves, partners with him who—in our listening for his word, in our believing his promises, in our being honest with him about ourselves and our own fears, and in our obeying him in humble submission—allow God's own life to be formed in us and "take flesh" from our flesh . . . just as Jesus took his flesh from a young woman who *believed* what had been spoken to her by God.

64. IF YOU WANT TO,
YOU CAN HEAL ME.

Mark 1:40-45

It's hard for us to imagine what it must have been like in Jesus' time for a person suffering from leprosy. In addition to the physical suffering caused by the disease, lepers had to live apart from everyone else. By law, they couldn't enter a town. They couldn't shop for food in the market place. And when they had a meal, they couldn't eat with anyone but other lepers. They weren't allowed to worship in the temple or a synagogue. As they walked along a road, if anyone else approached they had to cover their mouth with a hand and cry out, *"Unclean, unclean,"* so others would keep their distance.

According to the law, those who came in contact with a leper automatically contracted the leper's uncleanness, became contaminated, and so became outcasts too—until they went through a lengthy and expensive ritual cleansing.

Imagine this scene. We're with Jesus in the market place of Capernaum. His disciples are there too and other people are standing around, listening to Jesus talk. A ragged beggar comes to the edge of the crowd and begins to move toward Jesus. People turn, take one look at him, and leap back. Some even run away. We hear cries of *"Leper! Leper!"* and *"Unclean!"* Even the disciples pull back—though Jesus stands his ground and doesn't move. The wretched man comes right up to Jesus and falls to his knees at his feet. White, scaly flesh and missing fingers define the beggar as a leper. There can be no doubt at all. The disease causes an unpleasant odor, and everyone can smell it—though now no one but Jesus is nearer the man than ten feet.

From his place of abasement in the dust, surrounded by people with looks of revulsion (and curiosity) on their faces, the beggar lifts his eyes to Jesus' face and says, "If you *want* to, you can make me clean." Clearly, he didn't question the *power* of Jesus to heal him. He believed that Jesus could do what he needed. He only questioned the will of Jesus to do such a thing. He says, "If you want to . . ."

This leper had probably never met Jesus. He may have known nothing about him except that he had a reputation for being able to cast out demons and heal the sick. So the man took the risk of coming to find him.—Maybe Jesus would be strict about the Law. He didn't know. Maybe he was a Pharisee. Maybe Jesus would be offended that an unclean person dared approach him. The leper couldn't have known what would happen. But he came, and he said to Jesus, "If you want to, you can make me clean."

We can imagine that Jesus looked down at the man and then around at the crowd—who were all keeping their distance, fearful of coming in contact with this filthy "untouchable." Then Jesus reached down and put his hand on the man's disfigured, dirty face and said, "I do want to; be clean." Immediately the leper was healed, made clean.

Notice something here: Jesus, even if he wanted to help the leper, didn't have to *touch* him. He could have simply spoken a word, and the man would have been made well. He could have said, "I call on the Father to make you clean," or "It is God's will that you be clean."

To be effective, Jesus' healing power did not require physical contact.—But he *touched* this untouchable anyway. Coming in physical contact with a leper automatically contaminated Jesus. That was the law. The leper was cleansed, and now Jesus was *unclean.*—Or *was* he? Jesus didn't seem to think so.

The crowd heard Jesus tell the cleansed leper to find a priest and perform the correct ritual to be certified as clean and be able to re-enter society, but Jesus made no move to go along with him and find a priest for himself.—Why? Because he didn't regard himself as contaminated. On the contrary, he had absorbed the man's leprosy into himself and had given his own health to the leper. Instead of both being diseased, now *both* were whole and pure.—This was evident to everyone who was watching.

Here at the very beginning of the gospel—we're still in Chapter One of Mark—we see Jesus revealing the essence of his entire mission. We have a prefigurement of the cross. He came to take our sins, our uncleanness, our alienation, our pain, our grief, our sorrow all on himself. He *chose* to. He said, "I want to."

Who are our "lepers"? The actual disease may be disappearing, but we *do* have "lepers" of other sorts, don't we? And we don't want to touch them, either literally or figuratively. It's easy to make a short list of who might fit that category:

- People living with AIDS are the most obvious "lepers" these days.

- People with disfiguring diseases or even physical blemishes, like obvious birthmarks say that some people won't even look at them. The same is true for people who are morbidly obese.

- Homeless people, street people, bag ladies, everyone whose clothing or manner is other than mainstream, can find themselves isolated and treated as untouchable.

- Immigrants from Latin America, both legal residents and undocumented ones alike, report feeling cut off from the rest of us. They say that typical Anglos "keep their distance."

This week I read a piece about Michael Kirwan, who spent years working with homeless people in Washington, D.C. The story I read told about the beginning of his ministry. One winter night Michael brought down a gallon jug of split pea soup from his apartment to a group of homeless men huddled on the sidewalk near his building. He'd done things like that before—bringing them food or blankets. He put the jug of soup down on a cinderblock near the heating vent where the street people had gathered for warmth.

Michael says that no sooner had he brought the soup and put it down
than a rough-looking guy picked up the jar of soup and broke it over
his head. Instead of running away from this madman, which he might
ordinarily have done, Michael asked "Why did you do that to me?" It was
the first time he had ever *spoken* to any of these people, though he had
brought food to them before.

The man said Michael was doing nothing different from bringing food
to animals. He told him that he brought food, set it down as if putting it
in a pet dish, and walked away. The man said, "Why don't you stay and
talk to us. Visit with us. We won't bite."

So Michael began visiting with them. He said, "A barrier had been broken
down in my perception of who homeless people are. . . . Those men and
women on the street had feelings just like me. They wanted to be loved
and respected and listened to. They were glad someone cared about them,
but just giving them food and a blanket wasn't enough."

The leper said to Jesus, "If you want to, you can make me clean." Jesus
touched him and said, "I do want to. Be clean."

Most of us are glad to give money to help worthy causes—to feed and heal
and provide shelter for needy people. But God is inviting us to do more
than simply give money. *The gospel is calling us to reach out and touch people.*
Jesus had a hands-on ministry to lepers. We're called to the same work.

Who, in our little world is an outcast? Who's desperate for the human
contact of touch? . . . Is it someone dying from a disfiguring illness, who
desperately wants someone to sit by his bedside and hold his hand? . . . Is
it a lonely old person with no family still alive, just hoping that someone
might visit and give her a hug? . . . Is it a young person struggling with
his sexual identity, who's hoping for someone who'll talk to him about
his life, about how he feels, and not reject him?

The love Jesus offers is totally different from what the world offers. Jesus
reaches out to touch us and make us whole, make us clean, give us a new
beginning. He restores us to unity with God and one another. I'm glad
we hold hands as we say the Lord's Prayer in this service. No one should

be left out. We reach out and touch one another and draw together as those who have been touched and made clean by Jesus.

The leper who came to Jesus understood clearly that there would be no healing for him unless Jesus wanted to heal him. If we don't *want* to put ourselves into hands-on ministry, if we don't *want* to touch other lives, if we don't *want* to be the healing hands of Jesus among the social outcasts of our world, or among people who are unlovely or unlovable, then we will remain among those who merely *admire* Jesus, but can't be his *disciples*.

Someone needs *you* to touch them.
Someone needs *you* to listen to them.
Someone needs *you* to be with them.
If you want to, *you* can heal them.

65. THE FEAR OF THE LORD IS THE BEGINNING OF WISDOM.

Proverbs 9:1-6

One of my chief pleasures in life is reading newspapers. At our house we get the *Denver Post* every morning, and most days we stop somewhere and pick up both Aspen papers. Sometime during the day I read the *New York Times* on-line, but I usually start off with the *Post* at breakfast, then read a little more after lunch, and finish it up after supper—at which time I also read the local rags.

Of course, I don't read every word, but I scan the headlines, read the lead articles, sample the editorials, check out the baseball scores if it's the season, look at the business section to see what's happening with the economy and guess whether our retirement fund is growing or shriveling, then finally I read all the cartoons, even the ones that aren't funny. (Yes, I obviously have way too much time on my hands.) At least once a week—usually on Sunday—I'll take a look at some of the advice columns in the Lifestyles section.

By the way, it would appear that if you want guidance, all you need is a Sunday subscription to a big city newspaper. Ann Landers is gone, but we have her successor, "Ask Amy," along with good old "Dear Abby," to tell us how to handle awkward situations in love and marriage. And now there's also "Consejos" (which I think means something like "counsel" in Spanish) to guide people through the minefields of cross-cultural dating. Judith Martin, a.k.a "Miss Manners," is still around to give advice on what kind of thank-you notes to send for any occasion and to tell us when it's o.k. to eat pie with a spoon. In addition, there are columns for parents, teenagers, investors, weight watchers, hikers, bridge players, gardeners, and electronic gadget nuts. And I haven't even mentioned the daily horoscope.

The proliferation of advice and guidance columns in the papers and on line suggests that we who live in America today are people fundamentally uncertain of ourselves. We're not sure how to cope with life. We're anxious and looking for help.

Clearly, we have huge respect for brain-power. You need intelligence to succeed in our fast-changing Third Millennium society because there's a lot of new stuff to learn every day. We have our mantras, "Knowledge is power" and "The internet is the information superhighway."

So, bright people try to master as much information as possible. But the effort to keep up just makes us more anxious, because there's so much information, mis-information, and so-called informed opinion out there on the World Wide Web that most of us—even if we're well-educated—can't sort it out. Consequently, people seem more uncertain, edgy, and worried than they used to be . . . and hungrier for guidance.—It's as if we're saying, "Somebody please tell us how to handle this confusing world."

We admire brains. We collect information. We realize that knowledge is power. But the solution to our collective anxiety is to be found elsewhere—not in the mastery of facts or the pursuit of new technology, but in the *acquisition of wisdom.*

Every age and every civilization of the past has looked for wisdom, though some have searched for it more thoroughly and prized it more highly than others. The Hebrews, the Chinese, and the Greeks cherished wisdom. The Romans were more interested in law, engineering, and power politics. I've thought a lot about this, and I've concluded that American society has a more or less "Roman" approach to life.

Compare the Romans with the Hebrews. You may recall the Old Testament story of Solomon's prayer. Solomon had followed his father David as king of Israel. God asked the young king what he wanted him to give him.

Solomon didn't ask for riches or for power over his enemies. Instead, he asked for *wisdom*. Can you imagine Caesar doing that?

Our first lesson this morning came from the Book of Proverbs, one of the Wisdom Books of the Old Testament. It's the invitation of Lady Wisdom to all who are willing to listen to her. She says, "'You that are simple, turn in here.' To those without sense she says, 'Come, eat of my bread and drink of the wine I have mixed. Lay aside immaturity, and live, and walk in the way of insight.'" To have wisdom is "to walk in the way of insight." We want to live a centered and peaceful life in the midst of a rapidly changing, culturally polarized, and often confusing world. To do that, we need Lady Wisdom.

The Jewish tradition we find in the Bible, the tradition that shaped Jesus and trained Paul, understood wisdom as inherently practical. Wisdom showed how to live a good and meaningful life, especially in terms of various personal relationships—starting with God, and then moving down the social pyramid from the king to the aristocracy, to people superior to you, people subordinate to you, and your spouse, your children, your neighbors, and your servants. Wisdom showed how to deal with those who were stronger than you as well as those who were weaker.

The Book of Proverbs was a wisdom textbook for school-boys in ancient Israel. (Alas, there were no "school-*girls*" then, which is surprising since Wisdom was always portrayed as female. Maybe they thought girls came by their wisdom naturally, while boys had to be taught. The women in church this morning would probably agree with that.) The Book of Proverbs taught young Israelite gentlemen that the wise differ from fools in practical ways: the wise control their tongues and consider the power of their words; they also honor silence. They control their passions and practice moderation in all things. They learn how to work hard and be thrifty. And they have a goal for their lives. Above all, the wise grasp the truth of their own ignorance. They understand that they don't know it all.

A columnist I read sometimes said this week that wisdom in the Bible means more than shrewdness, "more than common sense, more than success in problem solving." It demands patience with oneself, and requires an effort to live with ambiguity. Wisdom recognizes that we don't live in a black and white universe where right and wrong are always self-evident.

I imagine just about all of you know the Bible verse that says, "The fear of the Lord is the beginning of wisdom," even if you don't know that it's Psalm 111, verse 10. For the Hebrew writers, the search for wisdom was the true quest of faith. The only way to wisdom was through a relationship with God grounded in awe. ("Awe" or "profound reverence" is the real meaning of the word "fear" when we say "the fear of the Lord is the beginning of wisdom.") And we don't practice fear of the Lord in order to win arguments or to prove that we're better than other people. Awe of God is the very beginning of wisdom. It opens the door to the practical understanding of how to live a meaningful life.

Awe of God, respect for God's Word, dread of offending him, response to his love, and eagerness to do his will are the starting point for human happiness and right relationships. In a time when we're anxious and edgy and looking for guidance, there's no more practical advice to give either our children or our friends than to tell them to seek the wisdom of God. It's more useful than a column in the newspaper, a hot new website, a self-help book, a guide to the stock market, or the latest guru to hit Aspen.

We Christians believe that the wisdom of God is summarized and incarnated in the person of Jesus Christ and is expressed in an awesome way through his Cross. Yes, through his Cross. Paul, who was shaped by the wisdom of the Hebrew Scriptures, called Christ "the wisdom of God and the power of God." He wrote in one of his letters, "I resolved to know nothing among you except Jesus Christ crucified . . . a message of wisdom among the mature, but not the wisdom of this world."

The imitation of Christ, who gave himself for those he loved, is the most practical wisdom anyone can share. We had a wedding here yesterday afternoon. The priest offers a solemn blessing of the bride and groom at the end of the service, and it starts with these words "Most gracious God, we give you thanks for your tender love in sending Jesus Christ to come among us, to be born of a human mother, and to make the way of the cross to be the way of life." This is wisdom: "the way of the cross is the way of life."

Do you want to have a happier family life? . . . *Walk the way of the cross.*
Do you want to get along better at work? . . . *Walk the way of the cross.*

Do you want to overcome your anxieties in this confusing age? . . . *Walk
     the way of the cross.*
Do you want to overcome your fear of death and start living an abundant
     life right now? . . . *Walk the way of the cross.*

In the Greek Church, before the reading of the Gospel at the Eucharist,
the Deacon cries out, *"Wisdom! Wisdom! Let us be attentive!"* The Good News
is wisdom, the best advice anyone can ever get—or give.

66. WE NEED A SAVIOR.

Christmas Eve
Luke 2:1-20

Last Sunday we had our annual Children's Christmas Pageant. It was lots of fun. It was a hoot, really, because we were welcoming new, walk-on pageant cast members right up to the very last minute. We told people to bring their neighbors' children, or family from out of town. All would be welcome; and they were. These extra kids, these "walk-ons" could be either shepherds or angels, because we have plenty of shepherd and angel costumes. Some say that this was our "best Christmas pageant ever," which reminds me of Barbara Robinson's book by that name. Perhaps some of you have read it.

The Best Christmas Pageant Ever tells the story of a church youth group that's putting on a Christmas pageant. There's just one problem: the Herdman kids. The Herdmans are the most misbehaved children in town, and they are all going to be in the pageant. The church people are outraged that the pageant director has decided even to let Imogene Herdman be Mary.—But wait a minute. There's a reason the angels came to the shepherds. Shepherds were dirty and difficult, yet they were the first to hear the news of Jesus' birth. Barbara Robinson made no mistake in giving the Herdmans a last name that has to remind us of shepherds.

If we read Luke's story of the birth of Jesus and pay attention to which characters appear most often in the story, we notice that although the Holy Child is the main character, there is at least as much and maybe even more in the story about shepherds than there is about Mary and

317

Joseph. (And the Wise Men aren't mentioned at all.) The herald angels were sent to announce the birth of the Son of God to some shepherds, and to nobody else.

Shepherds were not regarded as decent, upstanding citizens back in those days. They were smelly because they slept in the sheepfold with their animals. And they were notorious for working on the Sabbath. They were also suspected of pilfering lambs from the flock and giving the owner a false count of how many had been born. They were not allowed to be witnesses in court, because they were usually penniless and everyone assumed they could be easily bribed. Nice families didn't want their sons to grow up to be shepherds or their daughters to marry one.

Nevertheless, the Herald Angel appeared to just these people and said, "I am bringing you good news of great joy for all people: to YOU is born this day in the city of David a Savior, who is the Messiah, the Lord. This will be a sign for you: you will find a child wrapped in bands of cloth and lying in a manger." The good news of great joy is for all people, but the emphasis in this verse is on the pronoun "you". ". . . To *you* is born this day . . . a Savior." The Savior is born, not "to Mary and Joseph." . . . Not "to Israel." . . . But *"to you."* Christ was born for them. For shepherds! The "sign" of the baby lying in a manger was for them.—Why did the angel say that Christ was born for shepherds? . . . For dirty, poor, uneducated, disreputable hired hands? I think there's a mystical reason.

I think the shepherds in the Christmas gospel stand for both the physically poor (who have no worldly resources) and the poor in spirit (who recognize their own inner poverty). They are the group that Jesus later would say are "blessed, for theirs is the kingdom of God." They were people without pride, people who knew their own lowliness. They were the ones who most felt the need of a Savior. And they were the ones already primed to believe that God could do something totally new and unprecedented—which the religious authorities had already decided was impossible.

The shepherds stand for *those who know they need a Savior.*—But what *is* a Savior? And do we need one?

What do we need to be saved from? Let's try anxiety. Let's try fear. Many people are anxious or even frightened today. The future seems less certain than ever in our lifetime. Two years ago the economy plunged into the worst recession since the 1930s. The US auto industry was almost destroyed. Many other businesses closed their doors. The media tell us we're moving out of it, but millions of people are still out of work and that isn't going to change much very soon. People in our area who used to be able to make a living from one job now need to have two jobs.

Until recently our consumer culture offered its own secular salvation experience, but that disappeared with the recession for most people. Until a couple of years ago, if people weren't happy, or things weren't the way they wanted them to be, they could make themselves feel better by spending some money, getting some new toys.—It was like taking a drug. It didn't really offer a long-term solution, but it felt good for a little while. Now, however, most of us can't afford the consumerist culture's form of salvation.

The angels told the shepherds, "To you is born this day . . . a Savior, who is Christ the Lord." Are we ready to identify with the shepherds? Have the experiences of the last couple of years humbled us enough? Are we sufficiently poor or poor in spirit, now, to be able to recognize that we need saving? I think we are. And we don't need "a savior-*figure*," like a charismatic politician of either the left or the right. We need the real Savior, whose birthday is the reason we're here tonight. We need Jesus. And here are some reasons why, for us as a nation and for us as individuals.

On the national level, we need to be saved from a moral collapse rooted in self-indulgence and a pervasive sense of entitlement. We need to be saved from the kind of polarization that's eating away at our respect for each other, our shared sense of identity, and our consensus about what "the common good" really means. We need Christ the Savior to be born afresh in our nation, and give us a new vision for how to be our best selves, a vision we can learn from his own tolerance and compassion. This is the birthday of Jesus, God born among us, a human being—the most humane and gentle being the world has ever known. His gentleness and humanity can touch any heart, whether we're Christian, or Jewish, or Muslim, or claim no religion.

In the private realm, many of us suffer not only from economic anxiety, but from pains that stunt our souls: inconsolable grief, a concealed wound, spiritual emptiness, or a secret fear. These gnaw at our hearts. We try to keep up appearances, but many of us are masking agonies. We need a Savior who can touch the bruised places deep inside us and give us hope. False hope is advertised in every glossy magazine, but genuine hope is hard to come by. We need a Savior who can make it possible for wounded souls to look to the future with faith. We need Jesus. He said: "I have come in order that you might have life in all its fullness." He was talking about life *now*, not just in the sweet by-and-by.

Yes, we need a Savior, right here, right now. You do and I do. The herald angels are still singing, calling out to us, poor, lonely shepherds. We can hear them if we'll stop crying and listen: "To *you* is born this day a Savior . . . Christ the Lord." We can meet him tonight, just the way the shepherds of Bethlehem did, because he didn't come just that one time, long ago. He comes again, if we will turn to him and pray.

The timeless truth of Christmas is this: *God believes in us.* That's right. God believes in US. He risked himself on US. He entered our world as the dependent child of a peasant family, born to an illiterate girl from Nazareth twenty centuries ago, and he is still God-with-us—God who will never forsake us, even though we have gone after idols. We are precious in his sight. He believes in us, and *he loves us.* He loves us, and he will not give up on us.

The angels told the shepherds: "This will be the sign for you: you will find the child . . . lying in a manger." A baby found in so unlikely a crib was the sign which the angels said would prove the truth of their message.

I have an idea. Why don't you make a manger for Christ tonight in your heart, as you stretch out your hands to receive him in Communion? Let this reaching out be a sign from you to Jesus, a sign of your faith, a sign that you know the truth of the words we sing so glibly in a familiar Christmas carol: *"No ear may hear his coming, but in this world of sin, where meek souls will receive him still, the dear Christ enters in."*

67. GIVING IS GOOD, BUT WE MUST ALSO LEARN HOW TO RECEIVE.

Christmas Day
John 1:1-14

Christmas just *isn't* the same when there aren't any kids in the house. Joan and I did not race each other downstairs at dawn to empty our stockings and start ripping into our presents. In fact, people who did services at 4:30, 5:30, 8:00 and 11:00 on Christmas Eve don't race anybody anywhere at dawn on Christmas Day. Or even at 9:00. We do well to get dressed and have some coffee before going back to church at 10:00.

As we get older the whole gift-exchange thing is different, isn't it? I'm sure you've noticed that. For example: Joan might say to me, "I think I'd like a new '*X*' (insert whatever: coat, sweater, outfit, etc.—you know, 'girl stuff'). You can give me that for Christmas." And then I may say, "Well, I'd really like to have an '*X*' for my home office (insert whatever: computer, desk lamp, bookshelf, etc.—you know, 'bookish nerd stuff'), and you can give me that for my Christmas present." So we agree, and then we order the stuff on-line or by phone. Catalog shopping is cool. Pretty soon, Santa—disguised as the UPS man so as not to be trailed by hordes of children—brings just what we wanted, and we're both happy. In fact, sometimes we get our gifts a couple of weeks before Christmas. Like this year: Joan gave me a neat credenza so I could hide some of the clutter in my office. Of course, we do always have some little Christmas morning surprises in addition.

It's easy when there are just two of you at home. But when you have a family and you have a gift exchange, with everyone gathered around the Christmas tree, you have to remember that there is a serious art to receiving gifts. It may be more blessed to give than to receive, as our Lord quite rightly said, but it's very important to be a gracious and grateful receiver.

Have you ever given someone a gift and had that person—and I'm thinking of another adult here, not a six year old who had seriously wanted a skateboard but got pajamas instead—tell you in very explicit language, "That's not what I wanted"? Or, "What on earth made you get me that?" If such a thing has ever happened to you, how did it make you feel? Not too good, I bet.

One time, when I was in high school, I bought my dad a tie for Christmas. With my own money. It was a nice silk tie, a repp stripe—not something gross or gaudy. Dad wore a tie to work every day, so it wasn't an unreasonable gift choice. Not too creative, but not unreasonable. We were all opening our presents around the tree on Christmas morning, and it came time for dad to open his present from me. He undid the wrapping, held up the new tie, and said something appropriate, like "This is really nice. Thanks, son." Then he held it out to me and said, "But why don't you just keep it? *You* should wear it." And he put it over on my stack of stuff. Now, I don't think Dad meant to hurt my feelings, but that was not a good thing to do.

I didn't know what to say, and I was too big to cry. My gift had been rejected. I had tried hard to pick out a tasteful tie that Dad would like, but apparently he didn't like it.—I just said, "Well, o.k.," and kept it. It was a nice tie; I wore it to church. (That was back in the dark ages when even teenage boys wore ties to church.)—But I was still hurt. My gift being rejected felt like I was being rejected.

On Christmas Day, as opposed to Christmas Eve, the Church doesn't give us any part of the nativity story to read. We don't read about a decree going out from Caesar Augustus that forced Joseph and Mary to have to go to

Bethlehem. We don't hear about angels singing to shepherds. There's nothing about a baby "wrapped in swaddling clothes and lying in a manger." Instead, we hear the opening fourteen verses of the Gospel according to John. I think this is the most beautiful and eloquent text in the whole Bible. Speaking about Christ, the incarnate Word of God, he writes: "In the beginning was the Word, and the Word was with God, and the Word was God. He was in the beginning with God. All things came into being through him, and without him not one thing came into being. What has come into being in him was life, and the life was the light of all people. The light shines in the darkness, and the darkness has not overcome it."

The gospel writer goes on to say this about Jesus, whom he calls "the Word" and "the True Light" (and here I'm using a slightly different translation from the one you're probably familiar with): "He was in the world, and the world was made through him, yet the world knew him not. He came to his own home, and his own people received him not."

"He came to his own home and his own people received him not." When he wrote those words, John was thinking about the Jews, Jesus' "own people." Jesus was the Son of God, the Messiah, the True Light, God's unique gift to his Covenant People.—But "his own people received him not." He was not the gift they wanted. He wasn't the kind of Messiah they'd asked for. He wasn't what they'd been expecting. He was God's gift to them; but when he arrived, they rejected him. As it says, "They received him not."

Then John goes on to say: "But to all who *received* him, who believed in his name, he gave power to become children of God; who were born, not of blood nor of the will of the flesh nor of the will of man, but of God."

Christmas is about a Gift that's being offered you by God. It's the gift of his incarnate Son, God in our flesh.—What are you going to do with this Gift? Will you receive it warmly, with gratitude and profound respect for both Giver and Gift? Or will you say, "Thanks a lot, but this is really *not* what I want"?

The thing about this Gift Giver is that—in his loving patience and awareness of our immaturity—he is going to keep offering us his Gift, again and again as the years go by, even after we've rejected the Gift many times. He's persistent. This Christmas, next Christmas, and the Christmas after that, he'll offer us the Gift of the True Light, the Incarnate Word, his

Son, for as long as we live.—In fact, he doesn't just wait for Christmas to offer the Gift. The Gift is too important to be presented to us only once a year. The Gift is *always* on offer. Another way of putting it is to say: Christ is always standing there at the door of your heart, asking to come in.

He came to his own people long ago, and they did not receive him. He wasn't what they wanted. But to all who will *receive* him, welcome him, believe in him, he gives power to become children of God—that is, power to become his own brothers and sisters, members of his family. Could any gift be better?

It's Christmas morning. Maybe you haven't opened your presents yet. Remember: it's very important to know how to receive a gift—any gift we're given. But it's especially important for us to know how to receive the gift of Christ himself. If you haven't received this Gift warmly before, do so today. Even if you've said, "No thanks, I don't want this" a hundred times previously, come to the altar this Christmas Day, stretch your empty hands up to God, and say from your heart to the Giver: "Thank you, Lord, for this precious Gift. I receive him with gladness."

And the angels in heaven will sing.

Merry Christmas!